AF839871

Examining Net Zero

Examining Net Zero: Creating Solutions for A Greener Society and Sustainable Economic Growth

EDITED BY

ALEX DE RUYTER

Birmingham City University, UK

STEVEN McCABE

DoctorateHub, UK

AND

BEVERLEY NIELSEN

Centre for Brexit Studies, Birmingham City University

emerald PUBLISHING

United Kingdom – North America – Japan – India – Malaysia – China

Emerald Publishing Limited
Emerald Publishing, Floor 5, Northspring, 21–23 Wellington Street, Leeds LS1 4DL.

First edition 2025

Editorial matter and selection © 2025 Alex de Ruyter, Steven McCabe, and Beverley Nielsen.
Individual chapters © 2025 The authors.
Published under exclusive licence by Emerald Publishing Limited.

Reprints and permissions service
Contact: www.copyright.com

No part of this book may be reproduced, stored in a retrieval system, transmitted in any form or by any means electronic, mechanical, photocopying, recording or otherwise without either the prior written permission of the publisher or a licence permitting restricted copying issued in the UK by The Copyright Licensing Agency and in the USA by The Copyright Clearance Center. Any opinions expressed in the chapters are those of the authors. Whilst Emerald makes every effort to ensure the quality and accuracy of its content, Emerald makes no representation implied or otherwise, as to the chapters' suitability and application and disclaims any warranties, express or implied, to their use.

British Library Cataloguing in Publication Data
A catalogue record for this book is available from the British Library

ISBN: 978-1-83608-575-1 (Print)
ISBN: 978-1-83608-574-4 (Online)
ISBN: 978-1-83608-576-8 (Epub)

Printed and bound by CPI Group (UK) Ltd, Croydon, CR0 4YY

INVESTOR IN PEOPLE

Contents

Part Two
Empirical Examples of Practice
(Case Studies)

Part Three
Moving Forward

About the Editors

Alex de Ruyter is a Professor at Birmingham City University and serves as Director of its Centre for Brexit Studies. He brings a wealth of research experience and academic engagement in the areas of globalisation, regional economic development, labour market and social exclusion issues. He has published over 80 academic outputs in leading national and international economic journals and has been the Recipient of research funding, including being Principal Investigator in a British Academy-funded study on securing a successful transition to Net Zero in the West Midlands and Australian automotive sectors. He has also undertaken commissioned research for the West Midlands Combined Authority, Midlands Engine, Catapult and the British Council, looking that the impact on manufacturing in the UK and India of various 'disruptive' influences including Brexit, Covid, digitalisation and the challenge of transitioning to a green economy. He has undertaken numerous media interviews and is currently undertaking comparative research between the West Midlands and North East on the likely impact of Net Zero and digitalisation on the UK automotive supply chain and automotive workforce in addition to exploring working in the gig economy. He is a Fellow of the Regional Studies Association (RSA) and has also served as a Board member of the RSA, advising them on Brexit-related issues.

Steven McCabe is Professor and Pro Vice Chancellor, DoctorateHub. Previously, he spent 35 years as an academic at Birmingham City University where he taught management, business, economics and strategy to undergraduate and postgraduate students. He also supervised PhD students and taught research methods as part of their development.

Steven regularly writes and comments regularly in the national and international media on politics and the economy and has published ten texts on quality management, benchmarking, 'Brexit' and its economic and social impact, the green economy and manufacturing, house prices and India's progress since independence. Additionally, He has written extensively for edited texts examining economics and politics.

Beverley Nielsen is Visiting Professor at the Centre for Brexit Studies, Birmingham City University, having worked for the past decade as Executive Director at the Institute for Design, Economic Acceleration and Sustainability (IDEAS), a think tank based at the University. She has published books on diverse themes including Redesigning Manufacturing, Brexit Negotiations After Article 50, English

Regions After Brexit, Exploring the Green Economy, Green Manufacturing and India at 75. For the past decade Beverley has conducted economic analysis of the Birmingham Jewellery Quarter and has provided consultancy covering a wide range of specialised industrial clusters. She has served as an Expert Commissioner on the All-Party Manufacturing Group at the House of Commons, working for many years at the CBI in London, Brussels, Manchester and Birmingham. As a councillor in Worcestershire, she is focused on supporting local businesses and retains a strong interest in entrepreneurship having started community companies in outdoor activities and sustainable transport. Whilst working in industry, she was a Director of Aga Rangemaster plc and MD of Fired Earth.

About the Contributors

Carl Arntzen, Mechanical Engineering, joined Worcester Bosch in 1984 where he worked in Product Development for several years before moving into commercially oriented roles in Product Management and Marketing Management. Following national and international roles throughout the sales, marketing and service organisation, he was appointed as Managing Director in October 2011 and CEO for the whole Bosch Thermotechnology operations in the UK and Ireland in 2015. This includes the residential business operating under the Worcester Bosch brand. He is a Board Member of the Construction Product Association (CPA), the Energy Utilities Alliance (EUA) and the CBI Heat Commission.

Tom Bedford is Place Based Decarbonisation Manager for the Globe CIC. He's been driven for many years by the desire to make a positive impact on people and the planet, pursuing two sustainability degrees. Throughout, he focused on climate change and the net zero transition. Since completing these, he has worked on research, delivery and teaching to support the net zero transition. This has included overseeing the role out of major clean energy projects, completing research on the net zero governance landscape and training and supporting organisations across the West Midlands to decarbonise. Alongside his paid employment, he has several voluntary roles supporting communities to take positive action on the climate emergency.

Conall Boyle is Independent Researcher, formerly at Birmingham (UK) City University, and Lecturer in Economics and Statistics. Originally qualified as a Mechanical Engineer, his interests focus on the mechanisms for achieving social and political goals. In 2022, he co-authored *Stop House Prices Rising* with Steve McCabe.

Amy Burnett is a Research Fellow in Inclusive and Sustainable Enterprise at the Centre for Enterprise, Environment and Development Research (CEEDR), Middlesex University. She is also a Research Fellow at the Centre for the Understanding of Sustainable Prosperity (CUSP) and currently holds a British Academy Policy Innovation Fellowship. Her work focuses on the role of civil society groups and local government in promoting innovative sustainable development and supply chains. She also specialises in Monitoring, Evaluation, Accountability and Learning (MEAL) and communications, with extensive international and UK experience.

Jake Burnyeat is a Renewable Energy Professional with 18 years of experience covering renewable energy feasibility and development, finance, procurement, company and asset management and providing strategic advice. He has overseen Communities for Renewables' (CfR) organic growth and the £60 million accessed in the development of finance for community solar projects. Prior to founding CfR, he was Chief Operating Officer of Green Peninsula, an advisory company helping large corporations to develop and implement their own renewable energy strategies, including working with a major international retail and manufacturing company to develop and implement a Euro 1 billion wind power investment strategy. Before that, he worked for Ernst & Young Renewable team in Exeter. He is a Volunteer in a number of local energy enterprises CfR has helped to set up. He was awarded the 'Community Energy Champion' award by Community Energy England in 2018. He has an MSc in Renewable Energy Policy and Economics from Imperial College and a first Class MA in Social Anthropology from the University of St Andrews.

Michael Butler is Professor in Management, Head of Subject Group for Business, Management and Marketing, Lead of Organisational Behaviour Research Group and Member of Rhanbarth Management Board at Bangor Business School, Bangor University. He is on the Editorial Board of Complexity, Governance and Networks and *Asia Pacific Journal of Business Administration*. He publishes in leading management and organisation journals (*British Journal of Management, Human Relations, International Journal of Operations and Production Management, Journal of Management, Journal of Management Studies, The Leadership Quarterly, Organization Science* and *Public Management Review*). He is Founder/Director of The TRANSFORMATION Project (www.thetransformationproject.co.uk). His engaged scholarship (funded to c£1.5m) has been recognised (CMI and ESRC), and the OECD used his research to evaluate international policy implementation. In 2023, he was part of a CMI policy paper titled 'West Midlands Future Prosperity' which sets out how management skills can boost growth.

Kate Copeland-Rhodes is the Founder and Managing Director of The Globe Group CIC a non-profit dedicated to tackling climate change, which encompasses running The Globe Foundation, a community eco centre to establishing events such as the Midlands Climate Expo and Green Action Planning programmes. A passionate environmentalist with over 20 years of experience in project management, communications and environmental behavioural change programmes. As well as Globe, she helped establish and is Deputy Chair of Staffordshire & Stoke-on-Trent Climate Commission; she also sits as Deputy Chair on IEMA Midlands Regional Board.

Sharon Cronin, MSc in Marketing from the Technological University Dublin, has built on wide ranging experience in digital business transformation, energy management, information technology and the services industry to become Head of Marketing for Schneider Electric in Ireland before being promoted to Head of

Marketing Communications UK and Ireland. She is dedicated to driving brand relevance, consistency and engagement across all Schneider Electric touchpoints in the UK and Ireland Zone. Sharon leads a dynamic team responsible for crafting internal and external communications, executing marketing strategies, managing customer-facing events, overseeing Schneider Electric's UK&I Innovation Hubs and liaising with external agencies. She is a passionate Advocate for sustainability and biodiversity, committed to making a meaningful impact in local communities.

Rowan Crozier is CEO of Birmingham-based Brandauer, a 160-year-old metal pressing and stamping specialist that produces millions of parts that are sent across the world every week. The Loughborough engineering graduate, who is chair of the Make UK National Advisory board and Co-chair of the Industry Advisory Board for Birmingham City University, is a massive Advocate of developing the engineers of the future, putting in place a bespoke apprenticeship programme that currently accounts for 15% of the firm's workforce.

David Horsfall is Director of Property and Sustainability at Tyseley Energy Park. As a Chartered Surveyor, he qualified in Planning and Development and is passionate about creating high-quality sustainable places. He is currently delivering the development in Central Birmingham known as Tyseley Energy Park (TEP). Through collaborative partnerships with experts from academia, government and industry, Tyseley Energy Park will shape the way the City of Birmingham develops infrastructure for renewable heat and power, energy storage, clean transport fuels and advanced waste processing.

Holly Johnson has worked at Amtico for almost a decade and for the last three and a half as Marketing Director where she is responsible for a team of 35 design, marketing and brand professionals. Her role has a wide and interesting scope managing and implementing the product and marketing strategy globally for both the residential and commercial markets. Prior to that, she spent over a decade working for Midlands-based manufacturing brand, Aga Rangemaster, in marketing and brand management. She completed her degree in Marketing Management from the University of Derby where she also successfully attained her Chartered Institute of Marketing post-graduate diploma in Marketing and Management.

Mike Leonard is Visiting Professor, Manufacturing and the Built Environment, Birmingham City University (BCU), and has extensive senior leadership experience in building products manufacturing and housing. He is currently delivering primary research to support the transition to net zero, ensuring resilience in the built environment and frequently speaks at conferences and publishes material to shape future policy. A leader in the Birmingham City University "Centre for Future Homes" researching the Future Homes Standard through active Demonstrators, preventing overheating, enhancing indoor air quality, addressing the fire risk, reducing the use of single-life plastics, decarbonising the built environment and embracing the skills gap. In a period of unprecedented change, he believes that it is critical that we put customers at the heart of the journey and avoid unintended consequences.

Monica Mateo-Garcia is Senior Lecturer in Sustainable Built Environment and Lead of REFUoA13 at Birmingham City University. Architect by background, she has led and managed industry and publicly funded applied research projects related to zero-carbon homes, low-carbon refurbishment in buildings and healthy indoor environments. She is currently leading research in Future Homes Standard and post-occupancy evaluation. She co-leads the Centre for Future Homes at Birmingham City University.

Tony McNally is the Managing Director of Climate Change Solutions Ltd (est.2003). He jointly organised the first Midlands Environmental Business Conference NEC 1990 from which it was established and continues to date as the MEBC (Club). He was involved in organising the Pledge to the Planet and Tree of Life campaign, with John Talbot, David Middleton Jonathon Porritt, leading to and featuring in the UN Earth Summit Rio 1992. He is an Ambassador for the National Forest in the Midlands and co-founding detector HECE.

Julian Morgan is MD Founder and Technical Lead for KPM Marine and Scotseat KPM marine. He has an ONC in engineering, an Honours degree in Manufacturing from Brunel University (1987), an NSF scholarship in intelligent robotics and AI from URI/MIT (1985) and an MBA from Warwick Business (1989) where he specialised in Product development and future energy trends.

KPM Marine won the Queen's award for Innovation (2022), the SeaWork spirit of Innovation marine award three times for safety design and FSB international business of the year. He holds the world speed endurance record for 1, 2 and 3 hours S850 power boat, inspiring much of the design concepts used by the business. He is a Member of the Royal Institute of Naval Architects and a Fellow of the Lunar society. He also works with the West Midland Lieutenancy promoting the Kings award for Enterprise specialising in Sustainability and Innovation.

For over 30 years, he has specialised in the design and manufacture of safety critical products for the marine and automotive industries. He has worked for Phillips Research Laboratories medical division and consulted with organisations including Apple Computers, BAE Systems, Hewlett Packard and Psion to name a few in high technology and manufacturing.

Robyn Owen is Professor of Entrepreneurship and Sustainable Finance, Founder of GreenFin research cluster and Deputy Director of the Centre for Enterprise, Environment and Development Research (CEEDR), Middlesex University. Her research focus is green innovation finance and developing finance solutions for early-stage investment markets. She currently leads Middlesex University's Natural Environment Research Council Integrated Finance and Biodiversity research programme on SME Nature Positive Finance.

Rashmi Prakash is Experienced Educator with over 19 years of teaching prowess, catering to a diverse range of student-learners from ages 3 to 60. She equipped with a unique educational background – holding a Bachelor's in Accounting, MBA and a Masters in Interdisciplinary Studies focused on Education and Mathematics from UTD, Richardson, Texas. She recently earned a Doctorate in Educational Administration and Leadership Management from European International University, Paris.

Her journey involves a heartfelt commitment to community service, from constructing homes with Habitat for Humanity to supporting foster children, aiding animals at shelters and caring for seniors in old age homes. She is passionate about music, trekking and travel and totally invested in unearthing profound stories from history. She is an actively engaged educator imparting soft skills training to educational institutions and corporate sectors. Her notable achievements include earning award at Kalakari Film Festival for the best documentary on women empowerment & well-being, guiding a Special Education School to secure funds via the CSR Initiative at IIM/IIT Indore's i5 Summit and collaborating with India's Ministry of Women and Child Development for Professional Development initiatives for the field officers on site. She is always passionate about learning with avid learners, facilitating learning and nurturing a healthy mindset geared towards growth.

Vicky Pryce is Chief Economic Adviser at the Centre for Economics and Business Research (CEBR) and a Visiting Professor at BCU and King's College, London. She was previously Senior Managing Director at FTI Consulting, Director General for Economics at the Department for Business, Innovation and Skills (BIS) and Joint Head of the UK Government Economic Service. Before that she was Partner and Chief Economist at KPMG after senior economic positions in banking and the energy sector. She is a Fellow of the UK Academy of Social Sciences, a Fellow of the Society of Professional Economists, a Companion of the British Academy of Management, Chair of the Economic Advisory Council of the British Chambers of Commerce, and on the Advisory Group of the Better Statistics CIC. Her recent books include '*Greekonomics*: The Euro crisis and Why Politicians Don't Get It'; '*It's the Economy, Stupid*- Economics for Voters', with Ross and Urwin; '*Redesigning Manufacturing*' with Nielsen and Beverland and '*Women vs Capitalism*'.

Al Rainnie, Professor, has held Chairs at Monash, Leicester and Curtin Universities. He has researched in the area of work and employment for about 40 years and has published over 100 books, book chapters, journal articles and research reports. He was the founding Director of the Monash Institute for Regional Studies and Director of Research at both the Centre for Labour Market Studies at the University of Leicester and the Curtin Graduate School of Business in Perth, Western Australia. He has recently co-authored a report on skill and innovation commissioned by the Federal Chief Scientist for the Australian Council of Learned Academies.

Darryn Snell is an Associate Professor in the School of Management and Coordinator of the Work in Transition Research Group of the Business and Human Rights Centre and co-coordinator the Skills, Training and Industry Research Network at RMIT University, Melbourne. Forthcoming book Rainnie, A., Snell, D., & Dean, M. *Australia's regional and industrial future: Issues of militarization, manufacturing and climate change.* Taylor and Francis.

John Stott is a Chartered Member of the Energy Institute and worked in the electricity generation industry. He is very interested in finding ways of minimising climate change, and renewable energy is an important part of the solution.

He has invested in over 50 renewable energy projects and is well informed about renewable energy and, in particular, the technicalities of solar power. He has helped a community solar project with technical advice and helped a local business to purchase a solar power system. For 10 years, he promoted the low-carbon message by writing the green column in a local electronic newspaper.

Loukia G. Tsaprouni is a Professor in Biomedical Sciences with interests in the areas of Genomics and Epigenetics of common diseases, complex traits aiming at the discovery of molecular origins of human disease and the development of novel diagnostic and intervention strategies. She completed her PhD and Post-doctoral qualifications at Imperial College before joining the Wellcome Trust Sanger Institute as a Research Fellow. She joined Birmingham City University in 2017 as the School Research Director. Her research focuses on exploring epigenetic alterations and post-translational modifications implicated in respiratory diseases, with a specific emphasis on smoking- and vaping-related chronic obstructive pulmonary disease (COPD).

Foreword

As Chair of the Carbon Trust, a member of the UK Climate Change Committee since it was formed in 2008 and the UK's former Low Carbon Business Ambassador, I look back over the last 20 or so years of climate action in the UK with some satisfaction, given the progress in monitoring emissions, in establishing legally binding targets to reach both Net Zero by 2050 and in addressing biodiversity depletion through Net Gain. However, I am conscious of Lord Stern's warning that climate change is the greatest and widest-ranging market failure ever seen and a unique challenge for all our economies. And we have just experienced the hottest year on record, the 12 months up to May 2024, with global air temperatures 1.63° above pre-industrial levels. As I look ahead to the UK's Seventh Carbon Budget, which will set legal limits for net emissions of greenhouse gases in the period 2038–2042, I cannot help but be anxious about our current trajectory and the need for significant acceleration of action.

In 2023, wrong kind of records were broken – the highest global average temperatures, the hottest month on record and daily global temperatures briefly surpassing pre-industrial levels by more than 2 °C. Extreme weather events have become more frequent with consequences including forced migration and mass extinction. A recent survey of 10,000 young people conducted by universities across 10 countries showed that more than half of the respondents think humanity is doomed, three-quarters are frightened for their future and 4 out of 10 are reluctant to have children of their own. It is hard not to feel gloomy, but that won't help, we have to use this (almost literally) burning platform to motivate an urgent response.

The good news is that we can fix this, especially with the concerted efforts of global leadership and politicians working nationally and locally to deliver shared net zero goals. In the past, fossil fuels fuelled our progress, but at an increasing cost to our environment; we're now able to harness innovative technologies to power future progress through clean renewable energy. And whereas the Climate Change Committee previously highlighted that the costs of cutting greenhouse gas emissions by 80% by 2050 could reduce UK GDP by 1.5%, it's now considered that 100% emissions savings could have little impact on living standards and, indeed, could increase GDP through a growing green economy.

This book offers a lively and at times controversial commentary. Insightful analysis and a range of practical case studies demonstrate the ambition and commitment of many in business to reaching net zero and to passing on a more sustainable system to future generations.

Julia Elizabeth King,
Baroness Brown of Cambridge

Chapter 1

Introduction: What This Book Consists of

Alex de Ruyter[a], *Steven McCabe*[b] *and Beverley Nielsen*[c]

[a]*Birmingham City University, UK*
[b]*DoctorateHub, UK*
[c]*Centre for Brexit Studies, Birmingham City University*

Abstract

Climate change caused by an increase in greenhouse gas emissions poses a threat to species on earth. Such emissions have been caused by activities that have increased the rate at which greenhouse emissions have occurred due to the burning of fossil fuels and industrial processes in recent decades. Without urgent intervention, the ability of earth's citizens will be irrevocably altered. Hundreds of millions of people's lives will effectively become extremely challenging. Deaths due to starvation, lack of water, storms and flooding will increase. The magnitude of the crisis confronting humanity has resulted in means the formation of what's known as the 'Net Zero' target set by The Intergovernmental Panel on Climate Change (IPCC, 2024), a United Nations body consisting of global experts on climate change in 1994. This chapter explains why climate change has occurred, what its impact may be and how intervention by governments as well as all organisations and individuals catastrophe can be avoided. There is an overview of subsequent chapters contained in this book.

Keywords: Climate change; emissions; environmental threat; net zero; intervention; economic benefit

What's Causing Climate Change?

Climate change, defined by the United Nations Group (2024) for Climate Action as consisting of 'long-term shifts in temperatures and weather patterns', is almost universally acknowledged to be the result of human activity. In particular, the

Examining Net Zero: Creating Solutions for a Greener Society and Sustainable Economic Growth, 1–11
Copyright © 2025 by Alex de Ruyter, Steven McCabe and Beverley Nielsen
Published under exclusive licence by Emerald Publishing Limited
doi:10.1108/978-1-83608-574-420251001

burning of fossil fuels (coal, oil and gas) is the major reason for a noted increase in the average temperature of the earth following the industrial revolution which commenced, in Britain in the latter half of the 18th century, coal, a readily available resource, was used to heat water to produce steam. Producing steam provided a reliable supply of power to operate rapidly developing machines capable of producing goods at greater speed and reduced costs than hitherto possible. Mass production became the basis of the modern world we continue to enjoy over two and a half centuries later.

Burning non-renewable fossil fuels to produce energy, currently accounting for 80% of the world's requirements, and regarded as utterly essential to the effective functioning of every society has, in recent decades, contributed to an alarmingly rapid increase in what's are known as 'greenhouse' gases (Saplakoglu, 2019). Coal, oil and gas – created millions of years ago when dead plant matter was converted by heat and pressure – when burned produce over 75% of global emissions. Largely consisting of carbon dioxide (CO_2), representing around 90%, methane (CH_4) and nitrous oxide (N_2O) are also emitted by burning these fossil fuels. Notably, methane, produced by 'intensive' agricultural practices, waste management, energy use and biomass burning, though less prevalent than carbon dioxide, is 34 times more harmful.

Anyone who's been in a greenhouse when the sun shines will know it can be hot and uncomfortable. Unless cooler air is introduced, the heat will become increasingly oppressive. This is the effect increased greenhouse gas emissions are having on the earth. Heat from the sun is being trapped in the atmosphere. The result is global temperatures are increasing which disrupts the earth's complex interactive weather and ecosystems. As the earth becomes warmer, more water vapour is contained in the atmosphere. In turn, water vapour acts as a greenhouse gas creating a vicious circle by contributing to further warming.

The Impact of Climate Change

Though human beings are believed to have emerged around 800,000 years ago, the level of damage earth has suffered in the last 70 years is so great as to warrant an alternative era. What's known as the Anthropocene (human-centred) Epoch is characterised by the increase in greenhouse gases which, as we've experienced in the last 35–40 years, has resulted in extreme temperatures and weather patterns across the globe. Human activity in the Anthropocene Epoch, as well as increasing CO_2 levels to the highest level in 66 million years increased extinction rates, now running at well above the long-term average (Carrington, 2016). Levels of plastic and microplastic particles in waterways and the sea are 'now virtually ubiquitous' with attendant risks to long-term health (Carrington, 2016). The developing catastrophe that is climate crisis is cited as a major reason for a notable fall in oxygen levels in lakes across the world that's suffocating wildlife and creating a threat to drinking water supplies (Carrington, 2021).

The world's population has risen dramatically in the last 200 years from 1 billion to over 7.8 billion. As a direct consequence, there's been a corresponding rise in use of fossil fuel and consumption of the earth's resources. Growth in population, requiring prolific consumption of energy, food and a vast range of minerals essential in everything we do each day, is destructive to planet earth. Humanity's 'success' in survival and multiplication is, ironically, leading to the destruction of the only known planet in the universe capable of supporting life. Global warming, if allowed to continue unchecked, will make life considerably more difficult for many hundreds of millions of people who will be affected by rising temperature. Climate change will irrevocably alter ecosystems and natural habitats potentially affecting all life on earth.

Why Climate Change Poses Such an Existential Risk to Humanity

Earth is over 1°C warmer than it was prior to the industrial revolution and warmer than at any point in the last 100,000 years. If the production of greenhouse gases does not decline, the rise in the average temperature of earth will continue. What this will mean is a destabilisation of the delicate balance of the interconnected ecosystems that operate on earth IPCC (2014). Any alteration in one system influences all others. The consequence of climate change manifested by rising temperature will be a combination of outcomes potentially devastating to hundreds of millions of earth's citizens as the environment becomes increasingly inhospitable (Carrington, 2019). As we've seen in recent years, wildfires are more prevalent and spread more rapidly. Temperatures in the Arctic have warmed at least twice as fast as the global average meaning ice caps may eventually disappear (Milman, 2021).

Rising temperature increases heat-related illnesses and makes working outdoors more difficult. An increase in the incidence of 'wet bulb thermometer' readings has been experienced in many parts of the world. When a wet bulb reaches 35°C, humans are no longer able to cool themselves by sweating. Death from overheating can occur within hours, even among the fittest, but especially among the old, infirm and disabled. Currently, extreme temperatures are estimated to result in 5 million premature deaths each year. According to the United Nations, 'environmental factors' account for the deaths of some 13 million people annually. Altered weather will mean more diseases, place even greater strain on health care systems that, for the world's poorest, are inadequate at present. However, things could get a great deal worse.

A study led by the London School of Hygiene & Tropical Medicine (LSHTM) and published in The Lancet suggests that should the emission of greenhouse gases continue to rise at current rates, the effect on global temperatures could lengthen transmission seasons by more than a month for malaria and four months for dengue over the next 50 years (Zhao et al., 2021). Without action to reduce greenhouse gas emissions, the research carried out by LSHTM predicts up to 8 billion people could be at risk of malaria and dengue fever by 2080 (Dehghan, 2021). According to the United Nations, weather-related events have resulted in over 23 million people being forced to move every year (Dehghan, 2021). Such migration will only increase should the earth's average temperature continue to rise. Climate change will increase hunger and result in nutrition among the world's poorest, already insufficient, being undermined. Fisheries, crops and livestock are likely to be less productive. Increased temperature will reduce land available for grass to feed livestock and reduce yields of crops vital for food. Raised temperatures make external work, especially in agriculture, especially challenging.

It's not only humanity that will suffer from the impact of climate change. The rate of decline of species is one thousand times greater than at any time in recorded human history. It's believed that as many as a million species could become extinct within coming decades. The threat of forest fires, storms and more extreme weather coupled with a rise in invasive pests and disease will intensify such decline. Any increase in the average temperature of the earth will, according to the United Nations (Dehghan, 2021), cause a number of other devastatingly dire consequences.

Earth's weather patterns have altered in recent years and severe 'topical' storms have become more commonplace in many regions. Raised temperatures allow more moisture to be held in the atmosphere leading to extreme rainfall and flooding. Oceans that have become warmer increase the likelihood of intense dangerous cyclones, hurricanes and typhoons that may be potentially fatal and deadly to those affected. As oceans become warmer because of global warming and combined with melting ice from polar caps, their volume increases leading to sea levels rising. This means that many millions are forced inland. As well as the trauma induced, additional stress is placed on communities that must provide accommodation, feed them and provide water that may already be scarce. Moreover, as ocean absorbs greater levels of carbon dioxide, they will become more acidic which will threaten marine life and coral reefs.

However, while increased temperature and raised moisture in the atmosphere may cause storms and flooding in some parts of the world, water becomes scarcer elsewhere. Water shortages in already water-stressed regions result in a higher risk of drought. Water is, of course, essential to life and causes people to migrate with inevitable disruption (Harvey, 2020). Drought undermines crops yields leading to food shortages and starvation. It also causes ecological drought and increased vulnerability of ecosystems. Destructive sand and dust storms shift billions of tons of sand resulting in expanding deserts with reduced potential to cultivate land for food.

The IPCC and Emergence of Net Zero

The IPCC, formed in 1988 by the United Nations (UN) and the World Meteorological Organization, and currently consisting of 195 member countries, is a direct response to climate change. As its own website explains, it was 'created to provide policymakers with regular scientific assessments on climate change, its implications and potential future risks, as well as to put forward adaptation and mitigation options' (IPCC, 2021). Consisting of thousands of scientific experts from across the globe, its explicit purpose is reviewing all published research examining the likely consequences of 'human-induced climate change'.

Based on what amounts to an extremely rigorous review of extant research, the IPCC produces, every five or six years, 'Assessment Reports'. These reports contain a 'Summary for Policymakers' intended to guide thinking and, crucially, recommend collaborative and coordinated policymaking by all governments. To this end, and coinciding with the Assessment Reports, a Conference of Parties (COP) is held attended by delegates from participating countries that have signed the UN Framework Convention on Climate Change, an international treaty agreed in 1994. Significantly, in 1994, the IPCC identified immediate actions essential to arrest the rate at which emissions, particularly carbon, are produced.

As the IPCC reasoned, concerted and coordinated action by all countries needed to be implemented to reduce greenhouse gases required to limit the increase in average global temperature level to 1.5°C. This proclamation is standardly referred to as 'Net Zero' developed by the IPCC in Paris, the Paris Agreement. Critically, the IPCC (2024) has stressed with unerring consistency ever since – and with increasing alarm at the need for urgent action – cutting carbon emissions and other emissions is essential to ensure the earth's atmosphere can be protected and, eventually, allowed to recover. What was critical, the IPCC stresses, is that 'in order to avert the worst impacts of climate change and preserve a livable [sic] planet' a reduction of greenhouse gases, particularly carbon, must occur. Accordingly, the proclamation made in 1994 was that action to reduce greenhouse gas emissions would achieve a 45% reduction by 2030 and become net zero by 2050. As Oxford University's *Net Zero Climate* (2024) website explains, 'To "go net zero" is to reduce greenhouse gas emissions and/or to ensure that any ongoing emissions are balanced by removals'.

How Can Net Zero Be Achieved?

Faced with impending catastrophe, action is urgently required. It's utterly imperative that radical reduction in emissions of greenhouse gases occurs with as much urgency as possible. Though action by every individual is to be applauded, unless matched by collective endeavour across the globe, halting climate change will not succeed. Importantly, though CO_2 is emitted in every part of the globe, some countries produce a greater proportion, relative to population than others. Collective action is essential. Though not easy or cheap, the scale of the catastrophe means immediate intervention is not optional. Delay will merely ensure the likelihood of even greater catastrophe more likely. All governments, organisations, businesses and every individual must play their part.

In terms of activities and processes undertaken in any country, there will, of course, be variations in levels of contribution to greenhouse emissions. PCC (2024) data collected in 2010 present averages for global emission of greenhouse gas for six key activities:

- Electricity and heat production (25%)
- Agriculture, forestry and other land use (24%)
- Industry (21%)
- Transportation (14%)
- Other energy (10%)
- Buildings (6%)

The largest contributory sector, electricity and heat production, should be achieved using alternative sources which, as much as possible, are free from emission. The development of renewable energy by harnessing power from wind, solar and waves allows 'green' energy to be produced. Renewable energy is also possible through, for example, biomethane gas produced from organic waste.

Agriculture, forestry and other land use, producing 24% of greenhouse gases, marginally less than electricity and heat production, must be carried out using methods of production that do not rely on the use of nitrogen-based fertilisers. Reducing consumption of meat and dairy products, which require vast amounts of land to feed livestock, is regarded as essential.

Industry, which significantly contributes to emissions, must aim to produce, using green energy, goods that are free from waste. This requires all of those engaged in industry (manufacturing) across the globe, in all parts of the supply chain, to redesign processes utilised. Such redesign will include the extraction of raw materials and minerals through distribution and delivery. It is incumbent on consumers to demand goods made using green production methods. This is the central tenet of the 'Circular Economy'.

Transportation, accounting for 14% of global greenhouse gas emissions, includes all aspects of the way in which everything, both people and goods, moves from one place to another. It is estimated that 90% of energy used for transport regularly used, which includes cars, motorcycles, vans, lorries, buses, trains, trains, airplanes and shipping, currently uses fossil fuel. As such, this sector represents an immediate opportunity for change. International trade and tourism is currently carried out with an environmental cost. Collective action is needed to find ways to reduce the harm to the planet caused by transportation.

Other energy, representing 10% of the greenhouse gases emitted, though not directly associated with electricity or heat production, incorporates fuel extraction, refining, processing and transportation. Coordinated effort by all countries should seek ways to reduce the emission of greenhouse gases resulting from these activities.

Finally, buildings, essential for shelter and activities conducted under cover, account for 6% of global greenhouse gas emissions through the burning of energy, that is natural gas, to produce heat as well from cooking. Achieving a reduction in greenhouse gas emissions from newly constructed buildings through improved design and alternative fuels is already underway. However, in any mature economy, such as the United Kingdom, the overwhelming majority of the 'built environment' already exists. Consequently, an ambitious programme known as 'retrofitting' and adaption is urgently required.

An Economic and Societal Rationale for Action

According to the UN Environmental Programme (2021), a green economy is defined as a 'low carbon, resource efficient and socially inclusive'. Such an economy is based on the desire to achieve growth in employment, as well as income, through investment by the public and public sectors. It is explicitly based on ensuring future investment in all aspects of economic activity is achieved without any further increase in greenhouse gases and with, correspondingly, reduced waste in activities carried out. Additionally, decreased pollution, enhanced energy and resource efficiency, as well as prevention of degradation of biodiversity and ecosystems, are regarded as fundamental to achieving a green economy that will ensure the planet supports life for future generations. A greener economy achieved through a range of initiatives including Net Zero is not intended to replace sustainable development but, rather, to deliberately focus on the economic opportunities possible. As such there are three strands, 'Policy Mainstreaming', 'Economic Instruments' and 'Capability Building'.

At the time of writing, a report describes research showing that economic damage from climate change is calculated to be six times greater than previously believed (Bilal & Känzigcal, 2024). Crucially, the report's authors state every additional 1°C average increase in global temperature leads to a 12% decline in world gross domestic product. Given the collective output of all countries, gross domestic product (GDP), is estimated by the International Monetary Fund (2024) and published in its 2023 World Economic Outlook report, to be $105 trillion, this represents a phenomenal benefit that would accrue by proactively dealing with, and investing in, climate change.

A report published in *Nature* on the economic impact of climate change, 'The economic commitment of climate change', provides equally stark warning of the consequences of failure to act by governments in dealing with the threat (Kotz et al., 2024). Based on research carried out, the authors assert that average incomes across the globe will decrease by almost a 5th within the next 26 years compared with the level they'd reach in the absence of the effects of global warming. Though this report suggests that should net zero fall in line with accepted targets, the decline will be around 20%; if emissions continue to rise without action, the fall in income could be as high as 60% by 2010.

According to the OECD (Organisation for Economic Co-operation and Development) in *Towards green growth, A summary for policy makers* (2011), any framework to achieve a greener economy should be explicitly based on growth strategies that include two key objectives. Firstly, improving resource management and boosting productivity. Secondly, encouraging economic activity to take place where it is of best advantage to society over the long term. These should be achieved through innovation and collaboration. This will require economic growth which will be based on institutional and individual investment decisions informed by the desire to produce a future that is green. As OECD recognise, 'Advanced, emerging, and developing countries face different challenges and opportunities in greening growth, as will countries with differing economic and political circumstances'. Creating a greener future, in which Net Zero is fundamental to success, is only possible by the combination of policies implemented by government and incentives (financial or otherwise) provided to motivate a change in attitudes and behaviour.

Critically, as the OECD stresses, there is a clear connection between increased GDP used to measure economic progress generally enhancing the importance of 'natural assets to wealth, health and wellbeing'. Growth must be beneficial to the health, wealth and welfare of all citizens in all parts of the world.

This must include those who, traditionally, suffer the greatest inequality and poverty in, most especially, developing countries. The location of natural assets, largely in low-income countries, means that growth policies must be cognisant of the need to reduce local citizens' vulnerability to environmental risks and to increase their economic prospects.

Consistent with the attainment of Millennium Development Goals, the OECD contends a number of vital outputs should be achieved. This would include far effective and efficient methods of use of water, transport and, of course, production of energy which, as well as vastly improve poor health experienced by the world's poorest resulting from environmental degradation, would improve productivity and reduce the causes of climate change. In summary, implementing initiatives as part of Net Zero in pursuit of improving the earth's environment will immeasurably improve the quality of life for current and future citizens of this planet.

An Overview of This Book

Examining Net Zero – Creating Solutions for a Greener Society and Sustainable Economic Growth consists of three parts:

- Part One – Challenges/Opportunities and Issues Overview
- Part Two – Empirical Examples of Practice (Case Studies)
- Part Three – Moving Forward

The five chapters presented in the first part of this book provide a brief overview of theoretical perspectives of net zero. So, in Chapter 2, 'Circularity in Producing a Green Economy', BCU's Dr Steven McCabe examines what circularity means and what's required to successfully achieve the significant social, economic and environmental benefits offered by implementing net zero. In Chapter 3, Al Rainnie from Unisa/Curtin University and Darryn Snell of RMIT University in 'The Australian Net Zero Economy Authority: Limits and Possibilities' explore how the transition from an economy reliant on carbon is being achieved through the activities of a newly created Net Zero Authority. In particular, they describe the tensions that transition has engendered and how the aspiration of achieving Net Zero is being achieved. In Chapter 4, Dr Rashmi Prakash from Bengaluru City University, 'The Challenge of Net Zero: Evidence from the Indian Automotive Sector', explains the methods being used to achieve how net zero in the automobile industry in India. Emissions and the benefits of cleaner air for citizens are examined in Chapter 5, 'Unveiling the Interplay of Air Pollution, Genetics and Epigenetics' by BCU's Professor Loukia G. Tsaprouni. In an extensive examination of air quality based on her research, Loukia describes how by the advancement of preventive and therapeutic strategies, it's entirely possible to protect public health and achieve the promotion of sustainable environmental practices aligned with the objective of net zero. Finally, the last chapter in Part One, BCU's Professor Alex de Ruyter, Michael Butler and Rowan Crozier in 'Towards Net Zero: A Practical Transformative Leadership

Agenda for Manufacturers and SMEs', examines how a just transition to Net Zero is not only entirely sensible to ensure society does not suffer, particularly the poorest, but is economically logical.

Part Two of this book presents a number of case studies containing empirical examples of how initiatives actively implementing net zero are successfully being achieved. In Chapter 7, Carl Arntzen, CEO of Bosch Thermotechnology Ltd, in his chapter, 'The Green Economy – A Just Transition and Where to Go From Here – How to Decarbonise the Way We Heat Our Homes and Buildings in the UK?', explains what this involves using a diverse range of practical solutions including the manufacture and installation of heat networks, hydrogen boilers and in particular hybrids (boiler and heat pump). In Chapter 8, 'Schneider Electric Case Study', Sharon Cronin, Head of Marketing Communications, UK & Ireland, Schneider Electric, presents the approaches being used to achieve net zero by this company. In particular, she provides an overview of Schneider Electric's 'Zero Carbon Project', part of its commitment to minimising 'operational carbon emissions' by 2025. In Chapter 9, Holly Johnson, Marketing Director, Amtico, presents 'Amtico's Net Zero Journey So Far' in which she explains how a brand leader in luxury vinyl tiles (LVT) has developed a strategy that will enable this company to work towards net zero carbon emissions by 2040. Julian Morgan, Managing Director, KPM Marine Ltd in Chapter 10, 'KPM Marine Green Manufacturing for COP28', shows how a manufacturer producing essential services and refuelling for catamarans servicing wind turbines has created 10 design protocols reducing environmental emissions and planetary impact. As he explains, such protocols have delivered competitive advantage and lifetime energy savings for clients.

In Chapter 11, 'Tyseley Energy Park, East Birmingham, West Midlands UK', David Horsfall, Director of Property and Sustainability, Tyseley Energy Park, has actively worked with the University of Birmingham and Birmingham City Council in implementing clean energy innovations through new technologies. Using a range of currently active projects, David shows how collaborative partnerships have delivered sustainable solutions in the quest to achieve net zero. The theme of how cleaner energy can be produced and used is continued in Chapter 12 'The Role for Community Energy in the British Energy Mix' in which John Stott, Chair; Tony McNally, Director, Heart of England Community Energy (HECE) and as well as Jake Burnyeat, CEO of Communities for Renewables, describe how this is being successfully pursued by the HECE. In the concluding chapter of Part Three, Chapter 13, Tom Bedford and Kate Copeland-Rhodes of The Globe Group CIC have written about the 'Staffordshire and Stoke-on-Trent COP2024: A Celebration of the Possible'. Tom and Kate present their passionately held belief that there are seven key steps to enable businesses, stakeholders, funding organisations and local communities to operate effectively in the attainment of radically enhanced sustainability and net zero.

The final part of this book 'Moving Forward' includes five chapters describing what is needed to achieve action that is critical to ensuring the existential threat posed by climate change is avoided through successful implementation of net zero strategies. In Chapter 14, 'The Economic and Political Wisdom of Achieving Net

Zero', eminent economist and advisor Vicky Pryce with Steven McCabe consider the challenges for government in dedicating resources – most especially considerable amounts of money to achieve net zero and the dilemma this creates for political parties wishing to attract support from voters. In Chapter 15, 'Transporting Nations to Net Zero', BCU's Beverley Nielsen, an associate professor, explores ways in which there's potential for an holistic and circular approach to adopt through measuring embodied carbon, mineral and resource utilisation in transport production and use rather than emissions at point of use. How housing and accommodation, a significant contributor to carbon emissions, are examined in Chapter 16, 'An Evidence Based Pathway to Net Zero Ready Homes' by Mike Leonard and Monica Mateo-Garcia from BCU's Centre for Future Homes. As they describe, based on research carried out into ongoing housing developments, climate change through proactive carbon reduction is eminently achievable. In Chapter 17, 'Delivering Net Zero and Beyond: Addressing the Financing Challenges for UK Green SME Transition' coauthored by Professor Robyn Owen and Dr Amy Burnett from the Centre for Enterprise, Environment and Development Research (CEEDR) at Middlesex University Business School, research, they demonstrate that transition to a greener economy based on net zero requires a coherent public policy and regulation aligned to the knowledge of environmental risks and opportunities presented. They present a useable framework to achieve finance for net zero. Finally, Conall Boyle, who is a retired academic, in Chapter 18, 'The Elephant in the Net-Zero Room: Why Advocating Benign Population Reduction is Taboo', presents a provocative polemic to justify his belief that net zero requires population reduction as part of a coordinated global approach. In Chapter 19, 'Concluding Thoughts: An Impassioned Call for Intervention to Produce a Greener, Cleaner Future', we the editors of this book, posit what we believe is urgently requited to avert the rapidly developing existential crisis for humanity that is climate change.

References

Bilal, A., & Känzigcal, D. R. (2024). *The macroeconomic impact of climate change: Global vs. the macroeconomic impact of climate change: Global vs. local* [National Bureau of Economic Research, working paper 32450, May 2924]. https://www.nber.org/papers/w32450?utm_campaign=ntwh&utm_medium=email&utm_source=ntwg1

Carrington, D. (2016, August 29). The Anthropocene epoch: Scientists declare dawn of human-influenced age. *Guardian*. Retrieved May 10, 2016, from https://www.theguardian.com/environment/2016/aug/29/declare-anthropocene-epoch-experts-urge-geological-congress-human-impact-earth

Carrington, D. (2019, June 3). Climate crisis seriously damaging human health, report finds. *Guardian*. Retrieved May 17, 2019, from https://www.theguardian.com/environment/2019/jun/03/climate-crisis-seriously-damaging-human-health-report-finds

Carrington, D. (2021, June 2). Climate crisis is suffocating the world's lakes, study finds. *Guardian*. Retrieved May 16, 2021, from https://www.theguardian.com/environment/2021/jun/02/climate-crisis-is-suffocating-the-worlds-lakes-study-finds

Dehghan, S. K. (2021, July 8). Climate crisis 'may put 8bn at risk of malaria and dengue'. *Guardian*. Retrieved May 8, 2021, from https://www.theguardian.com/global-development/2021/jul/08/climate-crisis-may-put-8bn-at-risk-of-malaria-and-dengue

Harvey, F. (2020, November 26). More than 3 billion people affected by water shortages, data shows. *Guardian*. Retrieved May 12, 2020, from https://www.theguardian.com/environment/2020/nov/26/more-than-3-billion-people-affected-by-water-shortages-data-shows

International Monetary Fund. (2024). *GDP, current prices*. International Monetary Fund Website. Retrieved May 8, 2024, from https://www.imf.org/external/datamapper/NGDPD@WEO/OEMDC/ADVEC/WEOWORLD

Intergovernmental Panel on Climate Change. (2024). *Intergovernmental panel on climate change*. Intergovernmental Panel on Climate Change Website. Retrieved May 10, 2024, from https://www.ipcc.ch/

IPCC. (2014). *Climate change 2014 mitigation of climate change working group III contribution to the fifth assessment report of the intergovernmental panel on climate change*. Cambridge University Press.

IPCC. (2021, August 9). *Climate change widespread, rapid, and intensifying – IPCC*. Intergovernmental Panel on Climate Change Press Release. Retrieved May 4, 2021, from https://www.ipcc.ch/2021/08/09/ar6-wg1-20210809-pr/

IPCC. (2024). *For a liveable climate: Net-zero commitments must be backed by credible action*. The Intergovernmental Panel on Climate Change Website. Retrieved May 10, 2024, from https://www.un.org/en/climatechange/net-zero-coalition

Kotz, M., Levermann, A., & Wenz, L. (2024, May 17). The economic commitment of climate change. *Nature*, *628*, 551–557. https://doi.org/10.1038/s41586-024-07219-0

Milman, O. (2021, May 5). Global heating pace risks 'unstoppable' sea level rise as Antarctic ice sheet melts. *Guardian*. Retrieved May 6, 2121, from https://www.theguardian.com/environment/2021/may/05/antarctica-ice-sheet-melting-global-heating-sea-level-rise-study

Net Zero Climate. (2024, May 11). *What is net zero*. Net Zero Climate Website. https://netzeroclimate.org/what-is-net-zero-2/

OECD. (2011). *Towards green growth, A summary for policy makers*. OEDC.

Saplakoglu, Y. (2019, May, 14). *Carbon dioxide soars to record-breaking levels not seen in at least 800,000 years*. LiveScience Website. Retrieved May 12, 2019, from https://www.livescience.com/65469-highest-carbon-dioxide-levels.html

UN Environmental Programme. (2021, May 12). *Green economy*. https://www.unep.org/regions/asia-and-pacific/regional-initiatives/supporting-resource-efficiency/green-economy

United Nations. (2024, May 10). *What is climate change?* United Nations – Climate Action Website. https://www.un.org/en/climatechange/what-is-climate-change

Zhao, Q., Guo, Y., Ye, T., Gasparrini, A., Tong, S., Overcenco, A., Urban, A., Schneider, A., Entezari, A., Vicedo-Cabrera, A. M., Zanobetti, A., Analitis, A., Zeka, A., Tobias, A., Nunes, B., Alahmad, B., Armstrong, B., Forsberg, B., Pan, S.-C., … Li, S. (2021, July 1). Global, regional, and national burden of mortality associated with non-optimal ambient temperatures from 2000 to 2019: A three-stage modelling study. *The Lancet Planetary Health*, *5*(7), E415–E425. Retrieved May 13, 2021, from https://www.thelancet.com/journals/lanplh/article/PIIS2542-5196(21)00081-4/fulltext#articleInformation

Part One

Challenges/Opportunities and Issues: Overview

Chapter 2

Circularity in Producing a Green Economy

Steven McCabe

DoctorateHub, UK

Abstract

Using the earth's limited resources is essential as an urgent element in dealing with the existential crisis confronting humanity as a consequence of climate change. Circularity is based on production and society adopting a radically different approach to the way raw materials are used to produce goods developed societies consume. Primarily, the use of the earth's resources (raw materials) must be more carefully – and considerately –achieved in recognition of the impact that profligate exploitation has had in terms of pollution and disregard for the environment. Production systems should be designed to ensure that waste is vastly reduced and, eventually, eliminated. Crucially, goods should be designed to be used by consumers for as long as possible. Goods should incorporate the ability to repair them and, critically, that at the end of their effective life components can be recycled.

Moving from the traditional 'linear' model – 'take, make, throw away' – to one that is circular is essential as part of the quest to reduce carbon emissions. In explaining the historical development of the basis of why circularity is not only essential to protecting the planet from climate change, but also economically logical, this chapter explained that its theoretical foundations were first proposed in economist Kenneth Boulding who, in his 1966 essay, 'The Economics of the Coming Spaceship Earth'. Boulding's provocative arguments have been developed into the extensive advice and guidance presented by the Ellen Macarthur Foundation and summarised in this chapter. The circular economy will potentially achieve very significant social, economic and environmental benefits.

Keywords: Waste; production; consumption; recycling; reuse; environment; design innovation; economic wisdom

---

Examining Net Zero: Creating Solutions for a Greener Society and Sustainable Economic Growth, 15–24
Copyright © 2025 by Steven McCabe
Published under exclusive licence by Emerald Publishing Limited
doi:10.1108/978-1-83608-574-420251002

Introduction – The Origins of Circularity

In their overview of what the circular economy consists of, Ekins et al. (2019) explain that its theoretical and conceptual foundations are a good deal longer than many believe (p. 4). What's referred to as 'industrial ecology' became common within economic geography in the 1940s in analysing the consideration of where industries should be located to ensure efficiency of resources used and avoidance of waste. In the decades following the end of the Second World War in 1945, when recovery, reconstruction and increased production and consumption were regarded as priorities, reusing and recycling may have seemed relatively unimportant. However, the experiences of war, when production was dedicated to a constant supply of armaments and associated paraphernalia of engaging in conflict, meaning a shortage of many basic goods, had required millions to 'make do and mend'. Carrying out repairs was emphasised as part of a national collective effort. Basic foods which were rationed were used sparingly and waste was fed to animals destined to end up being eaten.

War followed by austerity arguably created the basis of a consumer society which, reliant on mass production to achieve economies of scale, eventually led to the acceptability of what's become a 'throwaway culture'. After all, in a culture which values novelty and newness, why would you bother to continue to possess and maintain devices, cars, clothes and all of the other things we're exhorted to purchase to improve our lives when replacements are freely available and, moreover, are considered vital to economic growth? The problem is that this leads to phenomenal waste both in terms of the goods themselves and, all too frequently, any packaging they come in. Though there were those who questioned the wisdom of such a system, their protestations were largely ignored.

One such voice was economist Kenneth Boulding who, in his 1966 essay, 'The Economics of the Coming Spaceship Earth', a text that, as Ekins et al. contend, is 'truly astonishing' in the fact that such a short paper was able to present the majority of principles upon which contemporary thinking concerning circular economy is based (Ekins et al., 2019, p. 5). However, and though its impact was not immediate, Boulding's analysis is now recognised as having identified the criticality of needing to consider preserving the earth's limited resources, what's now commonly called 'sustainability'. What Boulding posited was that in the future, the earth would become a closed economy – what he referred allegorically to as a 'spaceman' economy – in which 'without unlimited reservoirs of anything, either for extraction or for pollution [...] man must find his place in a cyclical ecological system', which is capable of continuous reproduction of material form even though it cannot escape having inputs of energy.

Humanity, he argued, would be forced to acknowledge that expending earth's precious resources and energy on the assumption they were limitless was erroneous. Rather, he stressed, governments should organise economies to ensure productive capability was radically altered. Crucially, Boulding inferred, such a shift would correspondingly require a better understanding of the consequences of individual behaviour by our use of everything we consume. In effect, what he believed almost 60 years ago is that collective behaviour would be vital to future generations' survival. Though Boulding didn't employ the expression, what he advocated, the importance of inculcating more circularity in our economies, is now accepted as financially logical as well as highly ethical in saving resources and the future of this planet.

From the 'Oil Shock' to 'Ellen's Way'

If the post-war period was a time of expansion and plenty, based on voracious consumption of the earth's resources, fuelled by cheap fossil fuels, the 1970s and the unforeseen spike in the costs of energy, notably of oil, caused profound shock. Though oil was primarily used as the basis of the fuel used to run power stations and the fuel used to run our cars, the oil shock of the 1970s demonstrated that the rapid increase in the price of such a commodity, not only caused economic turmoil and a rise in unemployment, it meant that governments and individuals recognised that using it more sparingly had a distinct advantage. Increasing awareness that oil is crucial in a vast array of taken-for-granted products and materials in developed countries added to the sense that change was needed.

In 1977, Walter Stahel, an architect and economist, made a submission to the European Commission with his coauthor Genevieve Ready, *The Potential for Substituting Manpower for Energy*, based on research examining whether the economy could operate in loops. In particular, Stahel, based on his work at the Product Life Institute in Geneva, sought to make a connection between the reuse of materials, reducing waste and positive outcomes for the economy including additional jobs and cost savings. Stahel believed that such an economy, one that we'd now describe as 'circular', is best considered a framework: as a generic notion, the circular economy draws on several more specific approaches that gravitate around a set of basic principles.

Stahel and Reday-Mulvey (1981) drew upon a developing zeitgeist in presenting an alternative model in which posited advantage could be gained through extending the life of products through better design to allow repair rather than continuing to exploit limited resources to make new ones. Crucially, their model incorporated recycling as integral to slowing down the requirement of resources and reducing waste. Stahel developed his ideas in a prize-winning essay in 1982, 'Product-Life Factor', in which he which referred to a 'spiral-loop system' emphasising the reduction of use of both limited resources and energy flow and environmental deterioration in a way that does not restrict the economic growth or social and technical progress. Employing the word spiral by Stahel, it may be argued, alluded to what became the circular economy. Indeed, it's notable that Stahel went on to author *The Circular Economy, A User's Guide* in 2019.

However, it's not until 1990 that Pearce and Turner in their text *Economics of Natural Resources and the Environment* between pages 35 and 41 more precisely define how circularity of use of resources can benefit the economy. Undoubtedly, appreciation of the importance of developing circularity within an economy really took hold in 2010 when Ellen MacArthur, who'd achieved fame for sailing around the word solo in a record-breaking time in 2005, created a partnership with the World economic Forum and including a number of large companies, that led to the Ellen MacArthur Foundation (EMF, 2024b, 2024c) which, as its website proudly proclaims, is a:

> [...] charity committed to creating a circular economy, which is designed to eliminate waste and pollution, circulate products and materials (at their highest value), and regenerate nature. It's an economic system that delivers better outcomes for people, and the environment.

In publishing three volumes of *Towards the Circular Economy* in 2013, the EMF ensured that the concepts first outlined almost half a century before gained prominence and recognition in the wider public and, more crucially, among governments. Each of the three documents provided a level of practical advice and guidance in what would be needed to achieve the aspiration of circularity:

- *Volume one: an economic and business rationale for an accelerated transition* including product case studies and economy-wide analysis explained the significant benefits for all economies through considerable 'net materials cost savings' and intended to engender 'economic activity in the areas of product development, remanufacturing, and refurbishment'
- *Volume two: opportunities for the consumer goods sector* focusing on how individual and collective behaviour can be improved by informed choices and increased demand for products (as well as food) incorporating recycled material that may be repaired and, of course, can easily be recycled rather than being sent for municipal waste
- *Volume three: accelerating the scale-up across global supply chains* which aims to reconcile the goal of scaling a circular model with the reality of a global economy through encouragement of recycling, reuse and remanufacture by complex multi-tier supply chains

Since 2013, EMF has striven to provide a wealth of material explicitly intended to encourage every person and organisation – whether in business or not-for-profit – to do everything possible to achieve the goal of greater circularity in our economies. As the next section will explain, the fundamental principles of circularity are simple. We should all strive to be part of it for the benefit of the planet but, equally, because it makes economic sense. As the EMF contends, making the adjustments will achieve a 'systemic shift that builds long-term resilience, generates business and economic opportunities, and provides environmental and societal benefits'.

There are, according to the EMF, three strands that are essential to produce a circular economy:

- Eliminate waste and pollution
- Circulate products and materials
- Regenerate nature

The first of these emphasises designing out the 'negative impacts of economic activity' that result in harm to health and natural systems by vastly reducing the release of greenhouse gases and other hazardous substances. Vitally, all pollution should be, wherever possible, eliminated though, of course, steady-state reduction may be the means to this end. The second is based on the preservation of 'value in the form of energy, labour, and materials'. Indeed, as the EMF contends, it's crucial to design for 'durability, reuse, remanufacturing, and recycling to keep products, components, and materials circulating in the economy (Ellen Macarthur Foundation, 2024a). Equally, it's stressed, circular systems embrace the incorporation of bio-based materials. This is entirely sympathetic with the guidance that it's using resources that cannot be renewed should be discontinued. Moreover, the EMF recommends, valuable nutrients should be returned to the soil to support regeneration as well as using renewable energy rather than, as has been the case since the beginning of the Industrial Revolution, fossil fuels.

What the Circular Economy Consists of?

Elimination of waste as well as pollution is one of the three tenets of a circular economy; the other two be to circulate products and materials and to regenerate nature. However, as data for waste disposal by local authorities in England, collected by DEFRA (Department for Environment, Food and Rural Affairs), show, recycling only accounts for just over 45% of waste. This is not a peculiarly British problem. The World Bank (2021) estimate that globally 2.01 billion tonnes of 'municipal solid waste' is produced annually. By the middle of this century, they estimate, this figure will increase to 3.4 billion tonnes, double the projected rate of population growth in the next three decades. Significantly, World Bank stress, high income countries though representing around 16% of the population of earth, produce 683 million tonnes, just over a third of global waste. Waste disproportionately affects the poorest in the world, especially when waste is sent to developing countries as an alternative to dealing with it where it's created.

Underpinning improvement through circularity requires two vital changes. Firstly, it's critical we use fewer resources through greater re-use and recycling which should logically mean less energy is required. Secondly, correspondingly, any energy generated in the future should be achieved through renewable (green) sources of power. In creating greater circularity, it's useful to distinguish between technical and biological cycles. Technical cycles are those in which the design of every aspect of what we consume is considered and sustainably enhanced. Many items are designed with very limited use before failure and obsolescence. Redesign should produce items in which use is longer, repair more economic and, where necessary, materials and components can be easily recycled. Packaging should be designed to reduce waste.

Biological cycles are concerned with the way in which materials are created through biological processes. Ideally, after use, they should be capable of being returned to their natural state by composting or anaerobic digestion. Food could be designed to ensure any waste can create energy or used to regenerate living systems intended to create food in the future. For example, in Singapore airline, food waste is converted into insect protein meal (Byrne, 2021). This equally applies to, for instance, timber which will eventually rot away and contribute to growth elsewhere.

Anne Velenturf, Research Impact Fellow in Circular Economy, and Phil Purnell, Professor of Materials and Structures, University of Leeds, in The Conversation, examine what a sustainable circular economy consists of (2020). As they assert, it's estimated that '99%' of what we buy is discarded within six months of purchasing. Velenturf and Purnell stress the importance of three objectives in successful implementation of a circular economy: Closing loops with energy from waste; Increased recycling; greater sustainability. Reducing burning of waste, though producing electricity, and greater recycling is crucial they argue. However, they acknowledge, recycling depends on the material.

Textiles, especially clothing, is a particular issue of concern. Given our propensity to buy clothes, on average a UK citizen purchases 26.7 kg each year (the highest in Europe), the fact a very large proportion is quickly discarded and incinerated rather than being recycled, reduced to 11% in 2019 from 17% in 2010, represents a lost opportunity. Velenturf and Purnell stress the absolute importance of ensuring textiles, as with all other products, are made of materials produced in a sustainable way and including as large a proportion as possible that's recycled. Though considered difficult, they point out that without action, even addressing plastic packaging recycling targets, 'more than 50 new recycling plants would be needed in England'.

In creating greater sustainability, the third of Velenturf and Purnell's objectives, there are 'opportunities' for new models of working to emerge. In seeking alternatives to the linear economy, they suggest, we'll embrace new ways of thinking about what's important. For instance, we will be more inclined to lease clothes rather than buying and disposing (Nazir, 2020). Additionally, there's likely to be the production of bespoke items people actually want and place greater value on, rather than the mass consumption of things we don't really need. There is a good argument that the impetus of urgent change will be the catalysts for innovation and creativity.

Critically, moving to a circular economy will create new jobs. Velenturf and Purnell contend that four times as many jobs are possible based on reuse, leasing, repair and remanufacturing than in waste treatment, disposal and recycling. This, they believe, offers the potential to 'generate local economic activity, helping to strengthen relations within communities'. A recent report by Green New Deal UK, a non-profit group, asserts that with sufficient stimulus intended to produce the sort of greener economy aligning with the principles of circularity, more than 1.2 million jobs could be created within two years and more than 2.7 million within a decade (Greene, 2021).

Economic Benefits of the Circular Economy

The Ellen MacArthur Foundation (2024b, 2024c) is widely acknowledged as the authoritative source of information and its website 'The circular economy in detail' is highly recommended.

Economic growth, it's stressed by EMF, is 'a combination of increased revenues from emerging circular activities, and lower cost of production through the more productive utilisation of inputs'. In effect, the logic of doing the same – potentially more – with reduced input is compelling. As commodity, prices have risen in recent years, particularly as a consequence of the pandemic and increased international tension and conflict, costs are passed on. There is economic logic, therefore, in seeking better ways to produce, use and, of course, recycle. As EMF, point out, enhanced design suggests considerable financial benefits are available:

- For complex 'medium-lived products' including the cellular phones and washing machines in the European Union (EU), 'the annual net-material cost savings opportunity' could be as much as $630 billion.
- For 'fast moving consumer goods', which would include the common household cleaning products we use on a daily basis, there's a 'material cost-saving potential' of up to $700 billion globally.

Crucially, as jobs are inevitably lost in traditional industries as a direct consequence of the quest to achieve a greener and cleaner economy, circularity has the potential to create alternative employment as detailed above. As EMF asserts, such jobs are likely to be created within all sectors of industry and particularly in small and medium enterprises 'through increased innovation and entrepreneurship, and a new service-based economy'. Moreover, as EMF passionately contends:

> The aspiration to replace linear products and systems with circular ones is an enormous creative opportunity. The benefits of a more innovative economy include higher rates of technological development, improved materials, labour, energy efficiency, and more profit opportunities for companies.

Achieving this objective will produce immense benefits through judicious design that explicitly avoids waste and pollution caused by carbon and other emissions equally harmful to the environment. As society collectively and consciously considers the way in it consumes products and food there's a direct payoff. As an example, the EMF describes, 'analysis indicates that the UK could reduce greenhouse gas emissions by 7.4 million tonnes per annum by keeping organic waste out of landfills'. Additionally, the reduction in chemical use to produce food, especially nitrogen, that's extremely harmful to the soil, could produce significant gain:

> Land degradation costs an estimated USD 40 billion annually worldwide, without taking into account the hidden costs of increased fertiliser use, loss of biodiversity, and unique landscapes. Higher land productivity, less waste in the food value chain, and the return of nutrients to the soil will enhance the value of land and soil as assets. Returning biological material back into the soil

> will reduce the need for replenishment with additional nutrients. Recovering all of the nitrogen, phosphorus, and potassium from food, animal and human waste streams globally could contribute nearly 2.7 times the nutrients contained within the volumes of chemical fertiliser currently used. This is the circular economy principle of regeneration at work.

Included on the EMF's website, an array of other benefits to both individuals and business is available. For the former, the following benefits are listed:

- Increased disposable income through reduced costs due to cheaper goods and services as well as a reduction in unproductive time as workers have access to enhanced and efficient transport and technology allows increased remote working
- Improved customer choice and access to bespoke products and services
- Reduced obsolescence and improved levels of service due to greater excellence
- Health and wellbeing is enhanced by healthier foods produced without pesticides and better air quality as a direct result of lower pollution and emissions

With respect to health, EMF claims it's estimated that a circular economy for food, 'catalysed by cities', has, by 2050, the potential to annually save 290,000 lives that would otherwise be lost because of outdoor air pollution.

For companies, the EMF website lists the following advantages by being part of the circular economy requiring a new approach to business based on alternative models, including a greater propensity to rent or lease their products and focused on long-term relationships in which there's an intense focus on the continual search for an opportunity to improve quality and service throughout the supply chain:

1. Collection and reverse logistics companies that support end-of-use products being reintroduced into the system
2. Product remarketers and sales platforms that facilitate longer use or higher utilisation of products
3. Parts and component remanufacturing, and product refurbishment offering specialised knowledge and services
4. Improved customer interaction and loyalty

Conclusion

Crucially, the sort of change needed to produce a circular economy will not be achieved without a radical shift in collective attitude and concomitant behaviour. In short, every individual must play their part. Government must take the lead in explaining what needs to be done and assisting in facilitating change and making finance available. In short, unless everything changes, there's a risk of failure. Vitally, all parts of society must interactively operate as a system based on the urgency of the existential challenge caused by the threat of climate change, but which seeks to inculcate innovation and creativity in search of solutions. We are as, as history attests, only limited by the constraints we place upon our imagination and desire to ensure earth continues to be the 'goldilocks' planet that so successfully sustains life.

References

Boulding, K. (1966). The economics of the coming spaceship earth. In H. Jarrett (Ed.), *Environmental quality in a growing economy, resources for the future* (pp. 3–14). John Hopkins University Press.

Byrne, J. (2021). *Singapore partnership looks to convert airline food waste into insect protein mail.* https://www.feednavigator.com/Article/2021/05/05/Converting-airline-food-waste-into-insect-protein-meal?utm_source=copyright&utm_medium=OnSite&utm_campaign=copyright

Ekins, P., Domenech, T., Drummond, P., Bleischwitz, R., Hughes, N., & Lotti, L. (2019). *The circular economy: What, why, how and where* [Background paper for an OECD/EC workshop on 5 July 2019 within the workshop series "Managing environmental and energy transitions for regions and cities"]. Paris.

Ellen MacArthur Foundation. (2013a). *Towards the circular economy, Volume 1: An economic and business rationale for an accelerated transition.* Ellen MacArthur Foundation, Isle of Wight, UK.

Ellen MacArthur Foundation. (2013b). *Towards the circular economy, Volume 2: Opportunities for the consumer goods sector.* Ellen MacArthur Foundation, Isle of Wight, UK.

Ellen MacArthur Foundation. (2013c). *Towards the circular economy, Volume 3: Accelerating the scale-up across global supply chains.* Ellen MacArthur Foundation, Isle of Wight, UK.

Ellen MacArthur Foundation. (2024a, October). *Circulate products and materials, Ellen MacArthur Foundation website.* https://www.ellenmacarthurfoundation.org/circulate-products-and-materials

Ellen MacArthur Foundation. (2024b, April 15). *Ellen MacArthur Foundation.* Ellen MacArthur Foundation website. https://www.ellenmacarthurfoundation.org/topics/circular-economy-introduction/overview

Ellen MacArthur Foundation. (2024c, April 26). *The circular economy in detail.* Ellen MacArthur Foundation website. https://www.ellenmacarthurfoundation.org/the-circular-economy-in-detail-deep-dive

Greene, T. (2021, April 20). Green stimulus plan could create 1.2m UK jobs in two years, research finds. *Guardian.* Retrieved May 8, 2021, from https://www.theguardian.com/environment/2021/apr/20/green-stimulus-plan-uk-jobs-green-new-deal

Nazir, S. (2020). *Primark joins United Nations' Fashion Charter to tackle supply chain emissions.* Retail Gazette. https://www.retailgazette.co.uk/blog/2020/10/primark-joins-united-nations-fashion-charter-to-tackle-supply-chain-emissions/

Pearce, D., & Turner, R. (1990). *Economics of natural resources and the environment.* Harvester, Wheatsheaf, Hemel Hempstead.

Reday-Mulvey, G., & Stahel, W. R. (1977, July 30). *The potential for substituting manpower for energy: Final report.* Geneva Research Centre, Commission of the European Communities, Switzerland.

Stahel, W. (2019). *The circular economy: A user's guide.* Routledge.

Stahel, W., & Reday-Mulvey, G. (1981). *Jobs for tomorrow: The potential for substituting manpower for energy*. Vantage Press.
Velenturf, A., & Purnell, P. (2020, April 6). What a sustainable circular economy would look like. *The Conversation*. https://theconversation.com/what-a-sustainable-circular-economy-would-look-like-133808
World Bank. (2021, April 7). *Trends in Solid Waste Management*. World Bank Website. https://datatopics.worldbank.org/what-a-waste/trends_in_solid_waste_management.html#:~:text=The%20world%20generates%202.01%20billion,from%200.11%20to%204.54%20kilograms

Chapter 3

The Australian Net Zero Economy Authority: Limits and Possibilities

Al Rainnie[a] *and Darryn Snell*[b]

[a]*University of South Australia, Australia*
[b]*RMIT University, Australia*

Abstract

Australia has struggled to escape its particular variant of the 'resource curse'. It has also had important economic, social and political ramifications. In this chapter, the authors consider how the recently announced Net Zero Economy Authority in Australia is progressing, but crucially, the authors want to put these developments into a broader context within which it exists. This context includes Australia's 'resource' curse challenges but also the emergence of a new state capitalism (Alami, 2023; Schindler et al., 2023) that has included a Future Made in Australia policy that involves advancing a renewable energy industry but also a militarisation of industry associated with the trilateral security partnership between Australia, the UK and USA (AUKUS). The authors begin by looking at the continued tensions between Australia's fossil-fuel dependence and efforts to combat climate change and lower greenhouse gas (GHG) emissions. The authors then track developments in the proposed structure and activity of the Net Zero Authority itself. Finally, the authors will review these developments in the light of the 'resource curse' and broader Australian government policy such as the AUKUS alliance and the 'Made in Australia' policy.

Keywords: Australia; resource management; renewable energy; zero emissions; fossil-fuel dependency

Examining Net Zero: Creating Solutions for a Greener Society and Sustainable Economic Growth, 25–34
Copyright © 2025 by Al Rainnie and Darryn Snell
Published under exclusive licence by Emerald Publishing Limited
doi:10.1108/978-1-83608-574-420251003

Introduction

> Australia's reputation in the clean energy sector is complex.
>
> We are global leaders in the R&D of certain technologies, particularly around solar photovoltaic technologies. Australia has one of the best renewable energy resources in the world and land mass. Yet much of our contribution to date is bound up in our reputation as a 'dig and ship' economy, where our mineral resources are mined and then sent offshore for processing and manufacturing, before returning as consumer goods. (SGS, 2024, p. 4)

Australia has struggled to escape its particular variant of the 'resource curse' which is also a curse of carbon 'lock-in' (Unruh, 2000). Australia is the world's sixth largest producer of fossil-fuel energy and the fourth largest fossil-fuel exporter, after Russia, the USA and Saudi Arabia. The total value of Australia's energy exports in the 2019–2020 financial year was $115.5 billion with exports of liquefied natural gas accounting for $47.5 billion, metallurgical coal $34.2 billion and thermal coal $20.4 billion (Burke, 2023). Any transition away from fossil fuels has significant economic, social and political ramifications. Nonetheless, the transition to a lower carbon economy is underway in Australia as it is in many other advanced economies. After decades of political 'climate wars' (Crowley, 2021) between Australia's major political parties, the recently elected federal Albanese Labor Government has prioritised the urgent transition to renewable energy and set a national goal of a 43% reduction of GHG emission by 2030 against 2005 levels and net zero by 2050 (Australian Government Department of Industry, Science, Energy and Resources, 2022). In response to the concerns of union, workers and communities in fossil-fuel-dependent regions, the Albanese Government announced the establishment of a Net Zero Authority to help manage the polarising and difficult transition process. This initiative has been considered historically important locally but also internationally with the Global Union Industriall (2023) declaring that the 'Net Zero Authority in Australia to ensure just transition for workers'. It is clear that just transition principles have informed aspects of the Net Zero Authority but as Rainnie and Snell (2024a, 2024b) have argued the original, radical, worker-centred focus of just transition has been largely replaced with regional diversification prescriptions and jobs and skills assistance programmes. In this chapter, we consider how the Net Zero Economy Authority in Australia is progressing, but crucially, we want to put these developments into a broader context within which it exists. This context includes Australia's 'resource' curse challenges but also the emergence of a new state capitalism (Alami, 2023; Schindler et al., 2023) that has included a Future Made in Australia policy that includes advancing a renewable energy industry but also a militarisation of industry associated with the trilateral security partnership between Australia, the UK and USA.

We begin by looking at the continued tensions between Australia's fossil-fuel dependence and efforts to combat climate change and lower GHG emissions. We then track developments in the proposed structure and activity of the Net Zero Authority itself. Finally, we will review these developments in the light of the 'resource curse' and broader Australian government policy such as the AUKUS alliance and the 'Made in Australia' policy.

Australia's Role in Contributing to and Combatting Climate Change

It is generally recognised that Australia has significant decarbonisation challenges. Among OECD countries, Australia ranks first as the highest emitter per capita (SBS, 2023). Australia's contribution to global carbon emissions as opposed to 'territorial' emissions is also significant due to its role as the world's third largest fossil-fuel exporter. According to the estimates of the University of New South Wales (UNSW) Australian Climate Accountability Project, the carbon emissions from Australian fossil-fuel exports are almost triple the emissions from the domestic use of fossil fuels (UNSW, 2024). The historical importance of fossil fuels for the local economy but also export earnings has meant national conversations about tackling carbon emissions have been dominated by economic, social and political concerns rather than environmental ones. When announcing emissions reduction targets, the Albanese Government looked to make Australia a renewable energy superpower which would bring investment, create jobs and regenerate regions. This was the vision put forward by Australian economist Ross Garnaut in Superpower Transformation (Garnaut, 2022). Not only was Australia well positioned to take advantage of available renewable energy resources (solar, wind, geothermal) but had vast critical mineral resources (lithium, magnesium, copper) needed for battery manufacturing and other renewable energy products. In other words, Australia was well positioned in a decarbonised world and the Albanese Government sought to accelerate the energy transition. As outlined by Greg Combet, retiring Chair of the Net Zero Agency (precursor of the Authority), in April 2024, the Albanese Government had a number of achievements in moving the Australian economy down this path including, inter alia:

- $20 billion to build the poles and wires required for Rewiring the Nation
- $2 billion programme to kick start green hydrogen production
- Multi-million dollar programme to develop critical minerals
- New vehicle efficiency standards

The $1 billion Solar Sunshot programme (Australian Renewable Energy Agency, 2024) which aimed to build up Australia's solar photovoltaic (PV) manufacturing capabilities could be added to this list along with several other State and Territory funded renewable energy projects.

The story, however, is far more complicated, and there are plenty of reasons to be sceptical about this Renewable Superpower Transformation. At the end of 2023, for example, The Climate Action Tracker released its report card on Australia. The Overview reported that:

> Despite a fresh start after a decade of inertia, the Australian government's promise to 'take the country forward on climate action' has failed to deliver. The government's overreliance on reported emissions reductions in the land sector obscures its continuous support for fossil fuels and lack of action beyond policies addressing emissions from large industrial facilities and the power sector.

The Overview concluded that:

> The government continues to endorse the expansion of the fossil fuel industry by supporting new carbon-intensive offshore gas field developments, permitting fracking, approving new coal mines, and creating regulations for CO2 sequestration beyond its borders, in contradiction with its stated climate goals.

Furthermore, the Government's Carbon Credit Scheme, described as a core pillar of Australia's climate change strategy, has been dismissed by the Australia Institute as a recipe for climate disaster. The same organisation reported that although some progress had been made in scaling back the huge subsidies that the fossil-fuel industry received under the previous Coalition government, total assistance to fossil-fuel producers and major users from all government departments only declined from \$11.6 billion in 2021–22 to \$11.1 billion in 2022–23. Total assistance still represents \$21,143 for every minute of the day (Campbell et al., 2023). Beyond conventional climate change threats, it has also been reported that Australia may be emitting more than twice the level of methane missions than are reported under the national reporting framework (Rae, 2024).

For those convinced by carbon 'lock-in' and 'resource curse' arguments, there continues to be plenty of evidence to support their claims. In May 2024, the Albanese government released its Future Gas Industry policy which included gas as part of Australia's energy mix until at least 2050. Under the policy, new gas fields will be opened to address local supply problems and support continued gas exports. This policy includes the controversial Scarborough-Pluto gas project in Western Australia which is predicted to emit almost 1.4 billion tonnes of greenhouse gases over its lifetime, currently more than three times Australia's annual emissions (Hare, 2024). These developments lend weight to those who have been arguing for many years regarding the 'capture' of organisations and institutions within and beyond state and federal government by the fossil-fuel industry (see Kurnelovs, 2024; Wilkinson, 2020) or at the bare minimum a case of 'having your cake and eating it to' (Hepburn, 2024). It is within this context that the Net Zero Authority needs to be located.

The Net Zero Economy Authority

Early Moves

In our earlier articles (Rainnie & Snell, 2024a, 2024b), we argued that, generally, unions supported the proposal for a Net Zero Authority as its aims were closely aligned with what they had been calling for over many years. However, there were concerns raised about the proposed authority's relationship to local communities and workers and the voice they would be provided in relation to the activities of the authority. The National Secretary of the Australian Manufacturing Workers Union (AMWU), for example, raised concerns that local communities and workers would be marginalised in the planning of community futures. The success of the Net Zero Authority, they argued, depended on worker and community buy-in:

> Without workers being consulted in its development, the authority will not be capable of delivering what it needs to – the confidence of workers that it will deliver justice for them in this transition. (Steve Murphy, National Secretary, AMWU cited in ABC, 2022)

In May 2023, the Albanese government announced a legislated Net Zero Authority to provide support for communities during the transition to a low carbon emissions economy. Former Labor minister Greg Combet was announced as the Chair of the new Agency (precursor to the Authority) with an advisory board that included academics, energy regulators, union leaders such as Tony Maher from the Mining and Energy Union, and Michelle O'Neill President of Australian Council of Trade Unions (ACTU), as well as executives from Rio Tinto Australia and BHP. The announcement gained broad support from, inter alia, the ACTU, Local Government, the Climate Council and the Australian Financial Review but how the Authority would carry out its activities remained unclear. As Rainnie and Snell (2024a, 2024b) noted regarding the early plans for the Authority, there were no details on the authority would work with other state authorities who were effectively performing these functions already or what role local government would perform. How local workers and communities would be empowered or disempower by the Authority's actions remained unanswered. In March 2024, the Albanese Government introduced legislation to establish the Net Zero Economy Authority. Under the proposed legislation, the Authority would be an independent statutory body housed in the Prime Minister's portfolio, whose responsibilities were to:

- Facilitate public and private sector participation and investment in emissions reduction and net zero transformation projects across Australia, including working with established investment funds.
- Support workers in emissions-intensive industries to access new employment, or acquire skills to improve their employment prospects, including an Energy Industry Jobs Plan to help workers in closing coal-fired power stations transition to new jobs.

- Support communities – including First Nations communities – to participate in, and benefit from, the economic shift to net zero emissions.
- Share information about Australia's transformation to net zero economy, educating communities and supporting social licence for the transition.
- Promote coordination and consistency across government policies and programmes (PMC, 2024).

According to Greg Combet's National Press Club speech, the aim of the Authority would be, inter alia, to help Australia become a renewable energy superpower with renewable energy generation being the key to Australia's economic transformation (Combet, 2024). However, questions still remained about what would be included in the Authority's 'net zero transformation projects'. Would new gas projects, or fossil-fuel projects that included carbon capture storage or even nuclear be considered alongside renewable energy projects? Certainly, some members of the advisory board are likely to be open to considering projects which are not specifically renewable energy projects including the Mining and Energy Union, BHP and Rio Tinto. How much attention would be given to supporting the resource industry in 'pivoting' to critical minerals was also an open question. In many ways, however, the aims of Authority aligned with Mazzucato's Mission Economy (2021) driven policy making with the government derisking private sector investment and promoting local small- and medium-sized enterprises. The approach would become clearer as it meshed with the emerging vision of the Governments' 'Future Made in Australia' strategy.

'Future Made in Australia' – From Solar Panels to Nuclear Submarines

At much the same time as the Net Zero Economy Authority was being set up, the Government announced its 'Future Made in Australia' initiative. Prime Minister Albanese argued that a 'Future Made in Australia' policy was needed in order to respond to the changing geo-political and post-COVID-19 environment. A 'Future Made in Australia' policy would 'mark out national interest' and 'boost productivity, improve competition and secure future prosperity' (Albanese, 2024). A key pillar of the Future Made in Australia would be the $15 billion National Reconstruction Fund which would 'support projects that create secure well-paid jobs, drive regional development, and invest in our national sovereign capability, broadening and diversifying Australia's economy' (Albanese, 2024). This announcement provided further evidence of a shift away from the market-oriented neo-liberal policies of the past three decades towards a new state capitalism (Alami, 2023; Schindler et al., 2023).

The reaction from the right-wing press, orthodox economists and the impeccably neo-liberal Productivity Commission were predictable. Claims these policies would distort markets with the government 'picking winners' and crowd out private investment were duly trotted out (for a critique of the 'orthodox' response, see Dodgson, 2024; Jericho, 2024). However, generally, reaction was more muted. Partially, this was due to a growing recognition that Australia had to do something to respond to development elsewhere which was threatening Australia's struggling manufacturing base and chances of developing a renewable energy industry. The USA's Inflation Reduction Act, which provided significant government incentives for renewable energy firms to set up in the USA, is one of the major threats. Treasurer Jim Chalmers, just before launching the 2024 Federal Budget, gave a speech noting that the nation faced challenges 'vastly different' from a decade ago. These included 'heightened geostrategic competition, an international system under continuous pressure, demographic change, greater risk of major shocks to supply chains, and a restructuring of global trade from the net zero transformation' (Hannan, 2024). He went on to argue that the government would use five tests to determine where and how it acts under the Future Made in Australia Policy:

> First, is the industry one where we can be competitive, and more productive?
>
> Second, does it contribute to an orderly path to net zero?
>
> Third, can it build the capabilities of our people and especially our regions?
>
> Fourth, will it improve Australia's national security and economic resilience?
>
> And fifth, does it recognise the key role of the private sector and deliver genuine value for money for government? (Chalmers, 2024).

The Future Made in Australia Act, however, was not solely about becoming a 'Renewable Energy Superpower'. Two streams of projects were identified for government assistance:

> A national interest stream, where domestic sovereign capability is needed to protect national security interests or ensure the economy is resilient enough to shocks. This would focus on only the most critical risks, not all risks.
>
> A net zero transformation stream, where industries support decarbonisation, and there is a reasonable prospect of a comparative advantage (Chalmers, 2024).

In this regard, the Future Made in Australia policy and the re-emergence of industrial policy in Australia more generally reflects a response to the polycrisis involving a militarisation of industrial policy, on the one hand, closely tied to AUKUS and the emergence of a New Cold War and decarbonisation and renewable energy superpower ambitions on the other (Dean et al., 2021, 2024; Rainnie & Dean, 2021; Rainnie & Snell, 2024a, 2024b forthcoming). It is within this context and that of the 'resources curse' that the Net Zero Economy Authority's concerns and operations will be shaped. The $1 billion proposed support for developing an Australian PV sector is dwarfed both by US investment underpinned by Inflation Reduction Act funding and is miniscule when compared to the $368 billion to be spent on developing nuclear submarine capabilities with AUKUS partners (Rainnie, 2023). What is also becoming increasingly clear is that the Net Zero Economy Authority will be driven by a 'Jobs and Growth' mantra in which investment in renewables will be encouraged and supported by the state but driven by (multinational) private sector organisations. The rationale behind these interventions will be as much driven by defence/strategic considerations as environmental concern.

Conclusion

The Net Zero Economy Authority is considered an important development within and outside Australia for managing energy transitions. What it actually does and how it comes to operate is still subject to considerable debate. The opposition parties are still considering if not it they will fully endorse the formal establishment of a Net Zero Economy Authority. The conservative Coalition Parties looks certain not to support it on the ground that it takes a 'Canberra-centric' approach to industrial transformation and runs the risk of duplicating existing government functions (How, 2024). The Green Party and Independents are likely to provide the necessary support required for the Albanese Government to get the Net Zero Economy Authority bill passed in Parliament, so it can begin officially operating. However, it will need plans, powers and budget to deliver a Net Zero Economy (Denniss et al., 2024) and in reality would need to prevent the development of new fossil-fuel projects. Given the Albanese Government remains committed to supporting new fossil-fuel projects, it is clear the contradictions inherent in Australia's 'carbon lock-in' and 'quarry mentality' will remain significant challenges for the Net Zero Economy Authority realising something that resembles a Net Zero Economy.

References

Alami, I. (2023). Ten theses on the new state capitalism and its futures. *Environment and Planning A: Economy and Space*, *55*(3), 76–79.

Albanese, A. (2024, April 11). *A future made in Australia*. Queensland Media Club. https://pm.gov.au/media/future-made-in-australia

Australian Government Department of Industry, Science, Energy and Resources. (2022). *Australia's nationally determined contribution communication 2022*. Australian Government. https://unfccc.int/sites/default/files/NDC/2022-06/Australias%20NDC%20June%202022%20Update%20%283%29.pdf

Australian Renewable Energy Agency. (2024). *Solar Sunshot*. https://arena.gov.au/funding/solar-sunshot/

Burke, P. J. (2023). On the way out: Government revenues from fossil fuels in Australia. *The Australian Journal of Agricultural and Resource Economics*, *67*(1), 1–17.

Campbell, R., Morison, L., Verstegen, P., Harrington, M., Adhikari, A., Scicuina, K., Simpson, E., & Anderson, L. (2023). *Fossil fuel subsidies in Australia 2023*. The Australia Institute.

Chalmers, J. (2024, May 1). *Address to the Lowy Institute*. Sydney. https://ministers.treasury.gov.au/ministers/jim-chalmers-2022/speeches/address-lowy-institute-sydney

Combet, G. (2024, April 2). *Address to National Press Club*. https://www.pmc.gov.au/news/address-national-press-club

Crowley, K. (2021). Fighting the future: The politics of climate policy failure in Australia (2015–2020). *WIREs Climate Change*, *12*, e725. https://doi.org/10.1002/wcc.725

Dean, M., Rainnie, A., Stanford, J., & Nahum, D. (2021). Industrial policy making after covid-19: Manufacturing innovation and sustainability. *Economic and Labour Relations Review*, *32*(2), 283–303.

Dean, M., Snell, D., & Rainnie, A. (2024, forthcoming) i5.0 and the future of work in manufacturing. In H. Pitts et al. (Eds.), *Routledge handbook for the future of work*. Routledge.

Denniss, R., Hemming, P., Gottschalk, A., & Ryan, M. (2024). *No jobs on a dead planet*. The Australia Institute.

Dodgson, M. (2024). *The productivity commission is well past its sell by date*. Acton Institute. https://www.actoninstitute.au/post/the-productivity-commission-is-past-its-sell-by-date

Garnaut, R. (Ed.). (2022). *The superpower transformation*. LaTrobe University Press.

Hannan, P. (2024). Labor to fast track foreign investment to help fund future industrial policy. *Guardian*.

Hare, B. (2024, June 3). The ultrapolluting Scarborough-Pluto project could blow through Labours climate target. *The Conversation*.

Hepburn, S. (2024, May 13). Australia can have a future for the gas industry, or meet its climate commitments – But not both. *The Conversation*.

How, B. (2024, May 14). *Coalition opposes Net Zero Economy Authority*. Innovation Australia. https://www.innovationaus.com/coalition-opposes-net-zero-economy-authority/?utm_medium=email&utm_campaign=Newsletter%201317%20-%2014%20May%202024&utm_content=Newsletter%201317%20-%2014%20May%202024+CID_dfe43ed4d3328ba60bc0a0c744a83716&utm_source=Email%20marketing%20software&utm_term=Coalition%20opposes%20Net%20Zero%20Economy%20Authority&utm_term=Coalition%20opposes%20Net%20Zero%20Economy%20Authority

Industriall. (2023). *Net Zero authority in Australia to ensure just transition for workers*. https://www.industriall-union.org/net-zero-authority-in-australia-to-ensure-just-transition-for-workers

Jericho, G. (2024). Funding Australia's renewable transition isn't 'picking winners'. *Guardian*.

Kurnelovs, R. (2024). *Slick: Australia's toxic relationship with Big Oil*. University of Queensland Press.

Mazzucato, M. (2021). *Mission economy : A moonshot guide to changing capitalism*. Allen Lane.

Mccafery, L. (2024, May 7). PM to announce funding for 'a new era of mineral exploration'. *News.com.au*.

Rae, M. (2024). Credibility up in smoke on 'astounding' methane results. *PerthNow*.

Rainnie, A. (2023). AUKUS and jobs. *Journal of Australian Political Economy*, *92*, 217–223.

Rainnie, A., & Dean, M. (2021). Post Covid-19 policy responses to climate change: Beyond capitalism?. *Labour & Industry*, *31*(4), 366–386. doi.org/10.1080/10301763.2021.1979448

Rainnie, A., & Snell, D. (2024a). Just transition in Australia – Depoliticization? *Contemporary Social Science*, *19*(1–3), 21–40.

Rainnie, A., & Snell, D. (2024b). Renewable energy and the promise of jobs, regional regeneration and first nations opportunities. *Labour & Industry, 33*(4), 403–421. doi.org/10.1080/10301763.2023.2289097

SBS. (2023). *How Australia compares to the rest of the world on CO2 emissions*. https://www.sbs.com.au/news/article/interactive-how-australia-compares-to-the-rest-of-the-world-on-co2-emissions/7oooxwnnm

Schindler, S., Alami, I., & Jepson, N. (2023). Goodbye Washington confusion, hello Wall Street Consensus: Contemporary state capitalism and the spatialisation of industrial strategy. *New Political Economy, 28*(2), 223–240.

SGS. (2024). *Towards a renewable energy superpower. Report prepared for Climate Action Network Australia and the AMWU*. SGS Economics & Planning/UTS Institute for Sustainable Futures.

Toscano, N., & Johanson, S. (2023, February 21). BHP set to sell more Australian coal mines as profit falls. *Sydney Morning Herald*.

Unruh, G. (2000). Understanding carbon lock-in. *Energy Policy, 28*(12), 817–830.

UNSW. (2024). *Australian climate accountability project*. https://www.humanrights.unsw.edu.au/research/australian-climate-accountability-project

Wilkinson, M. (2020). *The Carbon Club*. Allen & Unwin.

Chapter 4

The Challenge of Net Zero: Evidence from the Indian Automotive Sector

Rashmi Prakash

Bengaluru City University, India

Abstract

This chapter examines the challenges facing the Indian automotive industry in the pursuit of Net Zero. India is a major producer of passenger vehicles but traditionally has focussed on two-wheeled vehicles. However, Indian automotive manufacturers such as Tata and Maruti have established a presence internationally and India has become an FDI hub for global automotive MNCs keen to exploit its low production costs and large domestic market. The chapter commences with a brief overview of the Indian automotive sector. This is then followed by two mini case studies of Tata Motors and Maruti Suzuki that highlight practical measures that both companies have undertaken to promote Net Zero. Subsequently, the prognosis for electric vehicle (EV) uptake and associated regulatory issues in India are considered.

Keywords: Net Zero; India; automotive transition; case study; sustainability

Introduction

As businesses face up to the challenge of meeting Net Zero and transitioning away from fossil fuel reliance, the automotive sector as a key polluting industry must now transition towards zero-carbon technologies. For the most part, this transition has meant that the automotive industry has embraced EVs, demonstrating a clear commitment to environmentally friendly logistics practices.

Examining Net Zero: Creating Solutions for a Greener Society and Sustainable Economic Growth, 35–41
Copyright © 2025 by Rashmi Prakash
Published under exclusive licence by Emerald Publishing Limited
doi:10.1108/978-1-83608-574-420251004

By actively listening to customer needs and aligning with responsible consumers who prioritise environmental protection, the sector aims to navigate the path towards sustainability (Turner, 2019).

India is a key manufacturer of passenger vehicles (particularly two-wheeled vehicles) and, by 2022, had become the fourth-largest producer of cars in the world (OICA, 2023). In 1947, India gained independence, leading to the establishment of an automotive component manufacturing industry. The Ambassador, a model by Hindustan Motors, dominated Indian roads for the next two decades, alongside models from 'competitor' firms such as HM, Mahindra and Mahindra, Premier, and Ashok Leyland (Black et al., 2020). However, by the 1980s, Maruti Udyog Limited emerged as a strong competitor. During the late 1990s, open economy policies welcomed foreign parties, with Suzuki and Maruti forming a joint venture that soon came to dominate market share (Black et al., 2020). Simultaneously, the Indian government introduced mandatory emission standards known as 'Bharat Stage', aligning with strict European standards. These guidelines were enforced in major cities to reduce vehicle pollution. India maintains its position as one of the most densely populated regions globally and evidently caters to one of the largest markets not only in production but also in utilisation of vehicles.

As India enters a new century, technological advancements and heightened awareness have prompted the governing bodies to introduce various regulations and incentive schemes aimed at promoting sustainability within the automotive sector. This initiative made by Government of India (GOI) was aimed to strengthen India's automotive position globally. Recently though, the GOI has introduced schemes to boost manufacturing, infrastructure, and the adoption of electric and hybrid vehicles, whilst also encouraging circularity within the industry. As EVs have gained prominence, research and development efforts are expected to focus on improving battery technology. Innovations in materials, charging speed, and energy density are bound to drive the EV revolution. Lithium-ion batteries are crucial for EVs and renewable energy storage. As such, considerable efforts are being undertaken across countries to explore alternatives to lithium, such as solid-state batteries, to enhance safety, longevity, and sustainability (Ma et al., 2021). In a similar fashion, a reliance on rare earth raw materials has also spurred efforts to increase the recycling of battery components in the pursuit of a Circular Economy (see also McCabe in this volume).

In the material that follows, case studies of Tata Motors and Maruti Suzuki are provided in terms of their experience of transition to EV before a risk analysis of the sector is conducted. The chapter concludes with some recommendations for policy and practice.

Case Study Analysis

Tata Motors and Maruti Suzuki

Tata Motors has designed a few parameters that go on to define the sustainable measures that are being taken to ensure the consumers' expectations. First is that of Driving Net Zero: A target set for 2040 for Passenger-Vehicles Business and

2045 for Commercial Vehicle Business to achieve Net-Zero Emissions. With the help of science, the company is also looking forward to attain intermediate goals via focusing on science-based targets. In addition, Tata has also implemented measures to promote a Circular Economy within its production processes. For example, the company has committed to establishing responsible use of fresh water that is invested towards gaining water neutrality by 2030, disposal of waste and zero waste to landfill.

Tata is also seeking to promote conservation of natural resources and Biodiversity. It has been successful in creating water-body-based ecosystems around its establishments. These ecosystems support a rich variety of flora and fauna. Tata Motors strives to take on this initiative above and beyond its present state, using science to take on the challenge to propagate transformation (TataMotors, 2023).

Maruti Suzuki, in its 61-year journey, has evolved its mission to align with changing times. From the moment it introduced the iconic Maruti 800 in 1983, the company has spearheaded a revolution of change in the Indian automotive landscape. Driven by innovation and a commitment to excellence, Maruti Suzuki doesn't merely build cars; it strives to craft experiences for Indian roads. Recently, Maruti Suzuki made a significant alteration to its mission statement. The term 'Consumer' was replaced by 'Customer'. This change reflects the company's realisation that it needs to actively listen to and serve the requirements of the end-user. By making a notable change to 'Customer', Maruti Suzuki accentuates its sheer power to adapt and grow with the changing times to deliver value to every end-user choosing to drive their vehicles[1] (Maruti Suzuki, Sustainability Report – Corporate Environmental Report, 2023).

This shift at Maruti Suzuki has not been just about semantics; it's also about recognising the power of understanding and meeting the needs of each customer. With operations in various countries including India, Maruti Suzuki aims to invest time and efforts at the grassroots level in each community to understand their requirements. This initiative enables the company to embrace change and adaptability geared towards achieving success. In this context, the company also seeks to promote 'Sustainable Mobility'. Maruti Suzuki also seeks to craft experiences that matter. As the company moves forward, it aims to achieve carbon neutrality through electrification efforts. However, this step is not limited to EVs alone, as working to resolve the environmental challenges faced via gasoline-powered vehicles is also pondered upon.

Maruti Suzuki is also placing an emphasis on re-skilling, to create an adaptable workforce with the necessary skills base to successfully transition to Net Zero. Finally, Maruti Suzuki also seeks to enhance the human capital of their workforce. They seek to ensure that employees can express their concerns with regards to their job profile, training, and development requirements. They tend to install the motto of 'Don't turn away, Don't hide, Don't Lie' but choose to make right choices and develop their skills-set. Although this is a trial-and-error method meant to revise operations yet, the objective is to aid in streamlining the future processes for efficiency and productivity (Global Suzuki, 2023).

[1]https://www.marutisuzuki.com/

The Indian EV Market Going Forward

The automobile market in India now stands in the third place globally. India has showcased its capacity in this regard in FY2021–22 by producing 22.93 million vehicles, inclusive of all types – passenger, commercial, 2–3 wheelers, and quadricycles. The EV domain is expected to grow at 49% CAGR between 2022 and 2030, aiming for annual sales of 10 million vehicles by 2030 and helping to create 50 million job opportunities.[2]

In April 2020, the automotive sector witnessed significant changes due to the enforcement of stringent BS6 norms. Car manufacturers shifted away from diesel engines and explored alternatives such as petrol, CNG, and electric options. In 2023, the industry was found gearing up for the next phase of BS6 emission norms, known as BS6 2.0. Some vehicles already adhere to these updated standards. BS6-compliant vehicles are required to run on engines emitting low levels of NOx (nitrogen oxide) and particulate matter, meeting prescribed limits. This achievement is accomplished through technologies like Lean NOx Trap or Selective Catalytic Reduction. These measures ensure cleaner fuel combustion with reduced pollutants.

BS6 2.0 takes emission standards even further, demanding compliance not only in laboratory tests but also under real-world driving conditions. To achieve this, engines will need to undergo upgrades, and onboard self-diagnostic devices will assist in monitoring drivers' behaviour and traffic conditions in real time. The idea is to be able to cater to the masses with a promise to steer towards a cleaner mobility, that is driven by tech-advancements that garners environmental consciousness (Thornton, 2023).

In this context, NITI Aayog, in March 2019, established the National Mission on Transformative Mobility and Battery Storage. The Mission aims to promote eco-friendly, interconnected, shared, and comprehensive mobility in India through strategic policy actions and frameworks. In a further significant development, the FAME-II scheme underwent restructuring, resulting in a remarkable increase in the adoption rate of electric two wheelers – from 3.5% to an impressive 72% within just 11 months. Simultaneously, a ground-breaking initiative unfolded: the creation of the world's largest electric bus tender, encompassing 5,450 e-buses. This move led to a substantial 18–24% reduction in prices during the price discovery process.[3] The Mission's core functions include recommending strategies for transformative mobility, driving phased manufacturing programmes for EVs, EV-components, and batteries, and fostering cooperation among stakeholders to revolutionise mobility in India.

Clearly, fuel-efficient vehicles are the future of the automotive industry. Maruti Suzuki has been consistently on top of their game. Automatic cars like the Celerio, the industry's first Automatic Manual Transmission vehicle, bagged the 23.1 kmpl for both manual and automatic versions in 2013 itself. Tata Motors has also been

---

[2]Reducing carbon footprint in the automotive industry (grantthornton.in).

[3]E-Mobility: National Mission on Transformative Mobility and Battery Storage | NITI Aayog.

an avid participant in envisioning a bright future for the environment and living lives. In addition to the introduction of the largest range of green fuel-powered vehicles in heavy trucks, we set new benchmarks in India's rapidly growing pickup segment with the launch of the Yodha 2.0, Intra V20 bi-fuel, and Intra V50.

However, key challenges faced by the Indian automotive sector going forward include a lack of investment into sustainability initiatives, a lack of structure in terms of business proposals to promote sustainability, a lack of inherent alignment with government sustainability initiatives, and a lack of 'know-how' and appropriate skills sets (Capgemini Research Institute, 2022). As such, the automotive industry has been yielded into an arena of grave concern in India. Data suggest that, for every 1,000 people, there is a fleet of 33 automobiles that makes India as the 4th largest automotive market at the global level. Evidently, as one of the most populated countries in the world, India stands as world's third largest producer of GHG emissions and accounts for 90% CO_2 emissions from road transportations.

Risk Factors

As such, the automotive industry faces a significant challenge in being able to meet the required standards laid out by governing bodies in the domestic market and international settings. There are a number of different categories of risk facing the sector. The automotive industry faces substantial challenges in meeting the standards set by governing bodies both domestically and internationally. The sector encounters various categories of risk, including liquidity risks that impact its credit standing. The value for debt-securities, finance costs, and the ability to secure future financing options are also of serious concern to the reputation of the automotive industry. The automotive industry is also subject to risks associated with the automobile financing business. Deterioration in the performance of any of our subsidiaries, joint ventures, or affiliates could materially and adversely affect the outcome of the automotive industry, the operations, and financial performance (Annamária et al., 2019).

Although the awareness of making the required changes towards adapting sustainability is acknowledged, the automotive industry is deeply disturbed by the costs that they may incur to comply into, to address liabilities, keeping the environment, health, and abiding into the safety laws and regulations. The Reserve Bank of India has put in place a Prompt Corrective Action Framework. However, changes or uncertainty in respect of the LIBOR, IBORs, SONIA, and/or SOFR may adversely affect some financing options, Corporate Average Fuel Economy (CAFE) standards applicable to M1 category vehicles to demonstrate CAFE compliance for our Passenger Vehicles, changes to the European emissions tests of the Worldwide Harmonized Light Vehicle Test Procedure made models non-compliant with emissions limits subject to additional taxes, Corporate Governance initiatives and other binding regulations need to be adhered into by automotive industry players (Agency, 2014).

The automotive industry is also subject to risks associated with joint ventures and affiliates wherein they retain only partial or joint control. There are also risks associated with product liability, warranties, and recalls. Exchange rate and interest rate fluctuations and hedging arrangements could materially and adversely affect the financial books and working operations. Potential changes via mergers, acquisitions, and divestments may have a material adverse effect on future results and financial condition of the automotive sector. Transitional risk describes about the phase that is felt in the assembly line to apply the processes and procedures that go into defining the sustainability standards in production facilities. Should they fail to comply by the printed standards, there is a huge risk of missing out on making notable sales and end-up in paying heavy fines.

Undoubtedly, operational costs are significant in order to meet the requirements under carbon tax, GHG, and other systems. However, it's the consumer that defines the brand-market value w.r.t his/her personal experience based on the new product. This also dictates the investor relations and brand equity of the automotive industry. Finally, physical risks assess into the environmental changes that hinder or allow the automotive industry to look into viable alternatives for better suitability. Water resources also tend to dictate the shape of the automotive industry. The probability of experiencing natural disasters, unexpected calamities, and sustainable damage to the business site does lead to suspension of scheduled production, instigating losses in the near future.

Hence, the EV market and related opportunities may not evolve as anticipated. The industry is vulnerable to reduced demand for premium cars and all-terrain vehicles than automobile manufacturers with a more diversified product range, also impacted by terrorism, natural disasters, and epidemics, divulgence of confidential information, failures, or weaknesses in the internal controls could materially affect the financials, and market value of investments may fluctuate due to the volatility of the Indian securities market.

Conclusions

This chapter has provided a basic account of the goal of Net Zero and consequent impact on the Indian automotive industry as it shifts to zero-carbon vehicles, drawing on the examples of Tate Motors and Maruti Suzuki. It was found that whilst there is a clear recognition by the sector to effect transition and ensure environmental sustainability, there is a significant cost in doing so – potentially warranting further government intervention. The continued viability of the domestic automotive sector will, thus, form a major aspect of the Indian Government's goal to make India a high-tech global manufacturing hub. A major part of this goal, therefore, must be that all firms in the supply chain – especially SMEs – derive the maximum possible benefit from innovation and technology transfer (an area where Maruti Suzuki has been leaders for some time – see Sudan & Taggar, 2022).

References

Agency, E. (2014). *Climate change agreements*. Gov.uk.

Annamária, K., Pokorádi, L., & Johanyák, Z. C. (2019). *Risk analysis in the automotive industry*. Research Gate.

Autonewsreporter. (n.d.). *A brief history of automobile industry in India*. All about automotive Industry.

Black, A., Roy, P., El-Haddad, A., & Yilmaz, K. (2020). *The political economy of automotive industry development policy in middle income countries: A comparative analysis of Egypt, India, South Africa and Turkey* [ESID Working paper no. 143] https://eprints.soas.ac.uk/32972/1/Final%20ESID%20WP%20No%20143.pdf

Capgemini Research Institute. (2022). *Sustainability in automotive industry – An India perspective*. Capgemini Research Institute.

European Commission. (2023). *The green deal industrial plan*. The Green Deal Industrial Plan – European Commission (europa.eu)

Global Suzuki, G. (2023). *Suzuki sustainability report-2023*. Osaka, Japan.

IBEF & ACMA. (2023). *Automobiles*. https://www.bharat-mobility.com/img/pdf/IBEF-Automotive-OEM-Overview.pdf

Ma, J., Li, Y., Grundish, N. S., Goodenough, J. B., Chen, Y., Guo, L., Peng, Z., Qi, X., Yang, F., Qie, L., Wang, C.-A., Huang, B., Huang, Z., Chen, L., Su, D., Wang, G., Peng, X., Chen, Z., Yang, J., … Wan, L.-J. (2021). The 2021 battery technology roadmap. *Journal of Physics D: Applied Physics, 54*. https://doi.org/10.1088/1361-6463/abd353

Manish, S. (2023, August 7). *India Independence Act 1947, history, provision, impact and repeal*. Studyiq.com. https://www.studyiq.com/articles/india-independence-act-1947/

Maruti Suzuki. (2020). *Green product*. marutistoragenew.blob.core.windows.net. www.marutistoragenew.blob.core.windows.net/msilintiwebpdf/GREEN_PRODUCT.pdf

Maruti Suzuki. (2023). *Sustainability report – Corporate environmental report*.

Niti Aayog. (2019). *E-mobility: National mission on transformative mobility and battery storage*. New Delhi, New Delhi, India.

OICA. (2023). *Correspondents survey: World production of motor vehicles by country and region*. https://www.oica.net/wp-content/uploads/By-country-region-2021.pdf

Raju, V. (2024, March 8). Logistics trends to watch out for in 2024. *Indian Transport and Logistic News*.

Seetharaman, M., Sampat, M., Kashyap, P., Sagi, P., Agarwal, A., & Modi, V. (2023). *India electric vehicle report 2023*. Bain & Company.

Service, E. N., & Express, I. (2020, October 8). *Anand district: NDDB begins initiative for dairy farmers on manure management*. Vadodara, Gujarat, India.

Sharma, A., & Lobo, A. (2023, January 2). *Sustainability in automotive industry – An India perspective*. Insights, Expert Perspectives.

Simon. (2024, April 8). *Sustainable business practices (definition & 12 examples)*. Sustainability Success.

Sudan, T., & Taggar, R. (2022). COVID-19 induced supply chain disruptions and automotive industry: A case study of Maruti Suzuki India Limited and mitigation strategies. *Global Economics Science*, 35–52. file:///C:/Users/ID124562/Downloads/nadia,+GES-1095-v3i1-35-52.pdf

Tata Motors. (2023). *Annual report 2023*. TataMotors Group of Industries.

Tata Motors. (2023). *78th Sustainability report*. https://www.tatamotors.com/wp-content/uploads/2023/10/annual-report-2022-2023.pdf

Thomas Pohl, S. D. (2021, December 1). *How the automotive industry is driving toward a sustainable future*. Forbes.com.

Thornton, G. (2023). *Reducing carbon footprint in the automotive industry*. New Delhi. https://www.grantthornton.in/globalassets/1.-member-firms/india/assets/pdfs/reducing_carbon_footprint_in_the_automotive_industry_2023.pdf

Turner, L. J. (2019, September 19). *Zero carbon by 2050 is possible. Here's what we need to do*. World Economic Forum – Sustainable Development Impact Summit.

Wiki. (n.d.). Indian Independence Act 1947. *Wikipedia*.

Chapter 5

Unveiling the Interplay of Air Pollution, Genetics and Epigenetics

Loukia G. Tsaprouni

Birmingham City University, UK

Abstract

Air pollution poses a significant global threat to both human health and environmental stability, acknowledged by the World Health Organization as a leading cause of non-communicable diseases (NCDs) and a notable contributor to climate change. This chapter offers a comprehensive review of the impacts of air pollution on health, highlighting the complex interactions with genetic predispositions and epigenetic mechanisms. The consequences of air pollution to health are extensive, spanning respiratory diseases, cardiovascular disorders, adverse pregnancy outcomes, neurodevelopmental disorders, and heightened mortality rates. Genetic factors play a pivotal role in shaping individual responses to air pollution, influencing susceptibility to respiratory illnesses and the severity of symptoms. Additionally, epigenetic changes triggered by exposure to pollutants have been linked to respiratory health issues, cancer development and progression, and even transgenerational effects spanning multiple generations. As countries, including the UK, pursue ambitious targets for reducing emissions, ongoing research into the complex interplay of air pollution, genetics, and epigenetics is essential. By unravelling the underlying mechanisms and advancing preventive and therapeutic strategies, we can protect public health and promote sustainable environmental practices in the face of this pervasive global challenge.

Keywords: Epigenetics; genetic variants; air pollution; particulate matter; DNA methylation; histone modifications; respiratory diseases; COPD

Examining Net Zero: Creating Solutions for a Greener Society and Sustainable Economic Growth, 43–55
Copyright © 2025 by Loukia G. Tsaprouni
Published under exclusive licence by Emerald Publishing Limited
doi:10.1108/978-1-83608-574-420251005

1. Understanding the Impact and Challenges of Air Pollution in Health

According to the World Health Organisation, air pollution poses a major threat to health and climate and is the greatest environmental threat to health and a leading cause of NCDs. Air pollution refers to the introduction of any chemical, physical, or biological substance into the indoor or outdoor environment, altering the natural composition of the atmosphere. Origins of air pollution can be both natural and anthropogenic. Examples of natural causes include volcanic eruptions, wildfires, temperature variations, humidity, and dust storms, whilst common sources induced by men include household combustion of solid fuels, motor vehicles, and industrial emissions as well as agricultural facilities. These release a diverse array of pollutants into the atmosphere, including particulate matter (PM), nitrogen oxides (NOx), sulphur dioxide, volatile organic compounds, and heavy metals.

Nearly, the entire global population (99%) is exposed to air that exceeds the recommended pollution levels, particularly impacting low- and middle-income countries (WHO air quality guidelines, 2022). When considering clean air, there is a distinction between outdoor and domestic air quality (Poole et al., 2019). Outdoor air quality is affected by industrial emissions, vehicle exhaust, agricultural activities, and natural events. Domestic air is influenced by sources such as cooking, heating, cleaning products, and smoking that can release pollutants indoors, compromising indoor air quality. It is important to note that outdoor pollutants can infiltrate homes, further affecting indoor and outdoor air quality.

The health impacts of air pollution are profound and multifaceted, affecting various organ systems and contributing to a range of acute and chronic diseases. PM, especially fine particles (PM2.5), can penetrate deep into the respiratory tract, leading to respiratory infections, exacerbation of asthma, and chronic obstructive pulmonary disease (COPD). Prolonged exposure to nitrogen dioxide (NO_2) and ozone (O_3) is associated with cardiovascular diseases, including hypertension, stroke, and coronary artery disease. Furthermore, air pollution has been linked to adverse pregnancy outcomes, neurodevelopmental disorders, and increased mortality rates.

Certain populations are particularly vulnerable to the effects of air pollution, including children, the elderly, individuals with pre-existing respiratory or cardiovascular conditions, and socioeconomically disadvantaged communities. Children are especially susceptible due to their developing respiratory systems and higher respiratory rates, while older adults may have compromised immune function and underlying health conditions that exacerbate the impact of air pollution. Moreover, marginalised communities often bear a disproportionate burden of air pollution exposure due to socioeconomic factors such as limited access to healthcare, inadequate housing, and proximity to industrial facilities (Siddique et al., 2023).

To address the public health threat, the global scientific community is creating partnerships, initiatives, tools, and platforms aimed at reducing disease burdens associated with air pollution and contributing to short- and long-term efforts to mitigate climate change and implement a net zero clean air strategy (Munro et al., 2020). These efforts include the establishment of air quality standards, emission limits for industrial facilities and vehicles, and the promotion of clean energy technologies. Additionally, urban planning strategies such as promoting public transportation, implementing green infrastructure, and reducing vehicle traffic can help mitigate air pollution and improve air quality in urban areas. A key area that requires common international efforts and policy initiatives is addressing transboundary air pollution and mitigating global climate change, which exacerbate air quality issues (Grennfelt et al., 2020).

The severe repercussions of poor air quality on the population underscore the critical importance of public awareness and education in promoting community involvement and support for clean air efforts. By increasing understanding of the health hazards linked to air pollution and empowering individuals to take proactive steps, educational campaigns instigate behavioural shifts such as minimising vehicle use, practising energy conservation, and endorsing clean air policies. Finally, educational initiatives tailored to vulnerable groups can offer guidance on reducing exposure to air pollutants and accessing healthcare services. Examples of these in the UK include community workshops and seminars, school programmes, and mobile health clinics.

Despite the notable improvements in air quality over recent decades, urban areas in the UK continue to grapple with persistent levels of air pollution. PM, NO_2, and O_3 are among the key pollutants of concern, with exposure linked to adverse health effects. High levels of $PM_{2.5}$ have been associated with respiratory illnesses such as asthma and COPD, as well as cardiovascular diseases and premature mortality (Huang et al., 2021). Likewise, NO_2 exposure has been linked to exacerbation of respiratory conditions and increased risk of cardiovascular events. Vulnerable populations, including children, the elderly, and individuals with pre-existing health conditions, are disproportionately affected by air pollution in the UK, exacerbating health inequalities.

2. Exploring the Role of Genes in Modulating Responses to Air Pollution

Understanding the importance of clean air extends beyond its immediate impacts on respiratory health and environmental well-being. Research has shown that genetic predispositions may also play a role in how individuals respond to air pollution exposure.

Genes play a significant role in modulating the response of airways to clean air, influencing respiratory health and susceptibility to environmental pollutants. Several genes have been identified as key players in the physiological processes involved in airway response to clean air. Genes encoding enzymes involved in detoxification pathways, such as cytochrome P450 (CYP) enzymes and glutathione *S*-transferases (GSTs), play a critical role in metabolising and eliminating harmful substances from the airways. These genes facilitate the breakdown and clearance of airborne pollutants, thereby reducing their detrimental effects on respiratory tissues. Genetic variants to these detoxification enzymes have been linked amongst diseases other than those of respiratory nature with prostate cancer (Martinez-Gonzalez et al., 2020), orofacial clefts (Garland et al., 2020), papillary thyroid (Aschebrook-Kilfoy et al., 2012), and neurodegeneration (Molot et al., 2021).

Antioxidant genes, including superoxide dismutase (SOD), catalase, and glutathione peroxidase (GPx), help maintain redox balance in the airways by scavenging reactive oxygen species (ROS) generated in response to environmental stressors. By neutralising ROS and protecting against oxidative damage, these genes contribute to the preservation of airway function and integrity in clean air environments (Fitzpatrick et al., 2012).

Low air quality and exposure to environmental stressors induce inflammatory responses. Genes involved in the regulation of inflammatory pathways, such as tumour necrosis factor alpha (TNF-α), interleukins (ILs), and nuclear factor kappa B (NF-κB), influence the immune response of airway epithelial cells to clean air (Kaur et al., 2022). Regulation of inflammatory signalling is essential for mounting the immune response to airborne pathogens and pollutants while preventing excessive inflammation and tissue damage.

The impact of air pollution on respiratory mucosal immune responses has emerged as a significant theme in recent studies, particularly focusing on the disruption of oxidation–reduction (redox) homeostasis and the activity of the Aryl hydrocarbon receptor pathway (Vogel et al., 2020). Redox signalling and homeostasis involve a complex interplay of molecules, signalling proteins, and enzymes that regulate the balance between the production and breakdown of ROS and reactive nitrogen species (RNS) within and around cells (Mudway et al., 2020). The accumulation of these species beyond the cell's antioxidant capacity leads to oxidative stress, which influences various cellular processes, including mucus production, host defence peptides, antiviral responses, and cytokine production.

ROS are generated from both endogenous and exogenous sources. Endogenous sources include processes like oxidative phosphorylation in mitochondria, while exogenous sources include air pollutants such as particles, heavy transition metals, and reactive gases and organic compounds (Michaeloudes et al., 2022). Air pollution exposure triggers the production of intracellular ROS through xenobiotic metabolism, disruption of mitochondrial function, and increased levels of NOx. This increased ROS production is associated with various adverse effects on cellular structures and functions, including DNA oxidation and damage, lipid peroxidation, compromised membrane integrity, protein oxidation, and cell-cycle arrest or apoptosis (Thangavel et al., 2022).

Air pollution exposure also stimulates antioxidant defence mechanisms, involving scavenging antioxidant molecules and enzymes. When the respiratory system is stimulated by air pollution, it initiates a complex array of defence mechanisms to mitigate the oxidative stress effects. One crucial aspect of this defence system involves the activation of antioxidant pathways (Kelly & Fussell, 2011). Air pollution contains various reactive compounds, including ROS and RNS, which can induce oxidative damage to cellular structures and DNA if left unchecked. To counteract this oxidative stress, the body relies on antioxidant defence mechanisms.

One key player in this defence system is GPx, an enzyme that plays a central role in neutralising ROS and protecting cells from oxidative damage (Farhat et al., 2018). Glutathione peroxidase catalyses the reduction of hydrogen peroxide and lipid hydroperoxides to water and corresponding alcohols, respectively, using reduced glutathione (GSH) as a substrate. By scavenging these molecules, GPx helps maintain cellular homeostasis and protects against oxidative stress-related damage.

However, chronic or excessive exposure to air pollution and high ROS levels can overwhelm these defence mechanisms, leading to cellular damage and activation of signalling pathways such as mitogen-activated protein kinase and transcription factors like Nrf2 and NF-κB (Kahremany et al., 2021). This mechanism is associated with respiratory diseases such as asthma, COPD, and lung cancer.

Studies aiming to intervene in air pollution-induced ROS signalling and damage have explored compounds targeting different aspects of redox signalling or homeostasis. Compounds such as rosiglitazone, antioxidants like chebulic acid and gallic acid, vitamin D, and Nrf2 activators like resveratrol have shown promise in attenuating oxidative stress and inflammation induced by air pollution (Shin et al., 2020). *N*-acetylcysteine, which acts as both an antioxidant and a precursor in glutathione synthesis, has demonstrated protective effects against air pollution both in vitro and in vivo (Sharma et al., 2019). However, further research and development of interventions targeting ROS homeostasis in lung epithelial cells are needed for broader clinical applications.

Genes encoding proteins involved in mucociliary clearance, such as mucins and ciliary proteins, contribute to the removal of inhaled particles and pathogens from the airways. These genes facilitate the coordinated stimulation of cilia and the production of mucus to trap and expel foreign substances, maintaining airway patency and preventing respiratory infections. One key set of genes involved encodes proteins that contribute to the production and composition of mucus. Mucins, large glycoproteins, are a major component of mucus and are encoded by genes such as MUC5AC and MUC5B (Fitch et al., 2020). These genes are responsible for producing mucins that form the gel-like matrix of mucus, providing a barrier against inhaled particles and pathogens. Additionally, genes encoding proteins involved in the regulation of mucus production, such as the MUC genes transcriptional regulators, play essential roles in maintaining a balance of mucus secretion in the airways (Barnes, 2022).

Genes encoding proteins involved in the structure and function of cilia are critical for effective mucociliary clearance. Cilia are hair-like structures that extend from the surface of airway epithelial cells and transfer mucus and trapped particles out of the airways. Genes encoding components of the ciliary structure, such as dynein arms (encoded by DNAH5, DNAH11, etc.) and radial spokes, are essential for the proper assembly and function of cilia (Pedersen, 1990). Additionally, genes encoding regulatory proteins that control ciliary beating, such as CFTR (cystic fibrosis transmembrane conductance regulator) and FOXJ1 (forkhead box protein J1), are crucial for maintaining effective mucociliary clearance (Nguyen et al., 2021). In addition, genes encoding ion channels and transporters, such as ENaC (epithelial sodium channel) and CFTR, regulate the hydration and viscosity of mucus, which affects its clearance properties. To add to the complexity of the mucus secretion mechanisms, genes encoding mucociliary clearance-associated proteins, such as SPDEF (SAM pointed domain-containing Ets transcription factor), contribute to the coordination of mucus production and ciliary beating (Montgomery et al., 2020).

The role of genetics in airway pollutant responses encompasses a number of physiological and molecular mechanisms. Genetic factors influence how an individual will respond and include their susceptibility to respiratory diseases and the severity of their symptoms upon exposure. One key aspect lies in individual susceptibility to respiratory diseases. Genetic variants can predispose individuals to heightened sensitivity or increased risk of developing respiratory conditions. For example, genetic variations in genes encoding antioxidant enzymes, such as GSTs or SODs, can affect an individual's ability to neutralise ROS generated by air pollutants (Yang et al., 2023). Consequently, individuals with certain genetic variants may be more susceptible to oxidative stress-induced damage to the airways, leading to asthma, COPD, or bronchitis.

Variations in genes encoding cytokines, chemokines, and inflammatory mediators can influence the magnitude and duration of inflammatory reactions in the airways following pollutant exposure. Polymorphisms in genes encoding ILs or TNF-α have been associated with altered inflammatory responses to air pollution and increased risk of exacerbations in individuals with pre-existing respiratory conditions (Bowatte et al., 2016). It should also be noted that polymorphisms in genes involved in xenobiotic metabolism, such as CYP enzymes, can influence the bioactivation or detoxification of airborne toxins and contaminants (Dergham et al., 2012).

3. Unveiling the Epigenetic Impact of Air Pollution: From Immediate Responses to Transgenerational Effects

Epigenetics is the study of the effect that the environment can have on the genome. Unlike genetic changes, epigenetic changes are reversible and do not alter the DNA sequence, but they influence DNA expression (Zhang et al., 2020). Epigenetic changes are modifications to DNA that regulate whether genes are turned on or off. Epigenetic modifications include DNA methylation (DNAm), histone modifications, and non-coding RNA. DNAm involves the attachment of methyl groups to DNA leading to a gene being silenced or turned off. Histones are structural proteins in the cell nucleus allowing the DNA to wrap around them, therefore compacting the DNA tightly within the nucleus. Modification of histones by the addition or removal of chemical groups (i.e. methyl or acetyl groups) allows the DNA to unwind or wind leading to a gene being turned on or off.

Epigenetic mechanisms contribute to the epithelial response to pollution. Studies have shown alterations in DNAm and microRNA expression in response to pollutants, affecting pathways involved in transcription factor activity, protein metabolism, and cell adhesion (Mukherjee et al., 2021). These epigenetic changes are, therefore, linked with respiratory health and disease outcomes in response to air quality and pollution.

In the last years, DNAm has been extensively studied as an important modification linked to air pollutant exposure. Several studies have investigated the impact of in utero air pollution exposure DNAm by analysing placenta or cord blood samples. One study found a significant association between exposure to NO_2 during pregnancy and DNAm changes at specific CpG sites, notably in genes related to antioxidant and anti-inflammatory responses (Gruzieva et al., 2017). The study also validated these findings in blood samples from children aged 4 and 8 years, suggesting a potential role of NO_2 exposure in altering DNAm patterns associated with responses to ROS. Prenatal exposure to air pollution has also been associated with intrauterine growth restriction, with affected babies showing more significant DNAm effects compared to those with healthy growth (Cai et al., 2017). Studies have demonstrated lower birth weight and altered placental DNAm, particularly in genes like hydroxysteroid 11-beta dehydrogenase 2, associated with PM10 exposure during pregnancy, potentially leading to increased foetal cortisol exposure and reduced growth (Ghazi et al., 2021). Finally, a large randomised cross over trial performed in 2022 by Du et al. (2023) investigated genome-wide DNAm levels in traffic-related air pollution. The authors showed that after exposure to traffic-related air pollution, methylation levels at 68 CpG loci exhibited significant changes with 49 loci showing hypermethylation and 19 loci showing hypomethylation. The annotated genes associated were involved in pathways, including cardiovascular signalling, cytokine signalling, immune responses, nervous system signalling, and metabolism.

Transgenerational epigenetic inheritance can be defined as the acquisition of epigenomic traits on the DNA of one generation and their stable transfer to the subsequent generation through the gametes (Hanson & Skinner, 2016). Recent evidence suggests that air pollution exposure can induce epigenetic changes that may be inherited across generations (Shukla et al., 2019). For instance, studies have demonstrated that exposure to pollutants like PM, NO_2, and polycyclic aromatic hydrocarbons can lead to DNAm alterations in germ cells, affecting gene expression patterns in offspring (Gavito-Covarrubias et al., 2024). Animal studies have shown transgenerational effects of air pollution exposure on phenotypic traits, such as respiratory function and susceptibility to respiratory diseases, which may be mediated by epigenetic mechanisms (Real et al., 2021). This suggests that air pollution not only impacts the health of the exposed individuals but also has the potential to influence the health of future generations through transgenerational epigenetic inheritance. Further research is needed to fully understand the mechanisms underlying this phenomenon and its implications for human health.

4. Treatment Strategies for Air Pollution-related Diseases

Globally, 6.1 million deaths were attributed to air pollution in 2016 (Cohen et al., 2017). Of these, nearly 4.1 million deaths were attributed to outdoor air pollution and more than 2.5 million deaths were attributed to household air pollution. The massive burden of these numbers on health also has a significant effect in the local and international economies.

The intrinsic interplay between air quality and pollution, genetic predispositions, and epigenetic dynamics is highly complex and one that the scientific community is starting to address. We now understand that environmental factors can instigate epigenetic alterations, thereby reshaping gene expression profiles and influencing susceptibility to myriad diseases spanning from respiratory chronic conditions to autoimmune diseases and cancer as well as psychiatric conditions such as schizophrenia. Understanding the molecular mechanisms involved in the development of these conditions is paramount in developing treatments. It's also important in improving protection and prevention strategies.

Research in the development of next-generation compounds is underway that can specifically target symptoms associated with respiratory distress and alleviate symptoms. For example, medications targeting respiratory conditions like asthma and COPD can help manage symptoms and improve the quality of life for affected individuals (Adcock & Caramori, 2004). Additionally, advancements in medical technology, such as wearable devices and telemedicine platforms, enable early detection of respiratory distress and facilitate timely intervention, especially for vulnerable populations (Bousquet et al., 2019).

In addition to pharmaceutical interventions, research into the development of novel treatments for air pollution-related diseases is expanding. Clinical trials are underway to evaluate the efficacy of new drugs targeting specific pathways implicated in respiratory and cardiovascular conditions exacerbated by air pollution (Hansel et al., 2022; Raju et al., 2023). Studies are also investigating the use of anti-inflammatory agents to mitigate airway inflammation and reduce the severity of asthma attacks triggered by pollutants (Kelsen et al., 2021). Other pharmaceutical trials focus on antioxidants and mucolytic agents to counteract oxidative stress and enhance mucociliary clearance in individuals exposed to high levels of PM (Dailah, 2022).

Finally, advances in precision medicine hold promise for personalised treatment approaches tailored to individual genetic and environmental risk factors. Pharmacogenomic studies aim to identify genetic variations that influence an individual's response to air pollution exposure and inform targeted therapies. By understanding how genetic factors interact with environmental triggers, we can develop more effective therapies that optimise treatment outcomes and minimise adverse effects. Pharmacogenetic studies explore the role of genetic polymorphisms in metabolising pollutants and modulating inflammatory responses, offering insights into potential therapeutic targets for precision medicine approaches (Banerjee et al., 2019).

5. Summary

In the global fight against the detrimental effects of air pollution on health and economies, significant strides have been made in developing treatments and prevention strategies. Recognising the intricate interplay between air quality, genetic predispositions, and epigenetic dynamics, the scientific community has intensified efforts to address the multifaceted challenges posed by air pollution-related diseases. Importantly, the scientific community is recognising that, in addition to respiratory conditions and autoimmune diseases, air pollution can significantly influence well-being, psychiatric disorders such as depression, anxiety, and schizophrenia as well as neuronal degenerative diseases. As the UK is stepping up to the challenge of cutting emissions by at least 68% by 2030 on 1990 levels, and reaching net zero by 2050, the need to take a coordinated approach and continue research in air pollution and the impact it has in health and disease is not only important, it's vital.

References

Adcock, I. M., & Caramori, G. (2004). Kinase targets and inhibitors for the treatment of airway inflammatory diseases: The next generation of drugs for severe asthma and COPD? *BioDrugs*, *18*(3), 167–180. https://doi.org/10.2165/00063030-200418030-00003. PMID: 15161334.

Aschebrook-Kilfoy, B., Neta, G., Brenner, A. V., Hutchinson, A., Pfeiffer, R. M., Sturgis, E. M., Xu, L., Wheeler, W., Doody, M. M., Chanock, S. J., & Sigurdson, A. J. (2012, May 24). Common genetic variants in metabolism and detoxification pathways and the risk of papillary thyroid cancer. *Endocrine Related Cancer*, *19*(3), 333–344. https://doi.org.10.1530/ERC-11-0372. PMID: 22389382; PMCID: PMC3394851.

Banerjee, B. D., Kumar, R., Thamineni, K. L., Shah, H., Thakur, G. K., & Sharma, T. (2019). Effect of environmental exposure and pharmacogenomics on drug metabolism. *Current Drug Metabolism*, *20*(14), 1103–1113. https://doi.org/10.2174/1389200221666200110153304. PMID: 31933442.

Barnes, P. J. (2022, May 13). Oxidative stress in chronic obstructive pulmonary disease. *Antioxidants (Basel)*, *11*(5), 965. https://doi.org/10.3390/antiox11050965. PMID: 35624831; PMCID: PMC9138026.

Bousquet, J., Hellings, P. W., Agache, I., Amat, F., Annesi-Maesano, I., Ansotegui, I. J., Anto, J. M., Bachert, C., Bateman, E. D., Bedbrook, A., Bennoor, K., Bewick, M., Bindslev-Jensen, C., Bosnic-Anticevich, S., Bosse, I., Brozek, J., Brussino, L., Canonica, G. W., Cardona, V., ... Mobile Airways Sentinel Network (MASK) Study Group. (2019). Allergic rhinitis and its impact on asthma (ARIA) phase 4 (2018): Change management in allergic rhinitis and asthma multimorbidity using mobile technology. *The Journal of Allergy and Clinical Immunology*, *143*(3), 864–879. https://doi.org/10.1016/j.jaci.2018.08.049. PMID: 30273709.

Bowatte, G., Lodge, C. J., Perret, J. L., Matheson, M. C., & Dharmage, S. C. (2016). Interactions of GST polymorphisms in air pollution exposure and respiratory diseases and allergies. *Current Allergy and Asthma Reports*, *6*(12), 85. https://doi.org/10.1007/s11882-016-0664-z. PMID: 27878551.

Cai, J., Zhao, Y., Liu, P., Xia, B., Zhu, Q., Wang, X., Song, Q., Kan, H., & Zhang, Y. (2017). Exposure to particulate air pollution during early pregnancy is associated with placental DNA methylation. *Science of the Total Environment*, *607–608*, 1103–1108. https://doi.org/10.1016/j.scitotenv.2017.07.029. Epub 2017 Jul 27. PMID: 28724248.

Cohen, A. J., Brauer, M., Burnett, R., Anderson, H. R., Frostad, J., Estep, K., Balakrishnan, K., Brunekreef, B., Dandona, L., Dandona, R., Feigin, V., Freedman, G., Hubbell, B., Jobling, A., Kan, H., Knibbs, L., Liu, Y., Martin, R., Morawska, L., ... Forouzanfar, M. H. (2017, May 13). Estimates and 25-year trends of the global burden of disease attributable to ambient air pollution: An analysis of data from the Global Burden of Diseases Study 2015. *Lancet*, *389*(10082), 1907–1918. https://doi.org/10.1016/S0140-6736(17)30505-6. Epub 2017 Apr 10. Erratum in: Lancet. 2017 Jun 17;389(10087):e15. Erratum in: Lancet. 2018 Apr 21;391(10130):1576. PMID: 28408086; PMCID: PMC5439030.

Dailah, H. G. (2022, August 28). Therapeutic potential of small molecules targeting oxidative stress in the treatment of chronic obstructive pulmonary disease (COPD): A comprehensive review. *Molecules, 27*(17), 5542. https://doi.org/10.3390/molecules 27175542. PMID: 36080309; PMCID: PMC9458015.

Dergham, M., Lepers, C., Verdin, A., Billet, S., Cazier, F., Courcot, D., Shirali, P., & Garçon, G. (2012, April 16). Prooxidant and proinflammatory potency of air pollution particulate matter ($PM_{2.5\text{-}0.3}$) produced in rural, urban, or industrial surroundings in human bronchial epithelial cells (BEAS-2B). *Chemical Research in Toxicology, 25*(4), 904–919. https://doi.org/10.1021/tx200529v. Epub 2012 Mar 23. PMID: 22404339.

Du, X., Jiang, Y., Zhang, Q., Zhu, X., Zhang, Y., Liu, C., Niu, Y., Cai, J., Kan, H., & Chen, R. (2023, February 21). Genome-wide profiling of exosomal long noncoding RNAs following air pollution exposure: A randomized, crossover trial. *Environmental Science & Technology, 57*(7), 2856–2863. https://doi.org/10.1021/acs.est.2c05956. Epub 2023 Feb 9. PMID: 36757895.

Farhat, Z., Browne, R. W., Bonner, M. R., Tian, L., Deng, F., Swanson, M., & Mu, L. (2018). How do glutathione antioxidant enzymes and total antioxidant status respond to air pollution exposure? *Environment International, 112*, 287–293. https://doi.org/10.1016/j.envint.2017.12.033. Epub 2018 Jan 8. PMID: 29324239; PMCID: PMC5899033.

Fitch, M. N., Phillippi, D., Zhang, Y., Lucero, J., Pandey, R. S., Liu, J., Brower, J., Allen, M. S., Campen, M. J., McDonald, J. D., & Lund, A. K. (2020). Effects of inhaled air pollution on markers of integrity, inflammation, and microbiota profiles of the intestines in Apolipoprotein E knockout mice. *Environmental Research, 181*, 108913. https://doi.org/10.1016/j.envres.2019.108913. Epub 2019 Nov 14. PMID: 31753468; PMCID: PMC6982581.

Fitzpatrick, A. M., Jones, D. P., & Brown, L. A. (2012, July 15). Glutathione redox control of asthma: From molecular mechanisms to therapeutic opportunities. *Antioxidants & Redox Signaling, 17*(2), 375–408. https://doi.org/10.1089/ars.2011.4198. Epub 2012 Mar 9. PMID: 22304503; PMCID: PMC3353819.

Garland, M. A., Reynolds, K., & Zhou, C. J. (2020, November). Environmental mechanisms of orofacial clefts. *Birth Defects Research, 112*(19), 1660–1698. https://doi.org/10.1002/bdr2.1830. Epub 2020 Oct 30. PMID: 33125192; PMCID: PMC7902093.

Gavito-Covarrubias, D., Ramírez-Díaz, I., Guzmán-Linares, J., Limón, I. D., Manuel-Sánchez, D. M., Molina-Herrera, A., Coral-García, M. Á., Anastasio, E., Anaya-Hernández, A., López-Salazar, P., Juárez-Díaz, G., Martínez-Juárez, J., Torres-Jácome, J., Albarado-Ibáñez, A., Martínez-Laguna, Y., Morán, C., & Rubio, K. (2024, January 17). Epigenetic mechanisms of particulate matter exposure: Air pollution and hazards on human health. *Frontiers in Genetics, 14*, 1306600. https://doi.org/10.3389/fgene.2023.1306600. PMID: 38299096; PMCID: PMC10829887.

Ghazi, T., Naidoo, P., Naidoo, R. N., & Chuturgoon, A. A. (2021, November 5). Prenatal air pollution exposure and placental DNA methylation changes: Implications on fetal development and future disease susceptibility. *Cells, 10*(11), 3025. https://doi.org/10.3390/cells10113025. PMID: 34831248; PMCID: PMC8616150.

Grennfelt, P., Engleryd, A., Forsius, M., Hov, Ø., Rodhe, H., & Cowling, E. (2020, April). Acid rain and air pollution: 50 years of progress in environmental science and policy. *Ambio, 49*(4), 849–864. https://doi.org/10.1007/s13280-019-01244-4. Epub 2019 Sep 21. PMID: 31542884; PMCID: PMC7028813.

Gruzieva, O., Xu, C. J., Breton, C. V., Annesi-Maesano, I., Antó, J. M., Auffray, C., Ballereau, S., Bellander, T., Bousquet, J., Bustamante, M., Charles, M. A., de Kluizenaar, Y., den Dekker, H. T., Duijts, L., Felix, J. F., Gehring, U., Guxens, M.,

Jaddoe, V. V., Jankipersadsing, S. A., … Melén, E. (2017, January). Epigenome-wide meta-analysis of methylation in children related to prenatal NO2 air pollution exposure. *Environmental Health Perspectives, 125*(1), 104–110. https://doi.org/10.1289/EHP36. Epub 2016 Jul 22. PMID: 27448387; PMCID: PMC5226705.

Hansel, N. N., Putcha, N., Woo, H., Peng, R., Diette, G. B., Fawzy, A., Wise, R. A., Romero, K., Davis, M. F., Rule, A. M., Eakin, M. N., Breysse, P. N., McCormack, M. C., & Koehler, K. (2022, February 15). Randomized clinical trial of air cleaners to improve indoor air quality and chronic obstructive pulmonary disease health: Results of the CLEAN air study. *American Journal of Respiratory and Critical Care Medicine, 205*(4), 421–430. https://doi.org/10.1164/rccm.202103-0604OC. PMID: 34449285; PMCID: PMC8886948.

Hanson, M. A., & Skinner, M. K. (2016). Developmental origins of epigenetic transgenerational inheritance. *Environmental Epigenetics, 2*(1), dvw002. https://doi.org/10.1093/eep/dvw002. Epub 2016 Mar 6. PMID: 27390622; PMCID: PMC4933018.

Huang, Y., Zhu, M., Ji, M., Fan, J., Xie, J., Wei, X., Jiang, X., Xu, J., Chen, L., Yin, R., Wang, Y., Dai, J., Jin, G., Xu, L., Hu, Z., Ma, H., & Shen, H. (2021, October 1). Air pollution, genetic factors, and the risk of lung cancer: A prospective study in the UK Biobank. *American Journal of Respiratory and Critical Care Medicine, 204*(7), 817–825. https://doi.org/10.1164/rccm.202011-4063OC. Erratum in: Am J Respir Crit Care Med. 2022 May 15;205(10):1254. PMID: 34252012.

Kahremany, S., Hofmann, L., Eretz-Kdosha, N., Silberstein, E., Gruzman, A., & Cohen, G. (2021, November 24). SH-29 and SK-119 attenuates air-pollution induced damage by activating Nrf2 in HaCaT cells. *International Journal of Environmental Research and Public Health, 18*(23), 12371. https://doi.org/10.3390/ijerph182312371. PMID: 34886097; PMCID: PMC8656889.

Kaur, M., Chandel, J., Malik, J., & Naura, A. S. (2022, August). Particulate matter in COPD pathogenesis: An overview. *Inflammation Research, 71*(7–8), 797–815. https://doi.org/10.1007/s00011-022-01594-y. Epub 2022 Jun 16. PMID: 35710643.

Kelly, F. J., & Fussell, J. C. (2011, August). Air pollution and airway disease. *Clinical & Experimental Allergy, 41*(8), 1059–71. https://doi.org/10.1111/j.1365-2222.2011.03776.x. Epub 2011 May 30. PMID: 21623970.

Kelsen, S. G., Agache, I. O., Soong, W., Israel, E., Chupp, G. L., Cheung, D. S., Theess, W., Yang, X., Staton, T. L., Choy, D. F., Fong, A., Dash, A., Dolton, M., Pappu, R., & Brightling, C. E. (2021, September). Astegolimab (anti-ST2) efficacy and safety in adults with severe asthma: A randomized clinical trial. *The Journal of Allergy and Clinical Immunology, 148*(3), 790–798. https://doi.org/10.1016/j.jaci.2021.03.044. Epub 2021 Apr 16. PMID: 33872652.

Martinez-Gonzalez, L. J., Antúnez-Rodríguez, A., Vazquez-Alonso, F., Hernandez, A. F., & Alvarez-Cubero, M. J. (2020, August 15). Genetic variants in xenobiotic detoxification enzymes, antioxidant defenses and hormonal pathways as biomarkers of susceptibility to prostate cancer. *Science of the Total Environment, 730*, 138314. https://doi.org/10.1016/j.scitotenv.2020.138314. Epub 2020 Apr 30. PMID: 32388358.

Michaeloudes, C., Abubakar-Waziri, H., Lakhdar, R., Raby, K., Dixey, P., Adcock, I. M., Mumby, S., Bhavsar, P. K., & Chung, K. F. (2022, June). Molecular mechanisms of oxidative stress in asthma. *Molecular Aspects of Medicine, 85*, 101026. https://doi.org/10.1016/j.mam.2021.101026. Epub 2021 Oct 6. PMID: 34625291.

Molot, J., Sears, M., Marshall, L. M., & Bray, R. I. (2021, September 16). Neurological susceptibility to environmental exposures: Pathophysiological mechanisms in neurodegeneration and multiple chemical sensitivity. *Reviews on Environmental Health, 37*(4), 509–530. https://doi.org/10.1515/reveh-2021-0043. PMID: 34529912.

Montgomery, M. T., Sajuthi, S. P., Cho, S. H., Everman, J. L., Rios, C. L., Goldfarbmuren, K. C., Jackson, N. D., Saef, B., Cromie, M., Eng, C., Medina, V., Elhawary, J. R.,

Oh, S. S., Rodriguez-Santana, J., Vladar, E. K., Burchard, E. G., & Seibold, M. A. (2020, August) Genome-wide analysis reveals mucociliary remodeling of the nasal airway epithelium induced by urban PM2.5. *American Journal of Respiratory Cell and Molecular Biology*, *63*(2), 172–184. https://doi.org/10.1165/rcmb.2019-0454OC. PMID: 32275839; PMCID: PMC7397762.

Mudway, I. S., Holgate, S., Forman, H. J., & Kelly, F. J. (2020, May 1). Air pollution: Consequences for cellular redox signaling, antioxidant defenses and disease. *Free Radical Biology and Medicine*, *151*, 1. https://doi.org/10.1016/j.freeradbiomed.2020.04.030. Epub 2020 May 1. PMID: 32360614.

Mukherjee, S., Dasgupta, S., Mishra, P. K., & Chaudhury, K. (2021, October). Air pollution-induced epigenetic changes: Disease development and a possible link with hypersensitivity pneumonitis. *Environmental Science and Pollution Research*, *28*(40), 55981–56002. https://doi.org/10.1007/s11356-021-16056-x. Epub 2021 Sep 8. PMID: 34498177; PMCID: PMC8425320.

Munro, A., Boyce, T., & Marmot, M. (2020, December). Sustainable health equity: Achieving a net-zero UK. *Lancet Planet Health*, *4*(12), e551–e553. https://doi.org/10.1016/S2542-5196(20)30270-9. Epub 2020 Nov 5. PMID: 33160450.

Nguyen, J. P., Huff, R. D., Cao, Q. T., Tiessen, N., Carlsten, C., & Hirota, J. A. (2021, December). Effects of environmental air pollutants on CFTR expression and function in human airway epithelial cells. *Toxicology In Vitro*, *77*, 105253. https://doi.org/10.1016/j.tiv.2021.105253. Epub 2021 Sep 30. PMID: 34601066.

Pedersen, M. (1990). Ciliary activity and pollution. *Lung*, *168*(Suppl), 368–376. https://doi.org/10.1007/BF02718154. PMID: 2117139.

Poole, J. A., Barnes, C. S., Demain, J. G., Bernstein, J. A., Padukudru, M. A., Sheehan, W. J., Fogelbach, G. G., Wedner, J., Codina, R., Levetin, E., Cohn, J. R., Kagen, S., Portnoy, J. M., & Nel, A. E. (2019, May). Impact of weather and climate change with indoor and outdoor air quality in asthma: A Work Group Report of the AAAAI Environmental Exposure and Respiratory Health Committee. *The Journal of Allergy and Clinical Immunology*, *143*(5), 1702–1710. https://doi.org/10.1016/j.jaci.2019.02.018. Epub 2019 Feb 28. PMID: 30826366; PMCID: PMC10907958.

Raju, S., Woo, H., Koehler, K., Fawzy, A., Liu, C., Putcha, N., Balasubramanian, A., Peng, R. D., Lin, C. T., Lemoine, C., Wineke, J., Berger, R. D., Hansel, N. N., & McCormack, M. C. (2023, March 15). Indoor air pollution and impaired cardiac autonomic function in chronic obstructive pulmonary disease. *American Journal of Respiratory and Critical Care Medicine*, *207*(6), 721–730. https://doi.org/10.1164/rccm.202203-0523OC. PMID: 36288428; PMCID: PMC10037475.

Real, Á. D., Santurtún, A., & Teresa Zarrabeitia, M. (2021, June). Epigenetic related changes on air quality. *Environmental Research*, *197*, 111155. https://doi.org/10.1016/j.envres.2021.111155. Epub 2021 Apr 21. PMID: 33891958.

Sharma, K., Lee, H. H., Gong, D. S., Park, S. H., Yi, E., Schini-Kerth, V., & Oak, M. H. (2019, September). Fine air pollution particles induce endothelial senescence via redox-sensitive activation of local angiotensin system. *Environmental Pollution*, *252*(Pt A), 317–329. https://doi.org/10.1016/j.envpol.2019.05.066. Epub 2019 May 20. PMID: 31158660.

Shin, J. W., Lee, H. S., Na, J. I., Huh, C. H., Park, K. C., & Choi, H. R. (2020, May 13). Resveratrol inhibits particulate matter-induced inflammatory responses in human keratinocytes. *International Journal of Molecular Science*, *21*(10), 3446. https://doi.org/10.3390/ijms21103446. PMID: 32414118; PMCID: PMC7279174.

Shukla, A., Bunkar, N., Kumar, R., Bhargava, A., Tiwari, R., Chaudhury, K., Goryacheva, I. Y., & Mishra, P. K. (2019, March 15). Air pollution associated epigenetic modifications: Transgenerational inheritance and underlying molecular mechanisms. *Science of the Total Environment*, *656*, 760–777. https://doi.org/10.1016/j.scitotenv.2018.11.381. Epub 2018 Nov 28. PMID: 30530146.

Siddique, A., Al-Shamlan, M. Y. M., Al-Romaihi, H. E., & Khwaja, H. A. (2023, December 27). Beyond the outdoors: Indoor air quality guidelines and standards – Challenges, inequalities, and the path forward. *Reviews on Environmental Health*. https://doi.org/10.1515/reveh-2023-0150. Epub ahead of print. PMID: 38148484.

Thangavel, P., Park, D., & Lee, Y. C. (2022, June 19). Recent insights into particulate matter (PM2.5)-mediated toxicity in humans: An overview. *International Journal of Environmental Research and Public Health*, *19*(12), 7511. https://doi.org/10.3390/ijerph19127511. PMID: 35742761; PMCID: PMC9223652.

Vogel, C. F. A., Van Winkle, L. S., Esser, C., & Haarmann-Stemmann, T. (2020, July). The aryl hydrocarbon receptor as a target of environmental stressors – Implications for pollution mediated stress and inflammatory responses. *Redox Biology*, *34*, 101530. https://doi.org/10.1016/j.redox.2020.101530. Epub 2020 Apr 18. PMID: 32354640; PMCID: PMC7327980.

World Health Organisation. (2022). *WHO air quality guidelines and estimated reference levels*. https://www.eea.europa.eu/publications/status-of-air-quality-in-Europe-2022/europes-air-quality-status-2022/world-health-organization-who-air

Yang, Y., Zoulikha, M., Xiao, Q., Huang, F., Jiang, Q., Li, X., Wu, Z., & He, W. (2023, November). Pulmonary endothelium-targeted nanoassembly of indomethacin and superoxide dismutase relieves lung inflammation. *Acta Pharmaceutica Sinica B*, *13*(11), 4607–4620. https://doi.org/10.1016/j.apsb.2023.05.024. Epub 2023 May 26. PMID: 37969734; PMCID: PMC10638505.

Zhang, L., Lu, Q., & Chang, C. (2020). Epigenetics in health and disease. *Advances in Experimental Medicine and Biology*, *1253*, 3–55. https://doi.org/10.1007/978-981-15-3449-2_1. PMID: 32445090.

Chapter 6

Towards Net Zero: A Practical Transformative Leadership Agenda for Manufacturers and SMEs

Alex de Ruyter[a], *Michael Butler*[b] *and Rowan Crozier*[c]

[a]*Birmingham City University, UK*
[b]*Bangor University, UK*
[c]*C Brandauer & Co Ltd, UK*

Abstract

To deliver net zero, this chapter demonstrates the importance of linking different levels of analysis. Macro concepts like Net Zero need to be operationalised at meso- and micro levels so that individual firms, and the ecosystems they operate in, make the required changes to reduce carbon. However, such change is difficult to achieve because of the scale of activities involved. We draw on the manufacturing case study of C Brandauer & Co Ltd to reveal how they successfully pursued Net Zero and then went on to embed change in their supply chain. We also highlight the key role of a transformational leader to sustain purpose-driven change, a leader brave enough to share core knowledge with local competitors. The authors introduce the term 'sectoral transformation' to capture multi-level change within the geographical area of the West Midlands. The chapter finishes with policy implications so that more SMEs can follow this agenda for change, and so that Net Zero becomes a much-needed reality, not just a policy ambition.

Keywords: Net Zero; case study; entrepreneurial ecosystem; transformational leadership; SMEs; Triple Helix

Examining Net Zero: Creating Solutions for a Greener Society and Sustainable Economic Growth, 57–64
Copyright © 2025 by Alex de Ruyter, Michael Butler and Rowan Crozier
Published under exclusive licence by Emerald Publishing Limited
doi:10.1108/978-1-83608-574-420251006

Introduction

Part 1 of this edited volume has introduced the concept of Net Zero and then explored it through the lens of key attributes such as the Circular Economy and how industrial transformation should be linked to the essential goal of clean air. This was then followed by country case studies that have sought to examine challenges in the progress to Net Zero, by drawing on chapters on the USA, Australia and India. Accordingly, in this chapter, we seek to link macro-arguments on the progress to Net Zero to meso- and micro-level arguments about how this raises challenges for individual firms in terms of restructuring their operations, products and processes (namely, production processes) and skills base within an extant 'regional entrepreneurial ecosystem' (Roundy, 2021). However, we also seek to assess the challenge of Net Zero in terms of its transformative impact on organisational culture and the role of leadership thereof, both within individual firms and of promoting leadership and transformation across wider industrial sectors.

In an era of rapid technological change, heightened global competition and the shift to the Green Economy, gone are the times when an SME could operate with its head down, not looking over the parapet to assess market trends and emergent opportunities and problems. This problem is particularly acute for liberal market economies such as the UK, where in contrast to more coordinated market economies such as Germany[1], membership of connective organisations such as chambers of commerce that could provide market intelligence is not mandatory by law (Bennett, 2021). Thus, there is a real need for good leaders to act as boundary spanners and forge links within and across different sectors (a theme we return to below). In this context, we use the practical example of Brandauer PLC in the West Midlands to illustrate how a positive change agenda in the pursuit of Net Zero can be enacted within and between firms in a production network.

In so doing, this chapter provides a link between Part 1 of the book, and the business case studies in Part 2 from the UK West Midlands that follow. In the material that follows, we first explore the Brandauer experience of change and enabling wider sectoral transformation. We then follow this by an articulation of a wider sectoral transformation and place leadership agenda, with a clear view of informing government policy and business practice.

The Brandauer Experience

C Brandauer & Co Ltd (see https://brandauer.co.uk/) is a manufacturer of precision stamping tools and components that supplies the auto sector amongst others and exports to countries across the globe. Such companies have generally been established and run by engineers over the years. However, whilst engineers have obvious conceptual and technical skills, we argue that a good engineer

[1]https://www.frankfurt-main.ihk.de/servicenavigation/chamber-of-commerce-and-industry/about-us/chamber-membership-and-obligation-to-pay-fees-5277146

increasingly needs to have commerciality and communication skills in addition to technical knowledge. From an examination of the Brandauer experience, it is evident that a basic aspect of leadership is providing workers with the necessary autonomy and confidence to get on with the job. Moreover, the Brandauer experience suggests that transformational leadership is also about instilling a culture of questioning established practices and seeking continuous improvement to effect cultural change.

As such, a key challenge for firms in the auto supply chain (and it could be argued, for SMEs in general) is embedding a management culture that empowers workers to make decisions, ensures succession planning and gives workers the necessary skills, for which apprenticeships and degree apprenticeships play a key role. Over 13 years at Brandauer, the number of apprentices increased from a zero base to now comprise about 20% of the workforce. In concert with this has been a concerted push to create a succession level of workers just below the management team who are somewhere in between team leader and managers. The importance of succession planning also throws into the spotlight the importance of tacit knowledge (Natek & Lesjak, 2021) that is the informal knowledge embodied in an individual worker gained through having built up experience within the organisation (Natek & Lesjak, 2021). It also highlights the development of social capital, which Putnam (2001, p. 2) characterises at its most basic, informal level as consisting of a network where firms 'can easily develop reciprocity, and in which there can be gains'.

However, Brandauer see beyond their immediate company needs to also embrace viability for the wider sectors and regions in which they operate as part of promoting sectoral transformation and productivity enhancement. Spotting a gap in training provision, they developed their own in-house 20-week bespoke full-time programme in concert with, which they even offer to firms that might be competitors. As Rowan Crozier, CEO of Brandauer and co-author in this chapter comments:

> I've had people come to me and say 'why on Earth you sharing knowledge with your competitors?' Well, if I don't, our industry will be dead and of course I can charge them for it because there's a premium for well-founded knowledge to improve skills ... It's about being brave enough to use your own IP to the greater good, but also make some money at it along the way.

Moreover, the Brandauer experience highlights that good leaders of firms in the supply chain need to network with other players in the entrepreneurial ecosystem – that is, the whole spectrum of institutions linked to production in a given sector, all the way from universities and government agencies, through other firms in the sector (up and down the supply chain), and also consumer groups. Good leaders engage proactively with the sectors they operate in, to drive innovation and thereby help to bring about sectoral transformation. Effective leaders then, to reiterate, are Connectors across the entrepreneurial ecosystem and function as pro-active change agents to drive innovation, market growth and productivity enhancement. Similarly, they also embrace diversification and keeping ahead of the market.

As such, the Brandauer experience has been one of complete organisational transformation over the past decade, moving from a forced situation of reactive management and resulting poor morale to the current situation of being forward thinking, a lot more diverse and with a lot more autonomy, engaging with Net Zero challenges and thereby creating a completely different culture. Generalising from this, it is evident that a successful transition to Net Zero must involve businesses hiring managers that extoll environmental values, as they are the ones who can drive a shift towards eco-friendly production processes (Wang, 2019) such as that epitomised in the Circular Economy (see McCabe in this volume), and also be the drivers in terms of green product innovation (Wang, 2019).

Bringing It Together: The Role of Transformative Leadership Across Firms and Place

Evident then is that there is an explicit spatial dimension to industrial transformation and towards the pursuit of Net Zero in particular. Firms are inherently embedded in local and regional ecosystems (and, indeed, national and international), as first epitomised by Alfred Marshall in 1920 as 'industrial districts' (Marshall, 2013) and more latterly in the literature on clusters (e.g. Delgado et al., 2010; Porter, 1990), which in latter-day UK Government policy discourse on decarbonisation have come to be referred to as 'SuperPlaces' (Devine-Wright, 2022). Firms in clusters can derive benefits from knowledge spillovers and local sectoral specialisation (Brown & Mason, 2017). Such benefits may accrue to firms in the same sector in the form of Marshallian externalities or to firms in different sectors – that is Jacobean externalities (Brown & Mason, 2017).

Clearly, Brandauer operates within the West Midlands amidst an extant network of suppliers, customers and other firms. It also links extensively to other regional stakeholders such as government bodies and higher education institutions and, thus, can exploit innovations that arise in the realm of R&D and diffuse its own innovations across sectors by sharing intellectual property, to the mutual benefit of all businesses that it interacts with. Transformational leadership then occurs not only within the firm, but across firms, enabling a process of *sectoral transformation* – essential to the successful attainment of Net Zero. Brandauer, thus, operates effectively within a regional entrepreneurial ecosystem. There are inherent lessons here for other firms that may not be so effective at networking and boundary spanning.

In this context, place leadership theory has important insights to offer in terms of how businesses and other actors at various scalar levels have agency, or lack thereof, to make key decisions affecting their constituent economies (Beer et al., 2023; Grillitsch & Sotarauta, 2020; Sotarauta & Grillitsch, 2023). It also emphasises the nature of linkages between various regional stakeholders and, thus, emphasises the importance of formal (and informal) networks (Beer et al., 2023; Grillitsch & Sotarauta, 2020; Sotarauta & Grillitsch, 2023). In turn, this links to innovation theory and the extant concept of the Triple Helix, highlighting the importance of linkages between government, industry and academia. It is within this context that the effectiveness of an extant entrepreneurial ecosystem in a locality – and the effectiveness of leadership and management in individual businesses within it – should be evaluated. In turn, this warrants a particular focus on SMEs, as evidence suggests that compared to larger firms, they are less likely to be networked and, therefore, may not be benefiting from innovations arising elsewhere (De Ruyter et al., 2021, 2022).

Turning to policy implications, evident is a real need to ensure connectivity between actors in the entrepreneurial ecosystem so that the innovations that will help drive a successful transition to Net Zero lead to wider sectoral transformation. Connectivity can be enabled in many ways – such measures could include:

- Mandatory membership of organisations such as Chambers of Commerce or the Chartered Institute of Management, to enable businesses to keep abreast of market trends, be informed of (and learn from) best practice and wider issues that will affect their viability, and network directly with similar firms. Membership also provides a 'voice' for such businesses to air their concerns over key issues and, thus, help inform and shape government policy.
- A consolidation of regional bodies that serve to bring together stakeholders across the public, private and third sectors. Historically, this function had been enabled by regional development agencies in the UK (Pugalis & Bentley, 2013). However, since 2010, there has been a more fragmented geography with a diffusion of Local Enterprise Partnerships, Mayoral Combined Authorities and looser umbrella organisations such as the Northern Powerhouse and Midlands Engine. The roles of such bodies have often seemed opaque and confusing to business – particularly SMEs (James & Guile, 2014).
- The recruitment of 'supply chain champions' to advocate for a particular industrial sector and help build awareness of issues that will affect transition to Net Zero – particularly amongst SMEs in the supply chain, who may at best only have a partial knowledge of the impending changes that will affect them (De Ruyter et al., 2022). Indeed, SMEs are less likely to have the required organisational capability and employee skill base (motivation) to navigate the complex challenges associated with Net Zero (Singh et al., 2020).
- An enhanced emphasis on the creation of science parks and technology precincts, for those cases where co-location on a single site might enhance innovation (e.g. see Horsfall in this volume, for the case of the Tyseley Energy Park in Birmingham). Evidence (Lamperti et al., 2017) suggests that science parks can enhance patenting activities and R&D investments when research centres within the park are underpinned by strong university-industry linkages (Lamperti et al., 2017).
- An expanded adult education budget, devolved to the local/regional level, which will enable a more place-specific and proactive regional skills development policy (Corradini et al., 2023). Skills policy should thereby be conducted and controlled by that level of government that has the best market knowledge of training needs and skills gaps in a particular locality and region

(Corradini et al., 2023). It should also be targeted at those in sectors such as automotive facing the prospect of job loss as we transition to Net Zero, as evidence there suggests a distinct lack of company-provided training for such workers (De Ruyter et al., 2024).

Underpinning all these initiatives then is the need for an overall place-based industrial policy at the UK level (Bailey et al., 2019), which is cognisant of the changing geographies of production, and how government intervention can mitigate the negative effects of transition on particular regions with the emergence of a green economy (Devine-Wright, 2022). In this context, as Devine-Wright argues:

> [w]hat 'place' does is provide an ontological foundation for industrial decarbonisation that conceives technology deployment as an act of place-making. This foregrounds the locatedness of industrial facilities alongside host community lived experiences, emotional attachments and senses of identity (Devine-Wright, 2022).

Intimate to the notion of place-based policies is working with firms and communities affected by change. In this context, to return to our key argument, visionary firms led by agents of sectoral transformation can be key progenitors of wider change within a region.

Conclusion

In this chapter, we have sought to highlight the importance of transformational leadership as driving sectoral transformation, by drawing on the experience of Brandauer PLC as a benchmarking case study. In so doing, we distilled how macro-developments in the pursuit of Net Zero link at the meso- and micro-level to the decisions of managers within firms and the organisational culture they embed in securing a green transformation. Evident is that good leadership and management take place within a wider entrepreneurial ecosystem, whereby for this ecosystem to be effective, connectivity between its various participants must be ensured.

In the sections that follow the key lessons around green culture, collaboration and partnership, and the industry/government/HEI links evident in the Triple Helix are further explored through the business case studies in Section B. Here, we draw upon evidence and good practice from Bosch Thermotechnology, Schneider Electric, Amtico, KPM Marine, Tyseley Energy Park, Heart of England Community Energy and Communities for Renewables.

References

Bailey, D., Glasmeier, A., & Tomlinson, P. (2019). Industrial policy back on the agenda: Putting industrial policy in its place? *Cambridge Journal of Regions, Economy and Society*, *12*(3), 319–326. https://doi.org/10.1093/cjres/rsz018

Beer, A., Sotarauta, M., & Bailey, D. (2023). Leading change in communities experiencing economic transition: Place leadership, expectations, and industry closure. *Journal of Change Management*, *23*(1), 32–52. https://doi.org/10.1080/14697017.2023.2164936

Bennett, R. (2021). Institutional change in British chambers of commerce. In D. Sack (Ed.), *Chambers of commerce in Europe* (pp. 47–82). Palgrave Macmillan. https://doi.org/10.1007/978-3-030-62700-3_3

Brown, R., & Mason, C. (2017). Looking inside the spiky bits: A critical review and conceptualisation of entrepreneurial ecosystems. *Small Business Economics*, *49*, 11–30. https://doi.org/10.1007/s11187-017-9865-7

Corradini, C., Morris, D., & Vanino, E. (2023). Towards a regional approach for skills policy. *Regional Studies*, *57*(6), 1043–1054. https://doi.org/10.1080/00343404.2022.2031950

Delgado, M., Porter, M., & Stern, S. (2010). Clusters and entrepreneurship. *Journal of Economic Geography*, *10*(4), 495–518. https://doi.org/10.1093/jeg/lbq010

De Ruyter, A., Bentley, G., Hearne, D., Bailey, D., & Neilsen, B. (2024). A "just transition" for workers in the automotive sector? Survey evidence from the West Midlands. *Contemporary Social Science*, *19*(1–3), 199–222. https://doi.org/10.1080/21582041.2024.2353684

De Ruyter, A., Hearne, D., & Henry, I. (2021). *The resilience of advanced manufacturing supply chains across the Midlands*. https://www.midlandsengine.org/wp-content/uploads/Manufacturing.pdf

De Ruyter, A., Weller, S., Henry, I., Rainnie, A., & Bentley, G. (2022). *Enabling a just transition in automotive: Evidence from the West Midlands and South Australia*. https://bcuassets.blob.core.windows.net/docs/british-academy-just-transition-final-report-00273-132996712408502462.pdf

Devine-Wright, P. (2022). Decarbonisation of industrial clusters: A place-based research agenda. *Energy Research & Social Science*, *91*. https://doi.org/10.1016/j.erss.2022.102725

Grillitsch, M., & Sotarauta, M. (2020). Trinity of change agency, regional development paths and opportunity spaces. *Progress in Human Geography*, *44*(4), 704–723.

James, L., & Guile, D. (2014). Evaluating the transition from regional development agencies to local economic partnerships: The views of SMEs in the British West Midlands. *Local Economy*, *29*(3), 181–194. https://doi.org/10.1177/0269094214528773

Lamperti, F., Mavilia, R., & Castellini, S. (2017). The role of science parks: A puzzle of growth, innovation and R&D investments. *Journal of Technological Transfer*, *42*, 158–183. https://doi.org/10.1007/s10961-015-9455-2

Marshall, A. (2013). Industrial organization, continued. The concentration of specialized industries in particular localities. In A. Marshall (Ed.), *Principles of economics. Palgrave classics in economics* (pp. 222–231). Palgrave Macmillan. https://doi.org/10.1057/9781137375261_24

Natek, S., & Lesjak, D. (2021). Knowledge management systems and tacit knowledge. *International Journal of Innovation and Learning*, *29*(2), 166–180. https://doi.org/10.1504/IJIL.2021.112994

Porter, M. (1990). *The competitive advantage of nations*. Free Press.

Pugalis, L., & Bentley, G. (2013). Economic development under the Coalition Government. *Local Economy*, *28*(7–8), 665–678. https://doi.org/10.1177/0269094213506800

Putnam, R. (2001). *Social capital: Measurement and consequences*. Retrieved May 21, 2024, from https://visionaryvalues.com/wiki/images/Putnam_SocialCapital.pdf

Roundy, P. (2021). Leadership in startup communities: How incubator leaders develop a regional entrepreneurial ecosystem. *Journal of Management Development*, *40*(3), 190–208. https://doi.org/10.1108/JMD-10-2020-0320

Singh, S., Del Giudice, M., Chierici, R., & Graziano, D. (2020). Green innovation and environmental performance: The role of green transformational leadership and green human resource management. *Technological Forecasting and Social Change*, *150*. https://doi.org/10.1016/j.techfore.2019.119762

Sotarauta, M., & Grillitsch, M. (2023). Path tracing in the study of agency and structures: Methodological considerations. *Progress in Human Geography*, *47*(1), 85–102. https://doi.org/10.1177/03091325221145590

Wang, C.-H. (2019). How organizational green culture influences green performance and competitive advantage: The mediating role of green innovation. *Journal of Manufacturing Technology Management*, *30*(4), 666–683. https://doi.org/10.1108/JMTM-09-2018-0314

Part Two

Empirical Examples of Practice (Case Studies)

Chapter 7

The Green Economy: A Just Transition and Where to Go from Here – How to Decarbonise the Way We Heat Our Homes and Buildings in the UK?

Carl Arntzen

Bosch Thermotechnology Ltd, UK

Abstract

Bosch Thermotechnology is working to develop Net Zero, ethical manufacturing solutions so that the manufacturing of home heating products is not simply off-shored. With 85% of UK homes using gas boilers for heating, the challenges are considerable. Hydrogen is advocated as a solution, but the production of green hydrogen at a sufficient scale remains challenging. A tailored approach to decarbonising home heating is advocated by Bosch Thermotechnology, with electrification of new build homes, but, with a more cautious approach for existing homes drawing on a diverse range of technologies to suit individual and geographic circumstances including heat networks, hydrogen boilers, heat pumps (HPs) and, in particular, hybrids (boiler and HP). This approach contrasts with the UK government's focus on electrification and HPs as a near universal solution having set up the Clean Heat Market Mechanism (CHMM) placing obligations on boiler manufacturers to ensure they sell defined quantities of heat pumps from 2024, leading to fines where these targets are not achieved. The suitability of UK homes for heat pump technology is considered along with a phased hybrid solution. Hybrid HPs can deliver up to 80% carbon

Examining Net Zero: Creating Solutions for a Greener Society and Sustainable Economic Growth, 67–76
Copyright © 2025 by Carl Arntzen
Published under exclusive licence by Emerald Publishing Limited
doi:10.1108/978-1-83608-574-420251007

emissions reduction when compared to a 100% HP installation, for just 20% of the installation cost.

Keywords: Home Heating; HPs; hybrid HPs; retrofit; just transition; energy performance certificate; decarbonisation; multi-technology; biofuels; hydrogen

Introduction

Climate change and decarbonisation are the major challenges facing mankind during the remainder of this century and beyond. Having advanced human society in so many ways through the Industrial Revolution and made everyday comforts such as heating, hot water, cooking, dishwashing, laundry and motorised transport, accessible to the masses, we now have to confront the challenge of retaining such home comforts without destroying our planet.

Carbon-intensive fuels are a part of everyday life around the world. Oil, petrol, diesel, kerosene, natural gas and propane are all extracted and used in one form or another to fuel our cars, vans, HGVs, trains and aircraft and to heat our homes, offices, workplaces and buildings in general. We have become so reliant upon fossil fuels that it is difficult to imagine an industrialised world without them. But that is the challenge that confronts us if we are to prevent our climate changing to a point where it becomes unsustainable.

So how do we transition from where we are today to a carbon-free world, without foregoing our comforts and lifestyle, and without that lifestyle becoming too expensive and therefore inaccessible to the majority of society? And, how do we deliver the desired accessibility, whilst simultaneously providing energy security and stability? That is the challenge of delivering a *Just Transition*.

Delivering a Just Transition

Two areas within this challenge are transport and heating. In the transport sector, the transition to electric vehicles (EVs) is underway, and with respect to heating, the transition to HPs is in its infancy. In both sectors, the new electric technologies are expensive compared to their fossil fuel equivalents, so how do we make these technologies more affordable and hence more accessible, to support and manage the journey to Net Zero?

In both sectors, the UK Government is trying to accelerate the transition by placing obligations on manufacturers to sell targeted quantities of the new technologies each year, calculated as a percentage of their Fossil Fuel equivalents. In the case of the automotive sector, the policy is called the zero emission vehicle mandate, which compels car manufacturers to ensure at least 22% of the vehicles they sell in 2024 are electric (EVs). This target then increases each year until it reaches 80% by 2030. For every EV they fall short of the target, they will be fined £15,000.

In the boiler market, the policy is called the CHMM and similarly places obligations on boiler manufacturers to ensure they sell defined quantities of HPs in 2024 and beyond, calculated as a percentage of the boilers that they sell. The HP quota starts in 2024 at 4% of boiler sales (equivalent to 60,000 HPs) and then rises annually with the target of reaching 600,000 HPs sold in the UK each year by 2028. For every HP short of the target, the manufacturer will be fined £3,000.

Both these policies set out with good intentions to encourage the transition to low or zero carbon technologies, but the question is whether setting mandatory quotas on manufacturers represents and will *deliver a just transition?* Persuading Consumers to change their behaviour is always challenging but is the solution really to place financial obligations on manufacturers to essentially force consumers to buy things?

In general, households in the UK are very happy with gas boilers heating their homes, and the rhetoric around HPs is that they are big and expensive and don't keep you warm. Similarly, the rhetoric concerning electric cars is that the national charging infrastructure is inadequate and, therefore, you can't use them on long journeys, as you won't have anywhere to charge them. Both these challenges may be overcome in the future, but they aren't going to change overnight, and therefore, consumer nervousness and reticence will remain, at least for now.

But how do we instigate change? How do we persuade homeowners and consumers that they need to change in order to save the planet? Is the solution for our politicians to just keep setting targets? Or is the way forward about setting realistic policies? If our government devised policies rather than targets, would we move forward faster? If they defined policies, would they need targets? Since the targets they set are nearly always unrealistic and usually require millions of people to change their behaviour, do our politicians need to change *their* behaviour?

There is an old saying that 'you can lead a horse to water, but you can't make it drink'. In my experience, the 'Consumer is King'. If consumers don't want to buy expensive EVs or HPs, then no amount of government policy, advertising or salesmanship is going to make them. We need to come up with a Plan B!

Concentrating now on the Heating sector, how do we initiate and achieve a just transition, or in other words what is our Plan B?

UK Heating Market

The heating market in the UK is currently dominated by boilers. As can be seen from the pie chart below, almost 85% of UK homes are heated by a boiler of some type, predominantly natural gas boilers, but also included are LPG and oil boilers, for those properties not connected to the national gas grid.

Today, only 1.1% of UK homes are heated by HPs, which, therefore, illustrates the huge transformation required if we are to reach the Government's target of 600,000 HPs being installed in the UK each year by 2028.

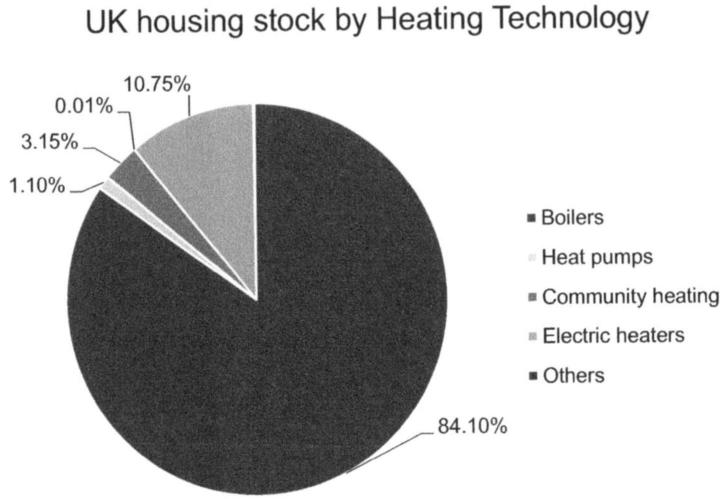

However, HPs are, in fact, a very mature technology and are much more prevalent in other parts of the world. They are essentially a refrigerator or an air conditioning unit working in reverse. The basic components are the same, but instead of providing cooling, they provide heat.

HPs operate at their optimum efficiency when running at relatively low and stable temperatures. A boiler typically operates at flow temperatures of around 80°C, meaning the radiators are relatively hot to touch and the system can achieve relatively rapid heat up curves. A HP typically operates at relatively low flow temperatures of 50°C and are, therefore, much more suited to well thermally insulated homes/buildings, where the internal ambient temperature does not fluctuate dramatically and they can, therefore, operate in a steady state, maintaining a stable temperature with only minor ambient fluctuations.

In terms of house construction, the thermal performance of a house is measured by something called the energy performance certificate (EPC). EPCs are a rating scheme that summarises the energy efficiency of a building and the building is rated between A and G; A being the most efficient, G being the least efficient. The EPC also provides tips on the most cost-effective way of improving the home energy rating.

Coming back to HPs, it is generally recommended that a house needs to have an EPC rating of C or above in order to be suitable for operating a low-temperature HP.

Below are two charts; the first shows UK housing stock by EPC rating, from which can be deduced that currently 45% of UK housing stock is theoretically suitable for a HP. The second provides more detail in terms of the EPC distribution across UK properties. These data show that only 12.2% of UK properties have an EPC rating of A or B, with a further 28.7% having an EPC rating of C, equating to 42% at Band C or above, which broadly correlates with the chart on the left.

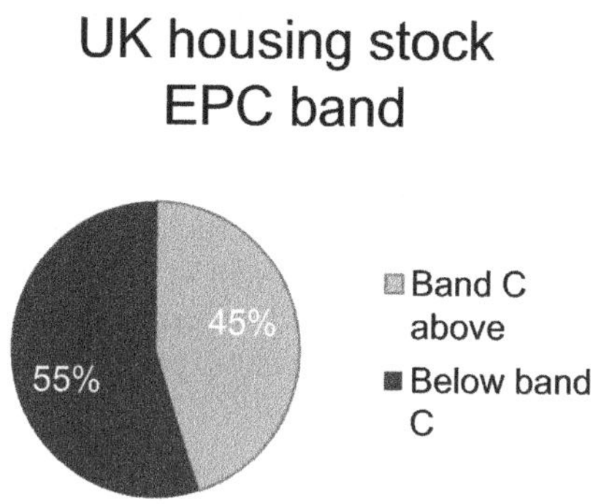

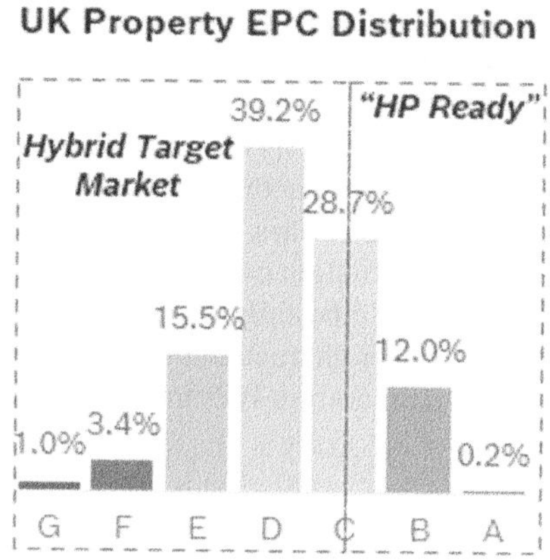

However, the EPC rating alone is not the only factor that should be taken into consideration when assessing the suitability of a house for a HP; other factors to consider are the building type (i.e. terrace, apartment, etc.) and the physical size, age and construction of the property. The table below provides further details on the distribution of property or building types in the UK, whether they are connected or not to the natural gas grid and, finally, whether their EPC rating is below C. This table again illustrates the mix and variation of property types in the UK, and the percentage with an EPC rating of below C, which will again have a bearing on suitability for deployment of a HP or not.

	Building Type	Converted Flat	Detached	Semi-Detached	Terrace
	Combi: 60% Heat Only: 30% Others: 10%				
On Grid	Total	975k	4,336k	6,512k	7,540k
On Grid	EPC Below C	69%	67%	69%	64%
Off Grid	Total	146k	952k	724k	594k
Off Grid	EPC Below C	75%	80%	82%	76%

*Easiest Hybrid Application

The final factor to consider is, of course, the weather or climate here in the UK.

In the UK, situated as we are to the west of the European land mass, at the eastern edge of the Atlantic Ocean and with prevailing westerly winds, we experience quite significant fluctuations in ambient temperatures throughout the year, particularly in the Spring and Autumn months but also increasingly in the Winter months. It is not uncommon to see temperature fluctuations of between 10°C and 15°C within 24 hours. If the property is not well insulated, then such rapid temperature fluctuation can be experienced inside the property, as well as outside. As HPs operate efficiently at relatively low and stable ambient temperatures, then this is another characteristic of the UK that emphasises the challenge of deploying low-temperature HPs into UK housing.

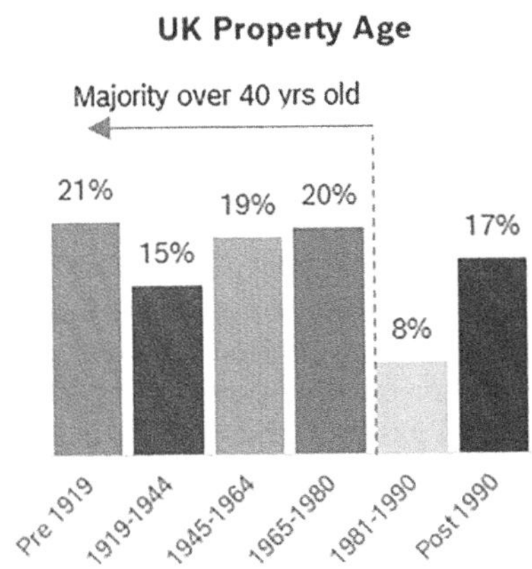

The UK has some of the oldest housing stock in Europe if not the world. As is shown in the chart above, the majority of our houses are over 40 years old, with high proportions of Georgian and Victorian housing, built with solid walls and single glazed sash windows. Very attractive aesthetically, but thermally extremely challenging to keep warm. In addition, 85% of UK homes are connected to the natural gas network, and as a result, the UK has become accustomed to gas boilers heating their homes, operating with relatively high flow and return temperatures in conjunction with relatively small and hot-to-touch radiators, delivering short and rapid heat up times, as referenced earlier.

Transition to HPs – A Multi-technology Approach

The transition to HP technology here in the UK, therefore, requires multiple changes in parallel:

- We need to improve the thermal insulation of our houses and install double glazed windows (if not already installed) in order to reduce heat losses from the building and associated fluctuations in ambient temperatures and enable a low-temperature radiator circuit to heat the house.
- We will need to install larger radiators in some rooms where necessary, to compensate for the lower flow and return temperatures.

- We will need to install a dedicated HP hot water cylinder to provide hot water for bathing/showering. If the property does not currently have a HW cylinder (e.g. if it has a Combi boiler), then space will need to be provided.
- And most importantly of all, we will need a change in behaviour from the consumer. The rapid heat up capability of a boiler is not achievable with a HP; therefore, the consumer has to change their behaviour and think more about sustaining a stable internal temperature with relatively minor adjustments to the ambient temperature. It is advisable to think ahead, monitor local weather forecasts and use the smart control systems within HP systems to effect subtle temperature changes.

These requirements to upgrade the fabric of the property often mean the cost of installing a HP is much higher than installing a replacement boiler. Combining this with the need to adjust behaviour in terms of operation of a HP, these are the challenges that are limiting the uptake of HPs right now.

So what is the way forward? How can we overcome these challenges and set ourselves on a pathway to decarbonising the heating of our homes?

I firmly believe the answer lies in a *multi-technology* approach. But what do we mean by a multi-technology approach?

It is becoming evident that the step from a heating system featuring a boiler to one involving a HP is too big a change to achieve in one step, for a large proportion of the houses in the UK. A better approach would be a more gradual transition using an interim solution – hybrid HPs.

Hybrid HPs

A hybrid HP, as illustrated in the below diagram, comprises a small HP featuring an outdoor unit and an indoor unit, operating in conjunction with a boiler of some description via an integrated control system that manages the operation of the two sources of heat.

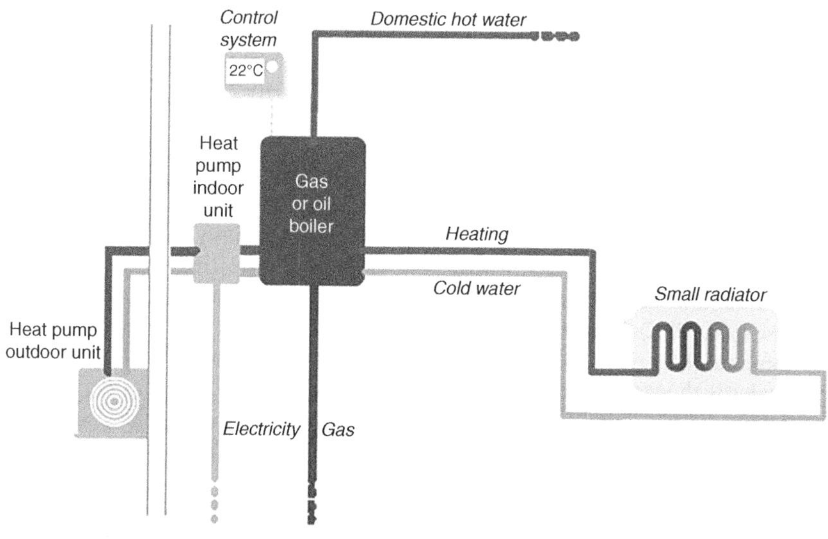

The boiler can be either an existing boiler or a new replacement appliance, running on natural gas, LPG or oil. If the existing boiler is retained, then the HP hybrid control elements can be added to the existing heating system.

Furthermore, if the new or existing boiler is a combination (Combi) boiler, then this eliminates the need for a dedicated HP hot water storage cylinder.

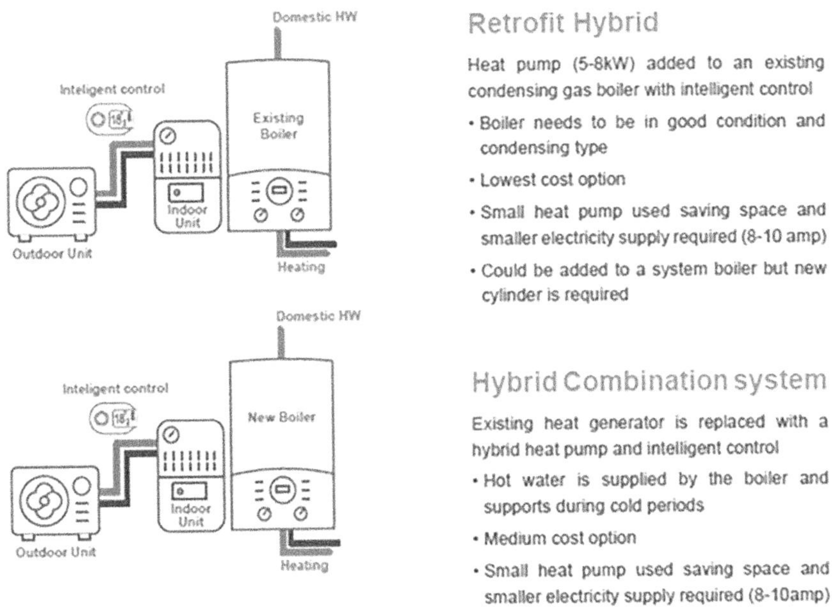

Based upon significant field trial data, gathered here in the UK, as well as in Germany and the Netherlands, it has been demonstrated that a hybrid HP can deliver up to 80% carbon emission reduction when compared to a 100% HP installation, for just 20% of the installation cost. The comparative installation cost is so low because a hybrid avoids the necessity to carry out fabric and radiator circuit improvements to the home upfront or at time of installation. This is because the hybrid has the backup of the boiler, so if sudden drops in ambient temperatures are experienced, then the boiler can operate to bring the property up to temperature quickly, and then the HP can maintain that temperature.

The hybrid solution, therefore, if sized correctly, essentially enables the homeowner to become familiar with operating a HP-based heating system for 80% of the time and become accustomed to the behaviour change that this entails. Because in the UK the number of days of sub-zero temperatures is relatively few, the home can be heated sufficiently by the HP for the majority (80%) of the time. The boiler is there to provide a backup if sudden drops in temperature are experienced, and potentially the hot water provision if the existing boiler is a combi boiler, and if the location of a hot water cylinder is a challenge.

The hybrid HP solution, therefore, enables the first significant step towards decarbonising the heating of our homes but at an affordable cost that enables the majority of UK households to take a first step towards decarbonisation.

Additional advantages could be derived via hybrid deployment if the UK ultimately decides to repurpose the natural gas network over to 100% hydrogen. Were the UK to deploy hydrogen hybrid solutions in a large proportion of UK housing, then this would attract the following advantages:

- Imagine hypothetically that the minimum standard in the UK is a hybrid installation.
- 100% HP systems are deployed wherever possible and financially viable, into properties that have an EPC rating of Band C or above.
- Where a hybrid HP is installed, the hybrid enables consumers to satisfy 80% of their heat demand via the HP but have the back up of a boiler if required.
- It enables consumers to become accustomed to and familiar with HP technology, and where possible facilitate the change in behaviour associated with low-temperature heating.
- Retrospective improvements to the fabric of the building can be made, as opposed to having to undertake this work upfront.
- The gas network is repurposed to 100% hydrogen in the future, but the capacity of green hydrogen required is significantly reduced because 80% of the heat load is covered by the hybrid HP.
- This provides huge advantages in terms of energy security because we are not totally reliant on one energy vector or another.
- Hybrids can also be operated via smart two-way communication systems, which means the hybrid appliances in people's homes can two-way communicate with the energy networks, enabling energy capacity management and, therefore, enhancing energy security. If the sun isn't shining and the wind isn't blowing, then rather than using electricity for heat demand, the network can switch over to hydrogen gas usage and vice versa.

The challenge for the future is to decarbonise the way we heat our homes and buildings, whilst simultaneously managing the security of energy supply. Hybrid HPs complement that ambition, by electrifying 80% of our heating and hot water demand, whilst providing the remaining 20% via a gas or oil boiler, which transitions in the near future to a hydrogen, biomethane or HVO boiler.

This transition enables consumers to become accustomed to the use of HP technology as a form of heat in their homes, enables an 80% reduction in carbon emissions immediately and then provides a time window for homeowners to improve the fabric and thermal efficiency of their homes. Eventually, the gas and oil boiler element of the hybrid is also decarbonised via the deployment of either green hydrogen or HVO or biofuels. This accelerates the decarbonisation of heat via a two-step approach, namely, boilers – hybrid HPs – HPs AND at an affordable cost to the consumer. The move to 100% electrification can be assessed and decisions can be taken at an appropriate point in the future.

In the meantime, hybrid deployment sets us on a journey and breaks the deadlock that currently exists. From gas heating systems of today to 100% HP systems is a big expensive step, requiring not only behavioural change relating to low-temperature heating but also significant expenditure in upgrading the fabric of the building through various insulation measures; this is too big a step for the vast majority of homeowners in the UK. Hybrids enable an interim step, buy us time to assess other alternatives, but achieve significant decarbonisation immediately, and at an affordable cost to the consumer.

Now that's what I would call a 'Just Transition'.

Chapter 8

Schneider Electric Case Study

Sharon Cronin

Schneider Electric, UK

Abstract

Schneider Electric's ethos to be 'the most local of global companies' includes promoting open standards and innovative partnerships, such as with customers Co-Op Live and the Tottenham Hotspur Stadium in the UK, along with 1,000 suppliers, to deliver Net Zero goals through their Life is On ethos. In 2005, they created their Sustainability Barometer delivering customer savings of 120 million tonnes in CO_2 emissions. Fifteen years after its launch and having enabled access to energy for 30 million people, they achieved a ranking as the World's most sustainable company in Knight's Global 100 ranking and have transformed energy management practices across their own sites including IntenCity as Schneider Electric's new flagship building located in the Scientific Polygon (Presqu'île) of Grenoble, France, and their Leeds UK decarbonisation programme. The Schneider Sustainability Impact (SSI) programme, 2021–2025, aims to deliver contributions across all the United Nations Sustainable Development Goals, including six long-term commitments to the environment, society, and economy, backed up by 11 global targets and accompanying local targets, as part of their focus on delivering a just transition. Schneider Electric introduced their 'Zero Carbon Project' as a demonstration of company-wide commitment to minimising 'operational carbon emissions' by 2025 and a Biodiversity Pledge promoting plan to protect and preserve nature and biodiversity. Early engagement at the design stage with clients has been essential. By explaining and demonstrating the opportunities for capturing and using technology and constantly evolving softwares, it is

Examining Net Zero: Creating Solutions for a Greener Society and Sustainable Economic Growth, 77–85
Copyright © 2025 by Sharon Cronin
Published under exclusive licence by Emerald Publishing Limited
doi:10.1108/978-1-83608-574-420251008

possible to unlock the efficiency of both project delivery and the operational energy performance of any building through its life cycle.

Keywords: Just transition; sustainability; energy management; net zero; resilience; climate strategy; scopes 1, 2, 3 emissions; UN Sustainable Development Goals; financial incentives; Biodiversity Pledge

Introduction

Schneider Electric is a French multinational specialising in electrification, digital automation, and energy management for homes, commercial buildings, data centres, infrastructures, and wider industry. Established in 1836, the company has, from the early 2000s, refocussed on the electric sector with a raft of acquisitions increasing their specialisation in the production of automotive and motion controls, data centre and transmission equipment, engineering, and industrial software controls.

With €34bn in revenues, 150k employees, the business is positioned as a global market leader building on its strong legacy in electrification and digitisation, working as a sustainability partner with their ethos as the 'most local of global companies' manifested through a multi-hub model. They trade in over 100 markets globally, providing solutions including accessing green electricity off-grid and working with local partners to make a positive difference to the environment and society.

Embarking on the Net Zero Journey

Schneider's mission to be a digital partner for sustainability and efficiency is central to their operations and as such they are strong advocates of open standards and partnership ecosystems, seen as essential to achieving Net Zero targets.

As climate concerns have become more pressing, Schneider has maintained a consistent focus on resilience and efficiency, both internally and with the increasing numbers of customers who have been approaching them to support them with their own sustainability transitions, seeking access to Schneider's expertise in working to deliver on the UN Sustainable Development Goals framework.

Launching a Sustainability Barometer and Programme

Schneider Electric's journey to Net Zero remains an ongoing work in progress positioned at the heart of their mission and ethos. They were the first company worldwide to report on this journey through their Sustainability Barometer, launched in 2005 and also positioning them as the first company to monitor their impact on the 'triple bottom line', people, planet, and profit, through the use of their 'Sustainability barometer'.

This approach led to the SSI programme and implemented to increase Schneider Electric's focus on fighting climate change and social inequality through 11 global transformations complemented by local commitments. It monitors their actions and impacts on the environment and the economy along with progress towards sustainable impact goals and undergoes scrutiny by auditors, a governance board, investors, customers, as well as peers, in and out of the industry.

As part of this, energy management has been taken very seriously with over 95% of facilities covered by an energy management system monitoring energy consumption focussed on implementing best practice and continual improvement to deliver further energy reductions. At the height of the energy crisis in 2022–2023, they ran an energy efficiency competition across the business with sites reducing energy consumption by over 1,600 MWh in 6 months, compared to the same time period the year before, delivering the equivalent of the average energy consumption for 110 homes in the UK. Their sites implemented digital monitoring systems, using excess heat from the compressors to warm other areas and running energy awareness campaigns.

Since 2017, Schneider has reduced energy consumption by 30% with a further 7% in energy savings between 2022 and 2023. Continuous assessment of further energy efficiency saving measures is ongoing. For example, at their Scarborough production site, they changed the operational management of the paint line by shifting the start and stop sequence, reducing total gas consumption at the site by 8.7% annually. In addition, sub-metering has been introduced in some facilities to deliver greater data granularity, highlighting further energy efficiency opportunities, for example, by being able to monitor whether energy is still being consumed when a line is no longer in production. The Leeds decarbonisation plan includes the installation of a heat pump as a significantly more efficient way to heat their facilities.

Scope 1 and 2 CO_2 emissions in the UK and Ireland have fallen by nearly two-thirds following energy efficiency measures. They have also switched from natural gas to electricity using a renewable electricity tariff. Ongoing decarbonisation projects continue to deliver energy savings. Specifically, they have committed to:

- Achieve carbon neutral operations (Scopes 1 and 2) by 2025, including CO_2 offsets. This is to be achieved through greater energy efficiency, electrification of fossil-based processes, renewable energy use and electric vehicles;
- Be 'Net-Zero ready' in their operations and make an absolute reduction of 25% of CO_2 emissions across all their value chain by 2030;
- Deliver an end-to-end carbon neutral value chain in 2040 (full Scopes 1, 2, and 3);
- Operate in a Net-Zero CO_2 emissions across the entire value chain in 2050.

Zero Carbon Project

Schneider Electric introduced their 'Zero Carbon Project' as a demonstration of their company-wide commitment to minimising 'operational carbon emissions' in 2025.

Launched in April 2020, it is focussed on their global supplier engagement and decarbonisation programme. In line with their Schneider Sustainability Impact targets for 2025, their aim is to support their top 1,000 suppliers through their own accelerated journeys to cut their CO_2 emissions in half by 2025 as these represent 70% of Schneider Electric's Scope 3 emissions, the bulk of all their CO_2 emissions.

Through the programme, facilitated by their sustainability consultants, environmental experts, and supply chain teams, Schneider Electric have placed all their expertise and knowledge in sustainability programmes at the service of their supply chain partners. They aim to evaluate their suppliers, assessing where they are in their decarbonisation journeys together with helping them to set goals to halve their CO_2 emissions. They plan to work with them to put in place roadmaps to achieve this and are delivering training, support, and solutions to enable the successful delivery of this programme. By the end of 2021, 91% of suppliers had already been trained and were working towards the decarbonisation of their operations as part of the Zero Carbon Project.

Climate strategies are also being developed with suppliers, with Schneider Electric assisting them in sourcing greener materials, such as bio-sourced or from recycled origin, along with appropriate certification. By assisting the delivery of higher energy efficiency in their own products and services, suppliers will reduce emissions produced during the use phase of all products sold. Schneider Electric also designs, sets up and manages these programmes for its customers, including delivery of the Energize programme developed for the Pharmaceutical Industry and overseen by their Sustainability Business Division.

Schneider Electric's Net-Zero commitment and roadmap includes their plan to decarbonise their full value chain across World Resources Institute Scopes 1, 2, and 3 emissions with this approach validated by the Science Based Targets initiative.

Scope 3 emissions are recognised as being 'the elephant in the room', given the lack of standardisation for commitments which they see as a risk which could bring any progress made so far to a halt. Nonetheless, the company aims to drastically reduce Scope 3 emissions and by embarking on their Net Zero Project they have already started to deliver a wide-ranging programme of training support to drive the targeted reductions.

Local initiatives include the electrification of their fleet and establishing a Carbon Fund. They planted 400 orchards between 2021 and 2023 and have pledged to plant a further 100 orchards in 2023–2024 in Ireland. They source 90% of electricity from renewables, with 100% of their primary and secondary packaging free of single-use plastic along with the use of recycled cardboard. In addition, they have launched their Zero Carbon Project with their top 1,000 suppliers.

Biodiversity Pledge

Accompanying their Net Zero Project, Schneider Electric undertook a Biodiversity Pledge promoting the Group's plan to protect and preserve nature and biodiversity in line with their commitment to Resource Efficiency. This involves:

- Quantifying and regularly publishing their impact on biodiversity. As part of this, they published the world's first end-to-end biodiversity footprint using the 'Global Biodiversity Score' tool, which calculates a company's biodiversity footprint across its entire value chain;
- Achieving net-zero biodiversity loss in their direct operations by 2030 and aligning biodiversity objectives with science;
- Developing solutions and technologies that contribute to the preservation of biodiversity, by optimising the use of resources over their entire lifecycle;
- Partnering with suppliers to eliminate the use of single-use plastics from packaging, the use of recycled cardboard, and helping them to sharply reduce CO_2 emissions;
- Partnering with NGOs and investment funds, and engaging employees and partners on local initiatives – such as ensuring that all of their sites deploy biodiversity conservation and restoration programmes and that sites located in water-stressed areas put in place water conservation plans.

As part of Act4Nature International, these commitments have been recognised as SMART, or Specific, Measurable, Achievable, Relevant, and Time-bound.

Schneider Electric pledge to deliver no net biodiversity loss in their direct operations by 2030 for Scope 1 activities and to align with the recommendations of international bodies (The Convention on Biological Diversity, The Science Based Targets Network) to preserve natural ecosystems and resources.

The business is also part of the Climate Group's EP100, RE100, and EV100 initiatives, setting respective targets for 2030 including:

- Switching to 100% renewable electricity by 2030 (RE 100).
- Doubling their energy productivity by 2030 against a 2005 baseline (EP 100).
- Replacing 100% of the Group's car fleet with electric vehicles by 2030 (EV 100).

'RE100', 'EP100', and 'EV100', respectively, refer to Renewables, Energy Productivity, and Electric Vehicles and are business initiatives run as part of the 'We Mean Business' coalition led by the NGO, the Climate Group. By inviting companies to join them, they aim to grow corporate demand for renewable energy, energy productivity, and electric transport, accelerating the transition to a zero-emissions economy, while helping leading businesses to reduce carbon emissions and to become more resilient whilst also increasing profits.

Leeds Case Study

At their Net Zero CO_2 site in Leeds, Schneider Electric deploy a green tariff and have installed solar panels on site. Both their Leeds and Scarborough sites have implemented energy efficiency measures, with a baseline Energy Performance Indicator established in 2019. By 2023, they intend to achieve 16% and 20% savings in energy use at these sites, respectively.

Energy efficiency and usage have been greatly improved. Strategies include installing a heat pump in September 2024 to eliminate gas usage. New solar panels are due to be installed on their extension and carports during 2024, adding to their current 1,400 m^2 array of photovoltaic panels. Additionally, to promote further energy efficiency, they will be implementing sensory lighting in all their office areas during 2024 with PIR lighting and insulation already in place.

Promoting greater biodiversity has also been prioritised at both these sites, with an external consultant conducting a biodiversity assessment, providing a 5-year action plan to improve biodiversity levels by 20%. Initiatives at the Leeds site include beekeeping, the creation of a recreation area within an orchard, and the installation of multiple green walls. Steps to reduce waste have included employees in Leeds embarking on their annual volunteering day at Middleton Park, removing litter and uprooting invasive Himalayan Balsam weeds.

Grenoble Case Study

The buildings sector is a key contributor to greenhouse gas (GHG) emissions, representing 35% of energy-related EU emissions in 2021 (EEA, 2023).

Schneider Electric's Grenoble site, known as IntenCity, has combined 13 separate sites into 4 Smart buildings to reduce their energy footprint. These support innovation and prioritise the well-being of 5,000 employees. They include 4,000 m^2 of photovoltaic panels; two wind turbines and onsite energy storage. The buildings use as much as 10 times less energy than for those with average European building specifications and are part of a microgrid partnership with any energy produced shared amongst neighbouring buildings and the city of Grenoble. They have reduced energy consumption in unoccupied spaces and ensured optimised air, lighting, heating, and blinds in shared spaces through their 'all digital' electric world.

Net Zero Project Partnerships

Tottenham Hotspur Stadium

The Background

In April 2019, English Premier League football club Tottenham Hotspur opened a brand-new, multi-use stadium, sport, and leisure destination at its home ground in London, N17. The 62,850-capacity stadium was built to host major sporting and non-sporting events, including NFL, rugby, concerts, and, naturally, Tottenham Hotspur football matches. With a strong local heritage stretching back to its establishment in 1882, Tottenham Hotspur Football Club is focused on supporting people, both on and off the pitch. They prioritise the curation of a memorable experience for their visitors as their number one priority, along with improving energy efficiency and addressing sustainability goals.

Schneider Electric worked with the club to bring their vision to life as part of their journey to build the most technologically advanced stadium in the world whilst simultaneously supporting their journey to net zero. The mission for Tottenham Hotspur Football Club has been to minimise the impact of their activities on the environment through energy consumption monitoring. Schneider Electric was appointed the Official Stadium Energy Management supplier installing their EcoStruxure Platform to monitor energy consumption across all the stadium's operations, using the data gathered to devise strategies for the delivery of greater energy efficiency. With energy waste representing the third-largest source of CO_2 emissions in the UK, at least 117 million tonnes of carbon dioxide emissions is generated through lost or wasted energy each year. Unless energy is managed efficiently, energy wastage cannot be detected, let alone reduced. As a signatory of the UN Sports for Climate Action Framework, Tottenham Hotspur is committed to halving its emissions by 2030, moving towards improving efficiency and sustainability whilst encouraging employees, suppliers, and partners to do the same. Investment in digital solutions has been a key part in delivering this so that energy wastage can be detected, analysed, and resolved in real time.

Solution

Schneider Electric's Building Operation management, Power Monitoring system, and Power Operations software platforms were installed on site working with their cloud-based Building and Asset Advisor programmes, providing real-time analytics to allow continuous control and monitoring of the systems integral to the stadium's smooth operations.

Using the Schneider Electric Power Monitoring Expert, the club can now monitor energy consumption across all of the stadium's operations and use data insights to inform operations to become even more energy-efficient. The EcoStruxure platform controls the mechanical plant, essential for the comfort and safety of visitors to the stadium. It also has full control of the stadium lighting system and can automate various lighting scenarios depending on the event taking place at the stadium and to reduce energy consumption where it is not necessary.

Collecting critical data using Schneider Electric's Building advisor and Asset Advisor analytics from sensors located around the stadium and linked to the cloud has been made to operate as simply as possible. This cloud-based analytics provides real-time monitoring of the stadium's vital infrastructure to ensure the safety of employees and optimise operations at Tottenham Hotspur Stadium. EcoStruxure has enabled the shift from preventive to predictive maintenance. Predictive maintenance means the stadium's facility managers can understand the current state of the equipment and infrastructure in real time so that maintenance updates can be planned and anticipated with minimal disruptions to business operations.

Result

Tottenham Hotspur has been named for the past four years as the Premier League's 'greenest club' following a study carried out by the UN-backed Sport Positive Summit.

The club remains dedicated to minimising the impacts of its activities on the environment. All electrical equipment at Tottenham Hotspur Stadium is powered by 100% renewable energy with zero Scope 2 emissions. Through technology powered by Schneider Electric, the stadium's LED lighting (including floodlights) is monitored along with high-efficiency building services systems to reduce energy consumption and minimise waste. Schneider Electric's solutions are integrated to support the stadium's unique features, such as the longest bar in Europe and the retractable pitch designed to enable the stadium to host a broader range of events.

On 19 September 2021, the stadium was home to the world's first net zero football match, #GameZero. Raising awareness amongst millions of football fans not just in the UK but globally, Tottenham Hotspur continues to take significant steps in the fight against climate change, highlighting the impact of major sporting events on our climate.

Co-op Live

Co-op Live is a new all-electric music arena which opened in 2024 in Manchester, UK. It uses a range of cutting-edge technologies to create a unique live music experience.

As part of Co-op Live's plans to become the UK's most sustainable venue, Schneider Electric was contracted as an official supplier for both the hardware and software for the electrical and building management systems and is also due to provide digital services and preventative maintenance throughout the venue to deliver a genuinely sustainable and people-centric facility.

The entire Co-op Live arena is 100% electric and is dependent on Schneider Electric's Power distribution products to ensure events go ahead and can handle the large electrical load when in operation. Ten percent of the site's energy is produced by photovoltaic solar panels installed across all the roof space of the arena.

The music venue is zero gas and uses alternative heat and cooling technology in the form of air source heat pumps controlled and monitored by Schneider's EcoStruxureIOT platform. It also includes a rainwater harvesting solution to capture and re-use the immense amount of rain which falls in Manchester! When the venue is NOT in use (event mode), the EcoStruxureBuilding Operation (BMS) is configured to change the site into setback mode ensuring it uses only the essential energy required to operate the occupied areas of the facility. Schneider Electric has also installed a PIR (presence) detection to set back the HVAC.

The case studies presented above have been challenging to implement, especially since contractors typically focus on purchasing at the lowest prices during the construction phase. This approach often overlooks long-term considerations beyond the capital expenditure period. This prevents some of the innovations from being implemented earlier, and if added at a later date, they often involve additional expense.

It remains challenging to convince end users that purchasing 'best in class technology' at the earliest stage pays off in the long run and integration of systems will release the data needed in the future to meet regulations and the highest industry standards.

However, as the case studies also demonstrate, with good relationships in place, it is possible. In the case of Co-op Live, it took 2 years in total from when Schneider Electric introduced to the project to the first order placed.

Lessons Learnt

Early engagement at the Design stage with clients is essential. By explaining and demonstrating the opportunities for capturing and using technology and constantly evolving software, it is possible to unlock the efficiency of both project delivery and the operational energy performance of the building through its life cycle.

However, in order to ensure that sustainability is at the heart of any organisation, it is critical to incentivise employees. Schneider Electric has linked sustainability performance to short- and long-term financial incentives for Group employees and the leadership team. Since 2011, annual short-term incentives for the Group's executives and about 58,000 eligible employees are linked to the SSI performance. From 2019, the weight of the sustainability criteria has increased from 6% to 20% in the collective part of the annual incentive, highlighting further the importance of ESG on Schneider Electric's business agenda.

Schneider Electric also offers long-term incentive plan share ownership opportunities to the Group's key talents and critical roles to align their rewards with the interests and experience of Schneider Electric shareholders. Similar to the short-term incentive, 25% of the award under the long-term incentive plan is subject to the achievement of sustainability objectives. From 2020, the long-term sustainability performance is measured through the Schneider Sustainability External & Relative Index, which is calculated by a combination of external ESG indices.

Reference

European Environment Agency. (2023, October 24). *Greenhouse gas emissions from energy use in buildings in Europe (europa.eu)*.

Chapter 9

Amtico's Net Zero Journey So Far

Holly Johnson

Amtico, UK

Abstract

Amtico, as a brand leader in luxury vinyl tiles (LVTs), is a 60-year-old design, manufacturing, sales and marketing business. As a plastics-based product manufacturer, the business undertakes energy-intensive production processes and has relied on fossil fuel-derived raw materials for decades. To assist on their journey to net zero, they engaged consultants and began harnessing the ingenuity, knowledge and insights of their entire workforce to develop four sustainability pillars. In 2023, they launched their first externally facing sustainability report, 'This is Where we Stand', reviewing actions taken during 2022 including, in full, their energy consumption, carbon footprint and product intensity ratios. In December 2022, the business launched Amtico Bio, a bio-attributed LVT option, starting to tackle the embodied carbon issue and demonstrating that the carbon footprint of their products could be effectively reduced. It relied upon deeper partnerships developed with their polyvinyl chloride (PVC) resin suppliers. To provide traceability and credibility, a further partnership was formed with the International Sustainability and Carbon Certification (ISCC), providing ISCC Plus certification and demonstrating strict auditing, and verification processes were in place for traceability of biomass consumption throughout the supply chain. In addition, far-reaching action plans have been put in place to reduce emissions in production and post-production, with recycling and working towards a circular economy at the heart of the company ethos. Amtico has also set an aspirational target to reach net zero carbon by 2040 as a demonstration of its commitment to reducing its impact on the environment and global warming.

Keywords: LVT; flooring; manufacturing; recycling; waste reduction; sustainability pillars; PVC; polymers; biomass-based; used cooking oil

Examining Net Zero: Creating Solutions for a Greener Society and Sustainable Economic Growth, 87–96
Copyright © 2025 by Holly Johnson
Published under exclusive licence by Emerald Publishing Limited
doi:10.1108/978-1-83608-574-420251009

Where It All Began

Amtico, as the brand leader in the LVT market, sells its products in over 130 countries, employing 640 in UK and Europe, with over 500 of these employees based in Coventry and Solihull in the UK's West Midlands. There is a further similarly sized operation in the USA, based in Atlanta. Amtico celebrated 60 years in business in 2024, marking this milestone with growth in sales to £250 million (end December 2023) with half of its sales in the USA, just over a third in the UK, and the balance in Continental Europe and Asia-Pacific.

The Amtico brand of luxury vinyl flooring was first introduced in 1964, operating as part of the National Plastics Division within the British textiles and chemicals company Courtaulds. Early development was led by a young chemist, John Harris, who as Amtico's first CEO was initially tasked with closing down a small loss-making subsidiary. Instead, John, ably assisted by other Courtaulds 'renegades', developed a unique method of manufacturing LVT from PVC, using high-pressure lamination techniques. PVC is a synthetic thermoplastic material with a carbon source derived from ethylene, which is traditionally derived from fossil fuels (crude oil). PVC and other polymers also use considerable amounts of energy to manufacture, posing immediate challenges to the firm when confronting net zero targets.

When John retired in 2003, he handed the reins over to Jonathan Duck, only the second CEO in Amtico's 60-year history. Jonathan explained that it has been quite a journey for Amtico, not only building an entirely new flooring market segment but also staying ahead of greatly increased competition as this particular type of flooring took off as Jonathan Duck explained:

> Amtico was sold by Courtaulds in 1995 to a management buyout. It pioneered the LVT market in the sixties, seventies and eighties. In 2006, the new management team led a secondary MBO (Management Buy Out) with a change of private equity investor. In 2012, Amtico became part of Mannington Mills, a much larger US-based flooring company, with great long-term vision and the ability to fully invest behind the business, including in the US where the true opportunities lay. As a result, there has been major recent investment in both our US and UK factories, more than doubling our manufacturing capacity in both sites. The investment here in our Coventry factory shows both our commitment to UK manufacturing and the strength and confidence we have in our product.

LVT is a durable, low-maintenance flooring tile made up of multiple different functional layers of PVC, compounded with plasticisers and stabilisers, which are compressed under pressure at a high temperature to create a hard-wearing type of flooring, almost indistinguishable from real wood or stone. The great advantage of LVT over the natural product is that it is much harder to wear, is unaffected by water, won't warp, chip or crack and since it is only a few millimetres thick, it is easy to install. Amtico LVT typically consists of five to six layers, including multiple backing layers, as well as two high-performance wear layers and a photographic film that offers either the appearance of real wood or stone or introduces a striking abstract look. Jonathan Duck further explained:

> We put a lot of effort into designing high fidelity woods and stones, which will look great year in, year out. We constantly update all our designs, including our abstract ranges, to stay right where the market is. Our proprietary production equipment also gives us a number of competitive advantages. These include excellent product strength, tight colour control and the ability to cut a whole range of tile sizes and shapes ... everything from parquet patterns to specialised logos. Finally manufacturing in the West, when most of our LVT competitors source from the Far East, lets us run a much shorter supply chain, better able to deal with the large number of product options we offer.
>
> Amtico is essentially a design business, a manufacturing business, and a sales & marketing business. Being great (and restless) at each of these three businesses, while linking them all together so they learn off each other, is what sets us apart. It has let us win in both residential and commercial markets ... and it is has let us grow internationally way beyond our UK origins.

Amtico, as market pioneers, built on their first mover market advantage for almost a decade until other companies appeared in the 1970s. Their current range has a number of collections including – Signature, Décor, Form, Spacia and Click Smart, each carefully positioned in the market to include different features. All flooring is sold with a long warranty in place and, in the case of their residential Signature collection, a lifetime wear-out warranty. Aftercare advisors offer vital support covering installation, maintenance, post-fitting and the technical aspects of how to maintain floors, helping ensure they last as long as possible, reflecting the company's ethos to ensure full and responsible use of the products it produces. Improving manufacturing productivity over the past two decades has been critical. Being able to get Amtico's UK and US manufacturing costs down to match Far Eastern sourced product pricing meant that the company could expand its manufacturing facilities in its home markets, at a time when many manufacturers were 'off-shoring' all production to lower cost economies. Amtico is proud of its British Manufacturing Excellence and continues to manufacture at the original site in Coventry. They work hard to connect design to manufacturing, facilitating and enabling innovative new designs, all of which are developed in the UK. Product renewal, combined with on-trend designs and high product quality, has consistently kept the business ahead of the competition.

The challenge for the coming decade has been identified as harnessing the same energy and commitment to address the challenges of becoming a sustainable, net zero manufacturer.

Background

Reaching net zero carbon emissions is a challenging undertaking for any business, particularly for a plastics manufacturing business like Amtico, where energy-intensive production processes and fossil fuel-derived raw materials have been used for decades. To do so within the time constraints applied by the UK Government, where all industries must reach net zero emissions by 2050, the company has devised a plan, by actively engaging their workforce and recognising the importance of sustainable action throughout their supply chains.

Setting About the Journey

In 2019, Amtico engaged an external sustainability consultancy, Simply Sustainable, to help them formulate their sustainability strategy and determine key priorities. By assessing the current sustainability landscape for Amtico, along with the LVT flooring sector, and conducting their first materiality assessment, they generated four areas of sustainability focus for the business which became Amtico's 'sustainability pillars':

- Climate action – To limit Amtico's impact on climate change and to work towards net zero carbon emissions through activities such as energy efficiency improvements and seeking alternatives to fossil fuel-derived raw materials
- Zero in on waste – To focus on waste generated throughout their entire value chain and to increase circular activities, from the flooring products produced to the packaging used
- Empowering people – To empower their workforce, focus on Diversity, Equity & Inclusivity, health & wellbeing, colleague development and to work with local communities to provide opportunities and give back through charitable partnerships
- Collaborate to innovate – To promote and incentivise innovative thinking across all teams, driving collaborations with external stakeholders and listening to experts to help achieve their mutual goals

Due to the coronavirus pandemic, they were delayed in launching their sustainability strategy, but in 2021, they launched their externally branded, *Responsible Foundations* strategy, informing customers of their four sustainable pillars. *Impact* was subsequently launched as their internally focussed sustainability branding as a means of engaging their workforce and providing a common identity and language in driving forward this strategy.

To deliver Impact, they assigned directors' responsibility as owners and sponsors for each of the four pillars and included a team of enthusiastic volunteers from across the business to support the directors, forming committees to discuss, develop and drive activity.

What Prompted Action?

Their initial drive for activity was very much a response to growing market demand and Amtico's desire to maintain its position as a leader in the LVT market. Their passionate workforce was also expressing a keen interest to do more on sustainability. Having consistently been a leader in design and innovation in LVT flooring, an approach which has sustained this leadership over many decades, the company found that given the increasingly visible impacts of climate change and growing consumer awareness, it was important to act. There was also the internal enthusiasm to go beyond the competition, and the pace of legislative requirements, to innovate in sustainability and maintain market leadership in this space.

Collaborative Partners and Market Reaction

In approaching sustainability and net zero strategies, Amtico were quite frank with themselves about not being experts in this area and keen to form partnerships with recognised expert consultancies, such as Simply Sustainable, who helped them create their first sustainability strategy. From 2023 onwards, another consultancy, Action Sustainability, also helped them further develop this strategy and their relationships with both consultancies assisted them in their corporate learning, insight and focus during their early sustainability journey.

In 2023, they launched their first externally facing sustainability report, 'This is Where we Stand', reviewing actions taken during 2022, sharing details from this with customers and stakeholders and covering their approach to sustainability, highlighting successes up to that point. The company reported on key sustainability issues including, in full, their energy consumption, carbon footprint and product intensity ratios. These measures provided a baseline for future years enabling them to map progress and demonstrate positive improvements are being made. They were clear in approaching this report about their intention to provide full transparency along with information on progress, even in areas which had not yet been actioned significantly to that point such as supply chain sustainability. Following on from this first report, areas highlighted, which required further action, have been used to create a new focus. One example of this was launching a sustainable procurement policy project in 2023 with Action Sustainability, in line with ISO 20400, to drive progress on supply sustainability.

Launching Amtico Bio

In December 2022, the business launched Amtico Bio, a bio-attributed LVT option, which rather than using fossil fuels to make the PVC, replaced them with renewable biomass-based feedstocks, representing a ground-breaking step for

Amtico on its sustainability journey. It demonstrated that by harnessing renewable design principles, the carbon footprint and embodied carbon within their products could be effectively reduced. This achievement relied upon deeper partnerships developed with their PVC resin suppliers, with Amtico being the first company in the UK to source bio-attributed PVC from their supplier. This PVC is made from used cooking oil, a waste product from the food production industry, or crude tall oil, a byproduct from the paper pulping industry, using certified sustainably managed forests. As this biomass fully replaces the fossil fuel feedstock for the PVC resin production, the CO_2 emissions created in the PVC resin production are reduced by more than 90%, providing customers with a greatly reduced carbon footprint option for their Amtico LVT.

Amtico Bio is chemically and physically identical to Amtico's standard LVT products and is produced using mass balance principles in the same way that renewable electricity is supplied to homes and businesses. For each order placed as Amtico Bio, the business sources the required amounts of bio-attributed PVC for that product, incorporating this into their existing manufacturing processes. This approach guarantees an equivalent amount of fossil fuel feedstocks, which are removed from their direct supply chain and replaced with renewable biomass. To provide traceability and credibility, another partnership was formed with the ISCC body, which provides their ISCC Plus certification, guaranteeing to customers that all stakeholders in the supply chain have followed strict auditing and verification processes for biomass consumption and production.

Amtico Bio is promoting mass balance, which is an important concept for the chemical industry in transitioning away from fossil fuel feedstocks and moving towards biomass-based (or circular) raw material feedstocks.

The Big Challenges Along the Way

One of the big challenges in creating their sustainability strategy has been gaining corporate buy-in throughout their workforce, as the business increasingly focuses on the delivery of its sustainability targets.

In 2021, they formed pillar committees, involving many colleagues keen to participate. However, they found the targets they were working towards were not always as focused as they needed to be, with some pillars, such as Climate Action, occasionally feeling overwhelmed by the scale of the challenges confronting them. As a result, in 2023, they completed a sustainability roadmap project with Action Sustainability to determine a highly focussed set of targets and objectives within each pillar for both near-term and long-term goals. For this project, workshops were held across the business to formulate a list of targets, supported by experts at Action Sustainability. By the end of 2023, they had finalised their roadmap across each pillar, grouping and prioritising targets into areas to be worked on by newly formed task forces. For example, under Climate Action, they formed three task forces with the following mission statements:

- *Energy and emissions* – 'Accurately understand Amtico's global emission levels and energy consumption, aiming to set stretch targets and focus reductions'

- *Energy alternatives* – 'Embracing innovation to seek sustainable energy alternatives and drive efficiencies throughout all operations'
- *Raw materials and product* – 'Embedding sustainability into the research, development, and sourcing of all materials, collaborating with innovative and knowledgeable partners'

The task force approach, although in its early days, is empowering individuals to drive activity with more clarity on targets through meaningful and deliverable actions.

Securing Funding to Enable Timely Progress

The driving force for action on sustainability at Amtico was very much driven by middle management recognising, through their various functions, how the company needed to do more and be clearer on the required objectives for the business. Their passion was presented to the board who agreed that a focus on sustainability should be actioned, and they subsequently funded the consultancy projects that led to the strategy development. The business has since invested dedicated resources into their sustainability strategy, with several roles in the business fully or partially dedicated to sustainability, including the appointment of a new Sustainability Manager. An agreed annual sustainability budget is now in place, with annual funding allocated to planned projects and agreed roadmap targets. It has become clear that to reach net zero emissions additional funding will be required to adapt manufacturing processes and further reduce emissions. These requirements will be driven by the task forces whose requests for capital expenditure, in line with roadmap targets, will be incorporated and assessed within upcoming annual budgets.

Overcoming Key Hurdles

One key hurdle to overcome has been maintaining corporate progress whilst staying ahead of consumer demands and expectations. To tackle this conundrum, Amtico has drawn on Elkington's Triple Bottom Line framework by focusing on People, Planet and Profit.

The company recognises the competing market expectations of customers wanting more sustainable products, but also, not always being willing to pay the increased price reflected in their design, production and distribution. They need to stay ahead of consumer expectations by offering more sustainable products and lower overall emissions, but if they increase prices to pay for these improvements too quickly, consumers may shift to their competitors if their desire for sustainable products is not on par with their price expectations. Therefore, to better understand consumer behaviours and motivations, the business has been conducting annual surveys, which include questions on customer attitudes to sustainable developments.

Amtico Bio was launched as an add-on option for consumers, where carbon emissions reduction is seen as a key priority and where they are prepared to pay a slight uplift for this option. As the business moves forward, they hope that the share of products specified as Amtico Bio will grow, as consumers ethical and sustainability motivations grow, either through shifts in societal attitudes or implementation of additional legislative drivers.

How Long Has the Journey Taken so Far?

The Amtico Sustainability Plan, developed from early actions taken in 2021, covers three main areas:

Production

- Amtico's factories in the UK and USA are certified to ISO 14001, the world's leading environmental management standard, with the company aiming to only work with suppliers who have the same certification
- Amtico has sourced 100% REGO-backed renewable electricity since 2021
- Lighting throughout Amtico's operations has been transitioned to lower-energy LED lighting
- Conserving energy through the installation of movement sensors and timers across Amtico's offices to ensure lights switch off automatically when areas are vacant
- Employing effective waste management policies enabling Amtico to reduce waste sent to landfill by 93% over the last 5 years
- Offsetting Scope 1 and 2 emissions using UN-approved offsetting schemes since 2019
  - Amtico recognises there are limits on this moving forward, and only 10% of emissions can be offset for companies claiming to be Net Zero by 2050, so offsetting is currently being used alongside initiatives to reduce consumption
- Developing a new shut-down procedure for plant equipment to ensure that energy isn't being consumed wastefully when not in production
- Installing more metres across all sites to gain more accurate energy usage data to target areas for improvement
- Recording Scope 3 emissions for the first time in 2021 (using spend-based modelling)
- Moving to a water bath annealing, to reduce energy consumption and scrap production in the plant and improve quality

Post-production

- All Amtico product boxes are made 100% recycled (and recyclable) cardboard and use water-activated bio-degradable tape for packaging now instead of plastic tape
- By manufacturing in UK factories, this reduces the fuel used to transport Amtico products to UK domestic consumers and, therefore, its overall carbon footprint
- Installing electric charging points on all sites and shifting fleet vehicles towards hybrid or EV cars

Recycling

- Recycling policy meaning customers can return any Amtico samples for recycling in reusable mailing envelopes
- Trials for taking back installer waste – 15 tonnes of LVT flooring collected and recycled in 2023. Reprocessing returned products into new Amtico flooring, or where this isn't possible, recycling the material into other downcycled products, such as traffic cones.

Other Accreditations

In addition to these environmental credentials, Amtico International also has a number of accreditations for other elements of its work:

- A+ and A ratings on the BREEAM environmental scale
- Membership of the DGNB and US Green Building Council; organisations committed to developing more sustainable built environments
- A+ rating on the French Indoor Air Quality Scale
- Holder of the FloorScore mark for low VOC (volatile organic compound) emissions and Eurofins Indoor Air Comfort Gold for all products
- Mandatory Streamlined Energy and Carbon Reporting for carbon emissions and energy consumption, now published in annual sustainability reports
- Mandatory Energy Savings and Opportunities Scheme has identified areas to save energy, some of which we have since implemented, with others planned in the coming years
- Approved as compliant with the ISO 9001 Quality Management standards in the UK
- Approved to the ISO 45001 Health & Safety standard to highlight Amtico's commitment to this important area
- Founding member of the ResiLoop recycling initiative in Australia

Lessons to Share

One of the major positives of their strategy and approach has been the workforce engagement and how this has evolved over time. For some businesses, a first step might involve hiring a sustainability manager to drive progress, perhaps against a backdrop of a disengaged workforce. However, by initially involving committed colleagues, and, in turn, establishing a large cohort of enthusiastic volunteers internally, they have been able to hit the ground running to deliver substantial improvements in a relatively short time period. Momentum, and maintaining this pace, is key. This, with increased business investment and visibility for their strategy, both internally and externally, should ensure continued progress is made at pace.

Future Goals

Amtico has a stated aspirational target to reach net zero carbon by 2040, deliberately setting a challenging goal – a full decade ahead of the mandatory government requirements of 2050, as a reflection of their genuine commitment. With their roadmap in place, they have clarity over the milestones they need to achieve and by when. The business is once again working with external experts to develop carbon reduction plans during 2024/25, along with progressing supply chain sustainability and devising circular solutions to their end-of-life product responsibilities.

Ian Lloyd, Operations Director, concluded:

> At Amtico, sustainability is more than just a buzzword – it's becoming a core principle embedded in every aspect of our operations. We are dedicated to minimising our environmental impact and preserving natural resources for future generations, a commitment demonstrated through reducing manufacturing waste, sourcing recycled materials, implementing energy-efficient production processes, and many more vital initiatives. By pioneering innovation and championing sustainability, we not only adhere to continuous improvement and best practices, but also strive to redefine industry standards for positive change.

Chapter 10

KPM Marine Green Manufacturing for COP28

Julian Morgan

KPM Marine Ltd, UK

Abstract

KPM Marine is at the forefront of wind farm service vessel interior build, providing essential services and refuelling for turbines. Designed as catamarans, usually 20–30 m long, they require several 1500 HP engines burning around 3,000 litres a day, 7 days a week. In designing the 2015 KPM Marine wind farm vessel, they created 10 design protocols reducing environmental emissions and planetary impact. Six protocols were used in all elements of interior build covering light weighting, elimination of volatile organic chemicals (VOCs), design for recyclability, ensuring end-of-life value (ELV), and reparability to extend product lifetime by 20 years. These protocols have delivered competitive advantage and lifetime energy savings for clients whilst protecting market share from larger international corporates and remain under constant review and development.

Keywords: Wind farm; service vessel; interior build; catamaran; green design protocols; light weighting; end-of-life value; repairability; volatile organic chemicals; environmental emissions

Introduction

Thirty years ago, whilst working on future-stating product development for an up-and-coming tech company, it dawned on me that environmentally I was the part of the problem. As such I studied the history of product development and stumbled across Edward Bernays, known as the 'father of public relations', who,

Examining Net Zero: Creating Solutions for a Greener Society and Sustainable Economic Growth, 97–105
Copyright © 2025 by Julian Morgan
Published under exclusive licence by Emerald Publishing Limited
doi:10.1108/978-1-83608-574-420251010

after the First World War, was tasked by corporations to address the problem of excess capacity leading to over production which would lead to deflation and economic collapse. His solution was to create Market Expansion Theory based upon creating 'want not need' derived from his uncle, Sigmund Freud's work, Psychoanalysis. Scrolling forward a hundred years, we live with the productive capacity of China and the Internet. This has led to Market Expansion Theory 'on steroids' or conspicuous consumption, the built-in obsolescence and fashion trends that keep global productive capacity gainfully employed. Soon after, I made it my mission to ensure the business that I was setting up was as environmentally conscious and sustainable as it could be with its products so I would become part of the solution.

KPM Marine

KPM Marine is a marine design and manufacturing company. We have been at the forefront of Wind farm service vessels that deliver the resource and technicians to the wind turbines. These vessels deliver between 12 and 24 technicians daily to service and refuel the wind turbines on a planned basis. The vessels range from 20 to 30 m in length and are predominantly made of aluminium, which makes them lightweight and 100% recyclable unlike composite vessels that are not.

However, for commercial and operational purposes, these catamarans need to travel fast by a principle called 'surface planning' to meet the economic imperative. To achieve this, there are usually two 1500 HP engines in each vessel which burn around a combined 3,000 litres a day, 7 days a week throughout the year. It takes a lot of power to be green.

Naval architects and Marine engineers recognised the importance of emissions reductions and the contradiction of CO_2 emissions, assessing a whole array of solutions including battery power hybrid and hydrogen as far back as 2015. But before we could consider any of these, there were two important milestones that needed to be resolved. Firstly, the hydrodynamics would make the hull more efficient and, secondly, the reduction of weight. Both in combination would mean that the power requirement would be lower, so smaller engines could be used generating less CO_2 and reducing cost. There is a principle called the 'Admiralty Coefficient' which states that for a 10% weight saving there is a 7% fuel saving and based on this benchmark, Andy Page of Chartwell, the lead naval architect, started work on the hull and vessel superstructure whilst KPM Marine set about reducing the interior weight. Moving forward, hybrid vessels are being constructed to these principles with hydrogen and hybrid engines being installed.

The Promise of Technology

When we are seeking improvement, human nature tends to look for the latest technology, materials, and systems to achieve our goals and bunny hop natural product lifecycle evolutions. The problem with this is the propensity for technical overreach, unproven technology, lack of understanding of cause and effect, integration to current systems and infrastructures, as well as not understanding the implementation/scalability of these technologies. With the rush to net zero by politicians and activists, many of these proposed solutions are not being assessed based on a robust Technology Readiness Level ranking, and in the worst cases, these technologies will not form viable commercial propositions, pushing green endeavours backwards and falling into the 'valley of death', never to be resurrected. A good example would be taking out the hybrid product life cycle which would be the natural bridge between Internal Combustion Engines and Battery Electric Vehicles. For commercial, and in some circumstances academic expediency, we discount the old and simple way of doing things, yet this approach would not attract grant/research funding through the array of new products and shiny 'stuff' proposed to excite new markets.

Knowing this, the team at KPM set about creating an environmental design protocol called Earthgain that was not only aggressive but also continued to challenge the status quo. Rather than address just weight, we decided to take a more holistic approach and included design for recyclability, extended life, repairability, elimination of plastic and VOCs, and increasing ELV. We called these the KPM Earthgain green design protocols.

For the 2015 wind farm vessel (known as boat 36), the KPM approach was to undertake a weight manifest and innovate ways of reducing weight but also meeting the full list of design criteria. Whilst we undertook this with every KPM interior product, even down to the exit sign, for the purposes of simplicity, we have used the seats as an example for which KPM Marine was consequently awarded the Queen's Award for Innovation 2022.

Protocol 1: Weight

Because of the harsh environment encountered at sea, the technicians needed to be protected against whole-body vibration and impacts. The existing solution to this point was to use suspension truck seats that would, on average, weigh 56–60 kg each. The initial KPM design team thought was to use composites to reduce the weight, but this would not have met the design protocols of recyclability, VOCs, and ELV. The KPM solution was found in the manufacturing techniques used in WW2 airplane construction using aluminium, rivets, and simple processes to create stress-induced structures that are incredibly light but also robust yet repairable. After development, contemporary design touches, and intensive crash testing, the KPM safety seats proved to be half the weight of the nearest truck seat with an average weight saving of 784 kg per vessel. This reduced weight allowed less structural requirement for the naval architects and the reduced weight of the KPM seats created significant fuel savings and reduced CO_2 emissions. By the time the same exercise was undertaken for all the KPM interior products, a net saving of 4,000 kg had been delivered through an overall 10% weight saving. Interestingly, the stressed aluminium technique to achieve the duty cycle ended up being lighter than the composite equivalent and much cheaper. We branded our construction 'made like a spitfire' (or Messerschmitt for our German cousins) since these exact techniques were being used some 70 years later but for peaceful purposes. Lighter weight equals less power, smaller engines, lower fuel bills, and fewer CO_2 emissions but more profit for operators.

Protocol 2: Elimination of VOCs and Plastic

All plastics and composites contain VOCs, and with the KPM factory being located 400 m from a school, the use of such materials and the emissions from composite moulding would be prohibited. Not only this but also composites would also violate our protocol 3 of recyclability and protocol 4 of ELV. The use of plastic was limited to one component, and the vinyl upholstery was replaced with reconstituted leather which is organic and recycled. Whilst more expensive as a covering, it is much harder to wear and satisfies the protocol of extended life, and we obtain a price premium. In summary, our objective was to find and specify materials to eliminate or reduce the following.

- Volatile organic chemicals.
- Forever chemicals.
- Plastic and dioxins.
- Air acidification.

Protocol 3: Design for Recyclability

The choice of using aluminium meant the seat structures could be totally recyclable. Whilst aluminium might seem to be a bad choice for the environment, it is one of the most abundant minerals in the world, and the power used to undertake the conversion is commonly supplied by hydroelectric power but once made requires 95% less energy to recycle into new aluminium. More importantly, with 75% of all the aluminium produced in history still in circulation, it is an infinitely recyclable and satisfies the ELV, protocol 4. The likelihood is that your frying pan was once a Spitfire! From the outset, KPM is designed with 95% recyclability and minimal plastic or VOC content. Further to this, the whole product range was designed to be repaired with a service life of 20 years. This was undertaken by a complete material review and new manufacturing techniques. KPM, when designing on the computer-aided design system, has access to Sustainability software, so can determine the CO_2 emissions, energy usage, water eutrophication, air acidification, CO_2 transport miles, material mining to end-of-life, for any component being designed by the click of a mouse. The design and specification are an iterative process until the best balance between function, duty cycle and environmental considerations is achieved. Currently, most KPM products are 96% recyclable by weight.

Protocol 4: ELV

To achieve high levels of recyclability, the materials specified need to have an ELV. If the material to be recycled is so abundant and costly to recycle the material becomes worthless. We have seen this with plastic and with 512 billion tonnes of waste plastic in the world, its value is not going to increase anytime soon, with several future generations having to contend with our pollution of their environment. However, if products are created with a high ELV, then the probability of the material being recycled increases exponentially due to the economics. As a simple test if you leave a bin of plastic containers and one of aluminium cans outside your house the aluminium will disappear within hours unlike the plastic that no one wants since it has no value. Manufacturers of products will shortly be entering a period where they will be responsible for the recycling of their own products and the cost of this, so it is in their own long-term interest to ensure they are maximising the economics of the circular economy and business model before legislation is created. KPM now market all their products as having an ELV, with a net economic gain rather than net cost of disposal, and this has been received by the market as a positive proposition. By using mainly aluminium, stainless steel, and brass inputs, these materials will always have value at end of life. Plastic does not. Will batteries in the future become the new plastic? This being the case, our legislators must be robust on policy before we repeat the same mistake but with a more pernicious group of elements. Considerations include:

- ELV – is it worth recycling?
- Will the material at end-of-life return to Earth?
  - Biodegrade.
  - Rust or corrode.
  - Be inert.
  - Aid biodiversity.

Protocol 5: Reparability and Lifetime Cost

All KPM products are made to not only be very reliable by design and through the choice of quality materials, but the company has also managed to engineer failure rates down to 0.03% on extended lifecycles of 20 years. This reliability and the ability to 100% repair any product produced has become a main marketing feature, unlike competitors that engineer products on a mean time between failure (MTBF) model, commonly known as planned obsolescence, enabling the sale of spares, maintenance services, or new products. It was decided that a product that would 'last' was a better long-term proposition rather than a short-term profit gain. Due to this one feature, it became evident that customers would pay a premium for this aspect of KPM products, and this has become a major differentiator of the company's brand and profitability. A quick win for the environment by designers and legislators is to extend the lifecycle of the product, stretching out the CO_2 cost of producing the product or the renewable machine footprint.

Protocol 6: Localisation

From the initial design stage, KPM designed all its products to include 90% local content by accommodating processes and capabilities within a 10-mile radius of the KPM factory in central Birmingham, UK. This allows KPM to reduce its

CO_2 footprint dramatically. Components and materials that had extended supply chains were avoided and alternatives were found, brought inhouse or developed with local suppliers. With the diminished UK supply base, this became a challenge but was possible. The most effective model is the factory-in-factory (FIF) model. For example, KPM is undertaking a process of inviting its key suppliers to move into a larger factory to supply KPM but also to operate with their existing customers. This symbiotic relationship not only reduces the travel but also provides strength in numbers by sharing resources such as lighting, energy, health, and safety but also equipment such as forklift trucks and delivery vehicles. As an example, each individual company would require four separate forklift trucks, whereas a FIF model would only require just one. This not only benefits the environment because of the carbon footprint required in the manufacture of three additional units, but economically, it makes sense as these forklifts would not be working at 100% capacity and the capital investment required is much lower due to the shared expense whilst also delivering reduced overheads, financial robustness, and security. This can be applied to all potential duplicated equipment and service capital costs from compressors through photo copiers and servers. This combined sharing of facilities is anticipated as having a very considerable effect on emissions and outputs.

Lower CO_2 Miles and Duplication

- Reduce extended supply chains and Just in Time.
- Lower demand for transport infrastructure and ULEZ costs.
- Lower pollution.
- FIF shared resource delivering less duplication.
- Machine CO_2 cost which is the CO_2 required to make the machine from prime material.
- Sustainable infrastructures.
- Optimal use of facility and capital equipment with increased revenue.

Protocol 7: 4 Rs – Repatriate, Recycle, Refurbish, or Repurpose

If a product is designed using the previous protocols, there is scope for the 4 Rs. As an example, in 2011, KPM supplied 700 seats and suspension units to a European Navy with no failures in the field. When the Navy in question wished to upgrade the suspension unit given new KPM technical developments in whole body vibration protection, KPM Marine offered to repatriate and buy the units back to conduct the 4 Rs. In this instance, the suspension units were refurbished and sold to customers in developing countries where affordability was of prime consideration. By Repatriating and Refurbishing, KPM democratised the product and afforded seafarers in developing countries whole-body protection. Not only was the life cycle of the product increased to 30 years, but KPM also made a second profit on the sale of the units. Only by using the previous protocols and design around the Earthgain principles was this possible. The saving to the environment is significant whilst being socially responsible.

- Repatriate.
- Refurbish – re-sell.
- Repurpose – re-sell.
- Recycle.

Protocol 8: Process and Facility

A good designer should be considering Design for Green Manufacture and using processes that have low energy requirements. For example, many of their products are manufactured using thin gauge aluminium and rivets just in the same manner as airplanes. With the structural design configured using the thin wall, there is as much as half delivered in weight savings and with no welding, nor any need for hydraulic power presses to bend the material, there is no intense energy requirement. Most of the tools can be manually operated saving a vast amount of electricity and cost, where power tools are required and then solar panels efficiently charge the batteries. With considered design, these processes can be scaled and required less capital investment, whilst the products, more importantly, attract a premium due to the fuel savings delivered.

- No VOCs or FEC by products.
- Low energy.
- By products usage (heat from foundry).
- Shared resource.
- Renewable.
- Re-purposed machinery.

Protocol 9: Extended Life

All products should be repairable over an extended life. MTBF should be used to increase life cycle and quality, not to determine the point of obsolescence to maintain sales demand. KPM products achieve a market premium for extended life where 'fit and forget' is the unique selling point consideration. Legislators, at some point, will surely create a tax vehicle to ensure that manufactures design products to extended life cycles, with a potential tax penalty. As such designers and manufacturers need to be accounting for this inevitability.

- No sealed units.
- No MTBF.
- No servitisation built in.
- Fit and forget.
- Low-warranty return rate.
- No built-in obsolescence.

Protocol 10: Digital Pollution

If the Internet was a country, it would be the sixth largest emitter and power user in the world, and on last estimates larger that the whole of Japan's energy needs. With the advent of Video Streaming, the Internet of Things, etc., these developments all require massive data centres that consume energy at an exponential rate. Every time we watch a movie, send an email, press a button, or use ChatGPT (10 times more energy required than a google search), there is an energy and environmental impact. As an example, an autonomous car will need to transfer 250 GBytes of data an hour to function. Scale this to 1 million cars and it becomes evident that there is not enough computer power to allow these cars to function. Also, 30 emails a day for a year is the equivalent of 1,000 miles in a family car.

KPM considered using real-time diagnostics on one of its products, where its only function would be to see how long it had run for, if at all, or it was broken. By the time the server energy and environmental cost was considered, it made our product less environmentally competitive when the environmental product declaration (EPD) was written due to its digital pollution footprint. KPM decided that making the product more reliable and failsafe was the environmentally responsible route to take, rather than gaining short-term competitive advantage on a feature that would detract from our quality and reputation. Why do you need an APP (digital application) to tell you that the product is faulty when, in fact, you could just have the peace of mind that the product does not go wrong. The imperative for many corporations is to sell servitisation, spares, or new product based on digital communication. However, for a Rolls Royce jet engine and complex machinery where maintenance for safety is imperative, then this level of data is of great value. But it is easy to question if household appliances need to be on the internet of things to really function effectively given the unseen environmental impact of such services.

In all the considerations made by product designers, they should be considering the digital impact of the following:

- Reduced energy.
- Reduced material.
- Eco web design.
- Reduce streaming.
- Reduce AI.

When KPM set out with these protocols and developed the products, their competitors laughed at them, but they are not laughing anymore. No more can business ignore the environmental aspects of their operations. By not pushing the boundaries and only focusing on the short-term profit imperative, expecting the taxpayer along with local authorities to clean up their mess or turning developing countries into their dumping grounds at little or no cost to themselves will no longer remain an option. The cost in the longer term will be much greater. Unless we have a clear understanding and address the simple quick wins, we will create a green industrial complex that benefits from taxpayer-funded incentives with no major delivery in terms of solving the problem. We are already seeing corporations using the green agenda for marketing purposes without making fundamental change but instead thinly veiled gestures which are treated like any other fashion trend. As legislation catches up so will taxation strategies including some of the predicted interventions included in this chapter:

- Manufacturers made to recycle own product.
- CO_2 import duties on miles travelled versus EPD.
- CAT – CO_2 added tax like VAT with difference between CO_2 inputs and CO_2 outputs. Tax is paid on the difference. This incentivises green design and lower processing cost.
- RAT – recycling added tax.
- Digital pollution tax per Gbytes used at source.

The message is, designers need to rewind societies' expectations through clever design and to make progress quickly companies can do very simple things that make a positive environmental impact, and not all these solutions require re-invention and new technology, but creative thinking. Fast forwarding to today KPM have customers saving £100,000 of pounds on fuel bills per year per vessel and KPM have dominated the windfarm service vessel market and the fast craft market globally. A small company based in Birmingham, by venturing to change its business model and the courage in challenging the status quo, has shown it can not only displace large international businesses but also benefit the environment. They now consider themselves to be part of the solution, and as they note, if they can do it, so can everyone else.

Chapter 11

Tyseley Energy Park, East Birmingham, West Midlands, UK

David Horsfall

Tyseley Energy Park, UK

Abstract

The Tyseley Energy Park's (TEP) mission is to transform clean energy innovation by stimulating and demonstrating new technologies, turning them into commercially viable systems contributing to Birmingham City Council's commitments to be Net Zero (NZ) by 2030.

TEP's development plan commits to delivering low and zero carbon power, transport, heat, waste and recycling solutions delivered through development phases: 10 MW Waste Wood Biomass Power Plant, a £47 million investment, supplies renewable electricity to Webster and Horsfall, the original site owner, along with tenants across this 17-acre site, providing the foundations for a distributed energy system. The Waste Wood Biomass Power Plant diverts 72,000 tonnes of waste wood from landfill with the sustainable power generated equivalent to 17,000 homes' requirements. Later, phases have seen the development of the UK's first low and zero carbon refuelling station with the hydrogen station supplying public and commercial vehicles with hydrogen for Birmingham's bus fleet. Partners on site are in the process of bringing forward a first-of-a-kind commercial scale electric charging station supply liquid fuels including drop in replacements for diesel such as hydrotreated vegetable oil (HVO) is also avaliable.

On site, the University of Birmingham has created a sustainable energy research and innovation centre that promotes innovation in waste, energy and low carbon vehicle systems across the West Midlands.

Within refurbished building on site, the Incubation Hub offers an integrated package of support to drive business growth amongst low-carbon

Examining Net Zero: Creating Solutions for a Greener Society and Sustainable Economic Growth, 107–113
Copyright © 2025 by David Horsfall
Published under exclusive licence by Emerald Publishing Limited
doi:10.1108/978-1-83608-574-420251011

energy businesses. This initiative has been developed in partnership with the University of Birmingham's Energy Institute's SME Engagement Programme.

Keywords: Energy park; clean energy; distributed energy system; zero carbon refuelling station; sustainable fuels; electric charging; hydrogen; HVO; research centre; fuel cells

The Story Starts Here

David Horsfall, Director of Property and Sustainability, at TEP (part of the Webster and Horsfall Group), explained how the development of the site evolved out of a consolidation strategy for Webster and Horsfall's 300-year-old manufacturing business. These early plans had, in turn, grown into a much bigger vision to develop a Green Energy Innovation Quarter across the Tyseley district, positioning Birmingham at the epicentre of the new green industrial revolution.

The family had been running the manufacturing business, Webster and Horsfall, producing and supplying wire and wire rope for 300 years with a history of innovation. With the general decline of UK manufacturing since the 1970s, their strategy had moved away from volume production and focused on high-quality specialist products which, in turn, had led to land becoming available which could be put to other uses. The business continues to grow too, with ongoing production consisting mainly of high-duty, spring quality carbon steel, silicon chrome and stainless steel wire-drawn to order.

David, speaking about the family business, explained how it had always been known affectionately as 'the works'. He and his brother, Robert, had grown up in Scotland, coming down to the factory for holiday jobs in their teenage years.

> My first experience of the works was as a teenager testing wire in a part of the factory called the music shop. I remember the place feeling vast with hundreds of people and huge machines clanking away all around you. I remember working with some big characters who had been there for many years and enjoyed telling stories about the factory in its heyday.

After leaving the school, David went on to pursue a career in the development industry, working for 10 years for developers in the North East of England and Scotland until he had a chance encounter with one of the directors of the family company which led him back into the Webster and Horsfall business.

> I had an idea about manufacturing sustainable insulation and wanted to explore if there was any scope to develop a production line at the works. The sustainable insulation idea didn't materialise, but it did lead to a follow up meeting with some of the directors

> who explained about the challenges faced by the business. On the back of these discussions, I was offered a role within the business with a focus on the land and property.
>
> The business faced major challenges with enormous overheads, buildings beyond the end of their useful life, a team of roofers trying to stop water ingress along with huge energy costs. All of this alongside a manufacturing business that was faced with an increasingly competitive global market meant that major surgery was required, and quickly.

Project 2020

From 2008, a team of people were assembled and tasked to come up with a strategy enabling the business to consolidate, without adversely impacting its customer base, along with a development strategy that would pay for any demolition and lead to the redevelopment of the site as a whole. This group was called 'Project 2020'.

The Project 2020 team would map out infrastructure and discuss process routes, demolition options and costing scenarios. It would meet every few weeks, and before long, it had started to have the basis for a plan. David said:

> This felt like a turning point as we went from a downward spiral to glimmers of hope and everyone began to unite around the plan. Everyone on the Project 2020 team had a unique skill set that they brought to the group and problem-solving and collective thinking was our 'superpower'.
>
> Our plans grew and where we did not have inhouse expertise we brought in a multi disciplinary team who helped to shape the development strategy. Before long we started to believe in ourselves and by 2010 we had outline approval for Tyseley Energy Park. This was a major planning application and a major step forward for us, setting out a five-phase plan with a new access road across third party land onto the A45. Our plans were also aligned with the vision that Birmingham City Council were developing for the area, centred around green tech, waste and recycling.

At a local level, Birmingham City Council had usefully produced the Tyseley Environmental Enterprise District (TEED) Framework for action in 2011, a non-statutory planning document that sought to direct inward investment towards Tyseley with a focus on the green technologies sector. There was, however, no national policy guidance on Green Energy Parks during this early development phase. David Horsfall believes that this would have helped, particularly where those energy parks require multi-stakeholder involvement from partners such as the local authority, the district network operators, utility companies energy companies and surrounding land and home owners, especially for the delivery of major infrastructure, such as district heating, microgrids and city scale low carbon transport infrastructure.

In 2017, Birmingham City Council usefully introduced a local development order which allows changes of use within the Tyseley Area without the need for specific planning permission or by enabling certain permitted development particularly in areas such as energy, waste, recycling and green technologies.

> The Tyseley Environment Enterprise District Framework for Action 2011 had helped with the delivery of the planning consent for the first phase of development for Tyseley Energy Park with the successful award of planning permission on 25th October 2012 for the waste wood biomass power station known as Birmingham Biopower Ltd (BBPL). Within three years BBPL had invested £50 million into the project which today produces 10MW of green power, diverting 72,000 tonnes of waste wood from landfill and supplying TEP and its tenants with green electricity.

With Birmingham Biopower under construction, Project 2020 turned their attention to the adjoining undeveloped phases of development.

> We had seen lots of innovative ideas put forward for phase 1 and we had also experienced the power of collective thinking as part of the Project 2020 group. This evolved into quarterly stakeholder meetings where we would invite key stakeholders and innovative businesses to our boardroom and give everyone the opportunity to pitch their ideas. By the end of the first year we were struggling to find a room big enough to hold the group. The meetings were lively and everyone was contributing, sparking off each other.
>
> Towards the end of 2015 we brought in a design team to capture the shortlisted ideas and this evolved into the low and zero carbon refuelling station that is on Tyseley Energy Park Phase 2 today. The low and zero carbon refuelling station was a first-of-a-kind for the UK and supplies public and commercial vehicles with a range of zero/low carbon, and cleaner fuels. These included hydrogen, drop-in biodiesels as well as commercial scale electric chargers.

By 2018, TEP was taking shape and the consolidation of Webster, and Horsfall's manufacturing operation was in its final phase of transition. Whilst this was considered a huge step forward, it had also become clear that there was still a long way to go with major challenges remaining.

> We were making big decisions on a daily basis with a fast-moving plan and it was becoming increasingly difficult to keep our extensive group of shareholders up to speed. In order for us to move

> forward we needed to streamline the decision-making process and bring full control to the board in charge of executing the plan and this required a management buyout (MBO). The management buyout was agreed and has allowed six of us to unite behind a strategy for the site and manufacturing business.
>
> The six of us have very different but complementary skills and specialisations. We can now make decisions quickly and this means we can pivot in different direction and we can be more agile than larger organisations.

2018 was also the year that they formalised their partnership with the University of Birmingham. Up until then, the University of Birmingham had worked alongside TEP as part of Birmingham City Council's Green Commission as well as Energy Capital's Energy Innovation Zone for Birmingham. Having built a strong working relationship over the years, a collaboration agreement was signed between TEP and the University of Birmingham binding them as partners into a shared vision to drive and accelerate the translation of world leading energy innovation at TEP with the intention of putting the city of Birmingham at the forefront of the green revolution.

By 2020, the University of Birmingham had created a sustainable energy research and innovation centre at TEP called the Birmingham Energy Innovation Centre (BEIC). The BEIC now delivers research, business support, systems integration across energy, waste and transportation systems sectors all in the one facility.

In addition to the BEIC, the University of Birmingham established the Tyseley Business Incubation Hub, providing support to climate-focussed start-ups with resources and expertise. The Birmingham Energy Incubation Hub offers an integrated package of support to drive business growth amongst low-carbon energy businesses. This initiative based at TEP has been developed in partnership with the University of Birmingham's Energy Institute's SME Engagement Programme, ATETA.

The aim of the energy incubation hub is to bring together the office and workshop space available at TEP with and the energy expertise and research facilities of the University of Birmingham. Businesses that become a part of this hub will drive transformational change in the generation, and use of clean power and heat.

Since formalising their collaboration with the University of Birmingham, TEP has built on the stakeholder engagement group that started in 2013 which is now known as the Co-creation group. TEP now brings together an evolving collaboration of passionate technology innovators, academics, scientists, project developers and proactive public sector bodies, all united around the theme of innovating to find solutions that will underpin the transition to low or zero carbon future.

TEP also works with partners to engage with residents and members of the local business community. Regular community engagement events are delivered by TEP to share information about projects and initiatives underway in the area and to hear from the community about their ideas and discuss how their business, school and the community might benefit from and contribute to activity underway across the TEED.

Key Hurdles

> Finding the right partners and securing the best funding options is our major challenge. Our 300-year-old family business is still operational but has had to undergo major upheaval as we have reconfigured the site to make way for Tyseley Energy Park. What's more, many of the buildings and much of the infrastructure is 100's of years old and requires major investment and creative problem solving. Overcoming these challenges whilst building a name for ourselves in a fast moving and volatile sector has taken a lot of effort and consistent messaging along with a large number of incredible partners who have got behind the vision for TEP. Today we are very proud to be part of a strategic alliances with University of Birmingham, Birmingham City Council and The Crown Estates working to define a clear identity for the area, reflecting the Council's overall commitment to net zero carbon. This partnership is set to leverage on key assets in Tyseley Energy Park as well as wider green and blue infrastructure, long-established transport routes, 230 local businesses, and will draw in exciting new low and zero carbon businesses.

Successes

We are proud that we have been able to turn around our 300-year-old manufacturing business and, in parallel, create an energy park that is leading the low carbon transition within Birmingham. We are committed to delivering low and zero carbon *power, transport, heat, waste and recycling solutions and we want to create a* legacy that sees greater engagement with and increased employment in low carbon industries.

Lessons

Creating that initial vision of what success might look like was key and this was closely followed by developing a narrative that helped us draw in others and kept us on track when we were going down blind alleys.

Assembling an eco-system and bringing in the right players was equally important. We had to be brutal at times. No passengers on the bus!

We also had to think long. This was never about making a quick buck and the world has changed in so many ways over the past 15 years, but we have stayed true to the early vision.

We try to visit other developments and businesses that are on a similar journey as much as possible to see best practice and to be inspired. We call these 'school day'.

We know that there is still a huge amount to learn from others, and we equally want to share the lessons we have learned over the years. Our capabilities continue to grow, along with our vision and appetite for bigger challenges!

Reflection

In reflecting on the changes that have taken place over the past 15 years, David noted:

> I am immensely proud to be part of an incredible team that have stabilised our 300-year-old family business and created Tyseley Energy Park. We have a long road ahead of us but our partnership with Birmingham City Council, the University of Birmingham and Co-creation partners presents huge opportunities.
>
> The Tyseley Environmental Enterprise District is now set to becoming the Green Energy Innovation Quarter for Birmingham and this has the potential to accelerate progress at TEP far beyond our original expectations and change the fortune of many businesses and homes in one of the most deprived areas of Birmingham. I believe that it is important to take stock and to reflect on how far we have come. That said we have no time to waste if we want to ensure that Birmingham is the epicenter of the new green industrial revolution.

Chapter 12

The Role for Community Energy in the British Energy Mix

John Stott[a], Tony McNally[a] and Jake Burnyeat[b]

[a]*Heart of England Community Energy, UK*
[b]*Communities for Renewables CIC, UK*

Abstract

Heart of England Community Energy (HECE) is 1 of 495 community energy companies with 331 MW of community-owned renewable electricity collectively generating 506 GWh renewable electricity, saving £3.35 million on energy bills, 143,000 tCO2e annually, powering 174,000 UK households and contributing over £21.5 million to community benefit funds (Community Energy, 2022). HECE's 15-MW array, comprising 60,000 solar panels, is located outside Stratford-upon-Avon generating renewable electricity since 2016, raising £17 million to make this possible and through surplus revenues over a 20-year period will contribute £6 million back into local communities. Small UK community energy companies face a wide range of challenges compared with policies elsewhere. The biggest hurdle for community energy companies in becoming a licenced energy supply company is the cost (IPPR, 2016). Gaining a grid connection is challenging with Ofgem estimating that between 60% and 70% of high voltage schemes never connect to the grid and a large backlog of green power projects has accumulated (Lawson, 2023). In Germany, where there is a 'Right to Local Supply' set-up, costs are proportional to the size of the energy organisation (Croner-i, 2022).

Whilst the Climate Change Committee has stated, 'it will not be possible to get close to meeting a net zero target without engaging with people or by pursuing an approach that focuses only on supply-side changes',

Examining Net Zero: Creating Solutions for a Greener Society and Sustainable Economic Growth, 115–127
Copyright © 2025 by John Stott, Tony McNally and Jake Burnyeat
Published under exclusive licence by Emerald Publishing Limited
doi:10.1108/978-1-83608-574-420251012

government's focus remains very largely supply-side focussed (Community Energy, 2022).

Keywords: Community energy; municipal energy; renewable electricity; electricity grid; generation; transmission; distribution; local supply; fuel poverty; energy imports

Introduction

The 2030 Climate Emergency aimed to contain rising global warming within 1.5 C. However, this tipping point was reached in 2023, recorded as the hottest year since the start of the industrial revolution. To redress this requires a dramatic scaling up to increase the availability of clean, green, and cheaper energy replacing carbon fuels. In light of the 200 GW registration queue (and more) awaiting UK National Grid approval, enhancing capacity through greater community energy generation and use, with minimal UK grid links, is proposed as an optimal solution.

Privatisation and Renationalisation

Privatisation in the UK has triggered great debate, and it would seem at best mixed, if not poor, results.

The energy sector in the UK underwent a transformation between 1979 and 1990 as 40 state-owned businesses employing 600,000 workers were privatised and the sector was split broadly into four components of generation, transmission, distribution and supply. Distribution systems are capital intensive, requiring overhead cables, switchgear, transformers, control systems and metres to enable the transfer of electricity from the transmission system to customers' premises. Supply businesses are engaged in the bulk purchase of electricity and its sale to customers.

The period after privatisation was followed by substantial losses of employment, especially in the decade from the mid-1990s where the electricity industry experienced job losses of up to 60%. This was accompanied by a decline in technical and maintenance staff and an increase in legal, marketing and sales staff. Job cuts were also experienced in low-skilled roles with increased demand for customer service staff, resulting in an increase in women entering the sector along with part-time and temporary working, outsourcing and self-employment (Broughton & Manzoni, 2017).

By 1994, it was reported that the majority of customers had not benefitted from privatisation in terms of pricing, with tariff customers effectively financing the privatisation. Additionally, domestic prices of electricity initially increased, relative to industrial prices, by about 5% more than expected (Domah & Pollitt, 2000). In contrast, the OECD has argued there is evidence that privatisation increased productivity at faster rates than those achieved prior to privatisation

(Holder S, OECD). However, with many redundancies following privatisation, this is hardly surprising and there is evidence that prices, as surely the main measure of improved productivity, have continued to increase with domestic bills adjusted for inflation increasing by 50% between 1996 and 2018 (Baines & Hager, 2021). Latest figures released by the government through its official Fuel Poverty Statistics for England (DESNZ, 2024) show *3.17 million households in fuel poverty in England,* virtually unchanged from 2022, when the number was 3.18 million, *despite a legal requirement for no households in England to be living in fuel poverty by 2030. Fuel-poor households now pay on average £417 a year more for energy than if they were living in a more efficient home and* 1.17 million households with children in England are in fuel poverty, up from 1.15 million in 2022 (National Energy Action, 2024).

Six big firms control 77% of the energy market for UK residents – Centrica the parent of British Gas, EDF, Energy UK, E.ON UK, npower, Scottish Power and Ovo, which recently acquired the retail arm of SSE. As a result, smaller suppliers, including municipal energy companies, have struggled to compete alongside these large, transnational and often foreign-owned companies, especially given the challenges posed by recent energy supply volatility since the Russian invasion of Ukraine, with Russia withholding natural gas from European markets, depletion of the Netherlands natural gas fields and the shortfall of energy provided by European wind power (Baines & Hager, 2021; Valentin & Steinfort, 2023).

As North Sea gas production declined, UK dependency on energy imports has grown, with gas being sourced from Norway, the Netherlands, Belgium, Qatar, the USA and Russia. With 86% of UK homes dependent on gas for heating and more than one-third of the electricity produced by gas plants, the country remained highly exposed in 2021 with over 30 small suppliers going out of business, consumers subject to 250% gas price increases and the government bailing out larger private energy firms through billions of pounds provided in support.

The grid companies, effectively in a monopoly position, have not invested as much into upgrading the system for renewable energy as is required for the country to hit net zero targets by 2050 although the same businesses have been widely criticised for extracting substantial amounts in dividends and interest. For example, National Grid shareholders took £1.4 billion out of the company in both 2020 and 2021 and a record take of £3.2 billion in 2017. The private generators similarly have not invested in renewables until public funding was provided and supply companies which also continued to extract dividends until the Tariff Cap Act of 2018 finally imposed a price cap on them during the May government (Hall, 2021).

These privatised companies have been described as sharing the characteristics of oligopolies – large profit margins, use of outsourcing and layoffs and billions extracted from the businesses in dividend payouts with the Office of Fair Trading stated as describing the energy businesses as a 'confusopoly', with deliberately complex price structures making it difficult for households to determine how any one offer fared in comparison with others (Hall, 2021).

In April 2022, the government announced it would renationalise the Electric System Operator, a division of the private energy company National Grid. In its place, a publicly owned Future System Operator is to be established during 2024, responsible for planning and distribution of the electricity system to prevent supply interruptions.

The Labour Party has proposed setting up Great British Energy, tasked with accelerating renewables investment with research by the think tank, Common Wealth, suggesting this could reduce electricity prices by £20.8 billion or £252 per household.

European Comparisons

In Germany, two-thirds of all electricity is bought from municipally owned energy companies, Stadtwerke, which own and run the majority of the distribution companies and have played a leading role in developing renewable energy electricity generation. Munich's Stadtwerke has supplied enough renewable energy to meet the needs of every household in the city since 2016 (Hall, 2021). A 'Right to Local Supply' has also been established, where costs for local community and municipal energy companies are proportional to the size of the energy organisation (Croner-i, 2022).

In France, two-thirds buy their electricity from EDF, majority owned by the French state, running the grids and generating most of the electricity. In Italy, a similar proportion of the population purchases electricity from AU a public company owned by the regulator.

Failures of UK Municipal Energy Companies

The experience of European municipally owned energy companies is in sharp contrast to the UK. Two high-profile English municipal energy companies which have failed in recent years include Bristol Energy and Robin Hood Energy. Both were founded in 2015 as not-for-profit energy companies – the former by Bristol City Council and the latter by Nottingham City Council. Both were involved in supplying gas and electricity to residential and business customers. Bristol Energy was established as part of the City Council's Climate Change and Energy Security Framework. Robin Hood Energy's primary role was to provide low-cost energy to households and address fuel poverty in Nottingham. Bristol Energy was sold in multiple parts in 2020 to Yu Energy, Together Energy and F&S Energy, with Together Energy ceasing to trade in 2022 and its 176,000 domestic customers transferred to British Gas. Robin Hood Energy's customer accounts were sold in September 2020 to Centrica, the parent company of British Gas.

Community Energy Companies

According to Community Energy England's (CEE) annual report, community energy projects in the UK had installed a total capacity of 331 MW by 2021, with 495 different groups helping to save £3.35 million from people's energy bills by investing in energy efficiency, providing advice to those in fuel poverty, creating jobs, and contributing over £21.5 million to community benefit funds (Community Energy, 2022). However, the government's recent reductions in subsidies for solar and wind power, and changes to other financial support mechanisms, have left the future of community energy highly uncertain. In 2021, 271 community organisations were involved in electricity generation projects across the UK. Twenty-three new electricity generation assets were installed, the lowest number since 2017 and a 32% decrease from the previous year. Survey responses gathered by CEE identified 80 stalled projects, totalling 68 MW stalled capacity, 53 of which were electricity generation projects and 19 were involved in energy efficiency. Whilst the think tank, IPPR, claim new financing models are beginning to emerge, including peer-to-peer lending, pension fund investment and municipal energy company funding, industry specialists are more cautious, emphasising that new community energy projects can no longer depend on subsidies for their survival and profitability (IPPR, 2016).

UK Community Energy companies doing any more than generating energy face a wide range of challenges compared with those based elsewhere. They must meet the same conditions as the main electricity supply companies for connecting to the grid, with the financial, technical and operational challenges involved in setting up a licenced energy supply company requiring at least £1 million investment simply to become a licenced provider (IPPR, 2016).

Whilst the Climate Change Committee has stated repeatedly that 'it will not be possible to get close to meeting a net zero target without engaging with people or by pursuing an approach that focuses only on supply-side changes', the PM's Ten Point Plan (HMG, 2020) and the National Infrastructure Strategy (HM Treasury, 2020) remain very largely committed to big ticket, technical, centralised, supply-side measures (Community Energy, 2022).

Heart of England Community Energy

HECE is located just outside Stratford Upon Avon and was established in 2016 as a community benefit society owning one of the largest community solar farms in the UK with a 15-MW array, made up of around 60,000 solar panels.

This not-for-profit community energy enterprise was established to bring the benefits of local energy to the Heart of England region, empowering local people and organisations by enabling them to invest in, control and benefit from local renewable energy generation. Structured as an asset-locked community benefit society, their ownership lies with their members, with the organisation governed by dedicated local volunteer directors and registered under the Co-operatives and Community Benefit Societies Act 2014.

They recycle their surpluses back into the Heart of England area by supporting local charities and projects with a positive social and environmental impact, whilst also supporting initiatives tackling climate change and poverty in developing countries. Over their 20 years in operation, they will have generated £6 million surpluses with these funds reinvested into the local area to support fuel poverty, community benefit and carbon reduction projects.

John Stott has been Chairman of HECE for 8 years, working in a non-executive capacity alongside founder non-executive directors (NEDs), Tony McNally and others, during this period.

John explained:

> Setting up HECE was not an easy process, particularly as grid connection costs are an inhibiting factor in setting up Community Energy Companies. Generally, these are set up to harness solar or wind power. More often than not, local people spot a place where panels could be placed and then set about raising the money. However, in the case of HECE we originated through a different route as our solar panels were put in place by developer but planning permission required them to put some of their solar farm into community ownership.

Operational day-to-day running of HECE and its solar farms are provided by Communities for Renewables CIC, who have also helped HECE raise around £17 million of capital through bank loans, social investment loans and community bonds to repay their higher cost construction finance. John Stott continued:

> We own three separate solar farms – all separate businesses in which the single shareholder is HECE. Our Solar Farms are locked into a feed-in tariff as a guaranteed price per KWh generated for 20 years and as we are in year eight, this makes us a very secure business with a further guaranteed price per KWh exported which is indexed annually and which we don't have to accept if we can get a better price on the market. In our case, the Feed-in tariff was secured by the developer who had secured funding through three big mortgages with Close Bros Bank. When we took on the three mortgages the developer required further sums, so a loan was taken on from Social and Sustainable Capital who try to put money into good community projects. The original mortgages only had a three-year term and during this time it was known we couldn't pay them off, so we refinanced with Triodos bank. This is still in place and is a 17-year term on a fixed interest rate around 3%. Given this, the only thing that would create a financial problem is asteroid strike or possibly a major localised grid failure which took a long time to fix!

HECE's power is exported via two large transformers over which they have no control, so if one or both failed, their export capability could be severely curtailed. They export everything they make; they are not able to sell their power directly to local consumers. Their export is taken up by aggregators, companies which enter into contracts with lots of smaller generators and behave like a larger power station.

> If we wanted to act like a power supply company to local residents, we would need a license, and this is prohibitively expensive. There are moves to change the rules on this though. We manage

> HECE as non-executive directors and none of us are paid in this capacity. All our surplus after capital and interest repayments as well as services by our asset manager go to social benefit as we are a not-for-profit. £17 million of capital was raised to build the solar farm and we will pay this off over 20 years.
>
> Our original model said we could put £30k a year into community benefit but this year we find we have £600k to invest in the community. This is because we have benefited from locking in low finance costs and high power price contracts during the energy crisis. Our revenues are around £2m a year. We anticipate £6m community benefit over the 20-year term of this project.

After this, their payments and income decrease, but the project should still be viable as most of their current income goes into paying off the loans.

Tony McNally, NED noted:

> There is an interesting dilemma for communities looking to set up solar farms and local energy generation. Most renewable energy requires large areas of land but the people who live in the countryside too often see the creation of a solar farm near to them as an imposition for the benefit of people in cities. Coventry City has just seen an application for 60k solar panels by Lenton's Lane Farm, which would have powered 7,650 homes in Coventry, but this was rejected after opposition from residents, and turned down by their planning committee on a vote of 3-2, being on green belt land.

Coventry City Council had proposed putting 65,000 panels, equipment and cabling on the fields with the solar farm in place for 40 years, generating 30 MW of electricity.

Dozens of objections were lodged with hundreds of people signing a petition against the proposal. Whilst planning officers had admitted the farm would cause harm to the greenbelt and the area's landscape, they judged that the benefits of the renewable energy generated would outweigh these potential harms (Nevett, 2024).

Tony McNally continued:

> The objections, however, were not in principle against solar power, which was my experience meeting local resident at the first public consultation meeting which I spoke with many residents there for 2 hours.
>
> The objections were firstly the impact from heavy vehicles associated from the site construction in a narrow residential lane and secondly, the loss of the sheep farmer's job and livelihood, building on green belt land with 60,000 solar panels, storage and substation.

John Stott added:

> A lot of these objections are irrational. The people who object say we are ruining the countryside, but planners won't allow a solar development unless it's well screened. At HECE we are managing the land to promote wildflower growth to help the insect population and wild mammals, so the two aims are not incompatible. There is a lot of misunderstanding of nature recovery and agriculture.

Tony McNally had submitted a set of proposals to Cllr George Duggins, Leader Coventry City Council (whose ward this solar farm was to be based in) on the need for ongoing discussion with the residents covering the following proposals:

(1) To include an exploration of the ways and means to minimise the disruption from the construction of the solar farm.
(2) To retain the sheep farm and the farmer by building the solar farm at a height that the sheep could take shelter in hot and rainy weather under the solar panels.
(3) To deliver social benefit by extending the 60,000 solar panels with a 'rent a roof' solar scheme on all the homes on both sides of Lenton's Lane, if not beyond, to be financed through the Power Purchase Agreement. This could also include a programme of energy efficiency particularly for those in fuel poverty generating local jobs.
(4) To restore the church that is used for community activities as part of the social benefit.

Tony in setting out options for the future, continued:

> Others are now looking at bringing together clusters of smaller sites and Climate Change Solutions, which was set up to encourage moving to a low-carbon future through facilitating partnerships, helped University of Birmingham students to map large clusters of buildings on Tyseley Energy Park which could potentially accommodate something of the order of 60k solar panels and this is now in progress through Birmingham City Council with Scottish and Southern Energy. On this site there is also scope for onshore wind – not given the current policy under the Conservatives who have remained opposed to this but given the potential for heat transfer from the canal as Grand Canal runs through this site providing an ongoing water source and all these could be brought together through a mixed decentralised community energy project.

Working with Communities for Renewables

Key to HECE's success has been the engagement of their experienced asset management team consisting of eight people from Communities for Renewables (CfR, cfrcic.co.uk) who work with the seven NEDs to ensure the 15 MW solar farm is run effectively and meets regulatory requirements. The NEDs take decisions around the strategic direction with CfR which provides company and asset management services to 50 MW of community solar across 7 diverse localities. Their services cover all aspects of managing the enterprises on behalf of the volunteer boards including daily performance monitoring;: management of O&M and other operations contractors; H&S oversight; book-keeping and financial administration; quarterly management and annual accounts; loan administration, compliance and covenant tests; company secretary duties and regulatory compliance; quarterly board reporting and meetings; community benefit funds management; business development; member registrar management and member communications. However, HECE is their largest client in terms of MW scale.

Policy Environment

One of the main challenges in establishing a facility similar to HECE will be the shortage of sites and grid connection challenges as there are very few places where it will be possible to install large scale solar. HECE note that they will always be on hand to help people where they want advice or any insights on setting up and running such a facility or the challenges of getting a connection to the grid.

The Grid has recently produced a report recommending more decentralised energy production which looks to simplify and optimise the opportunity for more bottom-up scenarios within gas and electricity network companies (National Grid ESO, 2022). They are focussed more than ever on understanding the regional insights for energy supply and demand out to 2050, recognising that a 'one-size fits all' approach across the country will not be adequate. The National Grid is looking to develop scenarios building on an understanding, down to local authority level, so they can reflect each local authority's unique journey towards Net Zero. This will be dependent on factors such as local policy, availability of resources, local ambition, proximity to infrastructure, demographics and building stock attributes. Tony McNally continued:

> The problem is very pressing for the country as outlined in an article in the Observer (Tapper, 2024) highlighting the challenges of getting a connection to the national grid are posing the country. Local development of badly needed homes is being held up as developers cannot get grid connection to power these homes. The National Grid's electricity systems operator (ESO) has pointed out that the connections queue has 'grown at an unprecedented pace'. UK power stations generate 75GW of power today and we will need an estimated 150GW by 2050 to hit net zero goals. The ESO has said the queue could reach the equivalent of 800GW by

> the end of 2024 – more than four times our needs - with developers able to jump the queue and those really need to build projects being effectively locked out. Being swamped with applications has made the current delays for grid connections even longer and the National Infrastructure Commission has recognised this problem and will be looking to make recommendations to overcome these issues shortly.
>
> It does remain challenging for the grid to take a more decentralised approach to energy generation as it was originally designed to export from large power stations to consumers and when small patches of energy generation are being put back into grid this provides other problems, so the grid needs to be electrically redesigned to get this to work.

To work through these challenges at West Midlands level, Climate Change Solutions recently established a West Midlands Bright Solar Future network hosted by PwC in February 2024. It was bringing together a wide range of interested representatives including the West Midlands Combined Authority, Birmingham City Council, Midlands Net Zero Hub, Greater Birmingham Chambers of Commerce, the National Farmers Union, Evo Energy, Solar for Schools and Birmingham City University. The senior officer present from National Grid made it clear that they were keen to work with UK Solar Taskforce, and this network recognised the importance of a distributed grid in future. It was recognised it would be increasingly important that where energy is generated locally it is also consumed locally to minimise engagement with the UK Grid, with this approach, depending on the specific project, capable of saving up to 60% of the total energy cost (Greenpeace, 2005, p. 31).

The UK has set a target for a 500% increase is solar power by 2035 to achieve 70 GW (1 GW can supply equivalent of 750,000 homes). It's established a Solar Task Force with a Road Map in preparation. Initial CCS local mapping of large south facing and flat roofs together with car park projects the potential for 12 million solar panels in the West Midlands. Given incapacity of the National Grid to facilitate this scale, they are currently supporting decentralised generation and consumption between large clusters of buildings with minimum interaction with the grid. There are thousands of these across the region that can deliver economies of scale, the creation new jobs, with businesses offering great potential for innovation and manufacturing. These large sites and clusters can include other renewable energy sources such as wind turbines, air, ground- and water-based heat pumps, hydrogen and fuel cells hydropower, smart systems, storage and EV charges, storage, etc., whilst maximising energy efficiency.

Tony McNally added:

> Creating a local energy grid is increasingly where the focus is – E.ON UK 15 year Energy Partnership with Coventry Council are planning an integrated low carbon city scale programme, There

> are ongoing discussions with larger industrial producers in the West Midlands including JLR which has signed up for three locations for solar arrays providing new off-grid energy power aimed to produce almost 120MW of renewable energy at their peak and commencing from end of 2026, with planning already having been granted for an 18.2MW ground-mounted solar array at the company's headquarters in Gaydon (Von Henning, 2024). Our hospitals and our two universities in Coventry and Warwickshire are assessing this option. The biggest consumers of energy in our city could be brought together in a cluster to start bringing together a local off-grid cluster and not without a lot of planning but this is the vision.

Charitable and Community Engagement

The HECE local directors wanted to use some of the surpluses from the solar farm to support local households struggling to pay their bills, so they engaged a local company, Act on Energy (actonenergy.org.uk) to do this. Once in place Act on Energy proposed a Complex Case Worker programme where HECE paid the salary for a specialist to help people in energy and fuel poverty. They found that often these people were experiencing other difficulties, with a lot simply unaware of how to claim their benefits. This was piloted as a two-year project, proving very successful as they met all the KPIs identified at the start of the project as illustrated by John Stott stating:

> This project comes to an end shortly and as it has been demonstrated to be a great success. Act on Energy don't require us to continue funding them as they now have two local councils in place to fund this programme, Stratford and Warwick District Councils.
>
> In addition, some time ago we discovered the Citizens Advice Bureau in South Warwickshire had some funding available to help people in hardship with no money in bank who needed support but they needed administration support to check that these people were in hardship, so we funded some additional administrator time and we have since added additional funding from HECE to enable this with many families subsequently assisted in this way.

The directors have also been able to provide support to other community energy projects assisting them in identifying hurdles and funding opportunities. John Stott continued:

> Solihull village community energy project was one such project where advice was provided. If you were a consultant this would be costing money but we have been able to provide this advice for free.

> Under the carbon reduction policy Communities for Renewables has developed a soft loan scheme, so if someone wants to put solar panels on a building, we can provide a loan for them to do this which they repay gradually out of the savings from the solar PVs on the building. If, in a given year, they save £1k on bills then we split that 50/50 until loan is repaid. We do this in South Warwickshire and nearby areas.

There is one exception to their focus on 'nearby areas' where HECE has been supporting Solaraid who market small solar systems to people living in off grid locations in Africa. They provide a solar lighting system which saves and involves selling this kit to the occupants, so they buy them on a HP scheme. This is handled in collaboration with Solar-Aid (solar-aid.org). As John Stott concluded:

> Our goals are to deploy more solar energy if we can find ways to do this and our asset manager is looking at ways of doing this and studying options. We need to find ways of wisely deploying these large sums of money which we are generating as surpluses. We are also planning for succession on the board so these projects can continue into the future.

References

Baines, J., & Hager, S. (2021, November 24). The UK energy sector must be brought back into public ownership as soon as possible, the collapse of Bulb is more proof that privatisation has been a costly and dismal failure for consumers. *The Guardian*.

Broughton, A., & Manzoni, C. (2017). *Employment in privatised utilities: A higher risk of precariousness?* Directorate general for internal policies policy department A: Economic and scientific policy, European Parliament IP/A/EMPL/2016-16 June 2017 PE 602.061.

Community Energy. (2022). *State of the sector report 2022, UK Report CES – Draft 9* (communityenergyengland.org).

Croner-i. (2022). *Assessing the benefits of community energy schemes, assessing the benefits of community energy schemes* | Croner-i (croneri.co.uk).

Department for Energy Security and Net Zero, Annual Fuel Poverty Statistics in England, 2024. (2023 data). *15 February 2024, Annual fuel poverty statistics in England, 2024* (2023 data) (publishing.service.gov.uk).

Domah, P., & Pollitt, M. (2000, July). *The restructuring and privatisation of the electricity distribution and supply businesses in England and Wales: A social cost benefit analysis*. University of Cambridge.

Greenpeace. (2005). *Decentralising power: An energy revolution for the 21st century*. Greenpeace.

Hall, D. (2021, September 23). If the UK's energy suppliers were publicly owned, would we be having this crisis? *The Guardian*.

HMG. (2020, November). *The ten point plan for a green industrial revolution building back better, supporting green jobs, and accelerating our path to net zero*. The Ten Point Plan for a Green Industrial Revolution (publishing.service.gov.uk).

HM Treasury. (2020, November). *National infrastructure strategy, fairer, greener faster, November 2020 CP 329 – National infrastructure strategy – Fairer, faster, greener* (publishing.service.gov.uk).

Institute for Public Policy Research. (2016, June). *Community and local energy: Challenges and opportunities*.

Lawson, A. (2023, May 23). Grid connection delays for low-carbon projects 'unacceptable', says Ofgem. *The Guardian*.

National Energy Action. (2024, February 15). *New official statistics highlight fuel poverty crisis deepening – As half of British adults turn their heating off, even when it's cold inside*. National Energy Action.

National Grid ESO. (2022). *Regional insights from the future energy scenarios*. NESO.

Nevett, J. (2024, March 1). *Plans for huge Coventry solar farm rejected amid concerns*. BBC.

Tapper, J. (2024, March 10). Council Leaders warn of 'infrastructure crisis' as lack of power also threatens green energy schemes and growth. *The Observer*.

Valentin, L., & Steinfort, L. (2023, October 12). *The United Kingdom going from failed energy privatisation to partial renationalisation*. Transnational Institute.

Von Henning, O. (2024, March 1). *Jaguar Land Rover to generate over 25% of electricity from solar, Solar Power Portal*. Jaguar Land Rover to generate over 25% of electricity from solar (solarpowerportal.co.uk).

Chapter 13

Staffordshire and Stoke-on-Trent COP2024: A Celebration of the Possible

Tom Bedford and Kate Copeland-Rhodes

The Globe Group CIC, UK

Abstract

The Globe Group CIC (Globe) was established as a not-for-profit dedicated to driving positive sustainable change mitigating the impacts of climate change and building resilience within communities. As a team of 26, consisting of staff and volunteers, they are based at their Eco Centre in Uttoxeter, Staffordshire. Having hosted the first ever Midlands Climate Expo & Sustainability Conference Climate Expo in 2022 and expanded this the following year by bringing together over 500 individuals and over 100 organisations to drive change, this highlighted the importance and impact of collaborative, cross-sector action. This was followed by efforts to create lasting change throughout their county by creating the first ever Staffordshire & Stoke-On-Trent Celebration of the Possible (COP). The case study highlights seven key steps to bringing together the partnerships, businesses, stakeholders, funding and local communities. This was built on the back of six years of steady growth at Globe and led to the COP Framework highlighting a potential vision of the future for the county agreed by the partnership with their vision informed by over 300 members of the Staffordshire and Stoke-on-Trent community and their oversubscribed COP Conference 2024 attended by over 150 from all walks of life keen to support the Staffordshire journey to greater sustainability and Net Zero.

Keywords: Community action; localism; resident engagement; climate change; environmental; social; climate expo; doughnut economics; social equity; COP

Examining Net Zero: Creating Solutions for a Greener Society and Sustainable Economic Growth, 129–135
Copyright © 2025 by Tom Bedford and Kate Copeland-Rhodes
Published under exclusive licence by Emerald Publishing Limited
doi:10.1108/978-1-83608-574-420251013

Background and Purpose

Having worked in climate action locally over decades, several issues emerged across Staffordshire and Stoke-on-Trent which have inhibited climate action. These included, growing concerns about climate change but a lack of agency, a lack of meaningful and structured regional action required in Staffordshire and Stoke-on-Trent together and concerns over inadequate climate and sustainability communications. To help alleviate these challenges, Globe was set up to create a collaborative movement empowering residents and businesses to build a sustainable future for the region supporting the creation of aligned, measurable and supported action.

Established as an independent non-profit dedicated to driving positive sustainable change by mitigating the impacts of climate change and building resilience within communities, Globe includes a team of 16 as a mixture of staff and volunteers, based within their Eco Centre in Uttoxeter, Staffordshire.

Following many queries from local people and businesses over a range of climate issues (e.g. how to gain planning permission for solar arrays, the actions local organisations should be taking and where to go for advice on renewable energy products and services) Globe decided to host the first ever Staffordshire Climate Expo in 2022 to creating a space for collaborative climate problem-solving. This enabled them to facilitate climate conversations to drive action and linking organisations to solution providers.

In 2023, they expanded to create the Midlands Climate Expo & Sustainability Conference, bringing together over 500 individuals and over 100 organisations to drive change. But in the final discussion of the day, a recent local graduate stood up and stated 'These events are amazing to learn and meet people across the sector, but how do we use the energy from today to drive real climate action?'. Thanks to words of this future leader, the Staffordshire & Stoke-On-Trent COP was born as a concept to create a collaborative movement empowering residents and businesses to build a sustainable future for the region helping anyone interested to overcome the hurdles through aligned, measurable and supported action.

The Globe team were convinced the answer wasn't a one-size-fits-all. Every person, street, town and community is different. Therefore, a tapestry of solutions is required recognsing the social, environment, economic and cultural context of each area. This approach relied upon communities coming together to build a new framework for change, not as a top-down decree but as a collaborative ecosystem, with local wisdom guiding each step. Welcome to the Staffordshire and Stoke-On-Trent COP project and the 7 steps they took to create their own place-based COP.

7 Steps to Create a COP

Step One: Find a Dynamic, Distributive and Innovative Leader

Finding the right leader is always a challenge. It has been noted that many leaders have accumulated power and status to secure their leadership and lock out challenge (Shaikh, 2020). But notably, economist Kate Raworth has singled out the importance of distributed leadership, especially if we are to collectively tackle climate change and to empower others as a means of enabling rapid and transformative collective climate action (Raworth, 2017).

Step Two: Convene an A-list Steering Committee

In helping to promote the distributed leadership model, a steering committee of local activists was formed, composed of people who know how their community works, its key assets and what really matters. For the Staffordshire and Stoke-on-Trent COP, the lineup included community infrastructure organisations, industry representatives tuned into the changing demands of business, a Climate Commission convening climate leaders across the region, academic institutions and faith groups representing deeply held values within the county.

Step Three: Research, Research, Research

The team were acutely aware that different places were embarking on similar journeys and conscious that there is learning to garner from others, no need to reinvest the wheel. Instead solutions should be pulled from successful places. This led to the a review of potential frameworks and ways to structure the COP, with so many to choose from we needed a broad framework that looked at the importance of interconnections and the levels of both social foundation and ecological factors. From this review, it was decided that Doughnut Economic would be the underpinning framework utilised for the COP. The COP Committee, then explored where this had been a successful approach in other areas, a notable example was Cornwall County Council. This county is committing to becoming carbon neutral by 2030 and is utilising innovative methods to drive change integrating new models of decision-making to increase transparency and deliver more inclusive decision-making (Turner & Wills, 2022).

To do this Cornwall created the Doughnut Decision Wheel to implement and develop their own version of similar local tools (Cornwall County Council, 2022). In creating the local COP we spent time working with leaders who were delivering such solutions to unpack how we could learn from their expertise, whilst also working with local people. Alongside external research local people was critical.

Step Four: Hear from the People

Doughnut Economics was found to be a useful framework to drive change. With applied models such as the 'Four Lenses Framework', already in existence to explore how their communities consider climate action. The tool created by the Doughnut Economics Action Lab is a means of developing ecologically safe and socially thriving local places (Doughnut Economics Action Lab, 2022). This tool enabled them to identify the needs of their community (local social), their local environment (local ecological), how communities interact with people globally (global social) and community impacts on global ecological life support systems (global ecological). Finally, it was important to understand what people wanted for their future. They met with people across Staffordshire and Stoke-on-Trent asking them to identify, 'how it could become home to thriving people in an ecologically thriving place, whilst respecting the wellbeing of all people, and the health of the whole planet?' (Doughnut Economics Action Lab, 2022).

Twelve workshops were held in total identifying some clear themes.

- **Food** – people wanted to source and consume locally grown, sustainable food.
- **Energy** – people wanted to access community-owned and generated energy, increasing levels of renewables and major improvements to the way the grid operates.
- **Health** – unsurprisingly people highlighted the need to access healthcare and preventative services catering to the needs of local people and enhancing well-being through the provision of spaces where they could interact with nature.
- **Travel networks** – greater access to public and active travel routes facilitating modal shift away from private vehicle ownership was prioritised.
- **Human networks** – collaborative spaces enabling greater connections and opportunities to celebrate successes within communities.
- **Social equity** – delivering a socially just transition where everyone's needs were met, not just those who could pay, whilst simultaneously addressing the root causes behind local crime.
- **Income and work** – supporting people in being able to secure meaningful, and well-paid employment along with opportunities to upskill and reduce needless consumption.
- **Education** – fit for the 21st century enabling people of all ages to connect with the natural world, shifting from academic to practical skills such as cookery or rewilding.
- **Political voice** – ensuring that all voices were heard enabling people to make and take decisions in their area.

Step Five: Share Your Insights with Decision Makers

Decision makers at grass roots level such as those overseeing neighbourhood watch groups or convening local charities were brought together with policy makers and professional bodies to create a truly mixed voice, to reflect on their findings and develop an understanding of what might be possible within certain timelines.

Step Six: Celebrate What Is Possible: Annual COP Conference

After the deliberative sessions, the COP team hosted their first Staffordshire and Stoke-on-Trent COP in 2024 sharing their early findings and highlighting the desires of local people. Critically local people thought it was essential to rebuild the social and human capital previously lost to the region and create a space for connection and collaboration.

Step Seven: Step into a 21st-century System

Their COP is seen as a 10-year framework and platform for action that begins with 'an ambitious vision of tomorrow' which aims to become a reality through the networks, skills and bonds created across throughout the COP process.

Partners and Supporters

A an important takeaway is the pivotal role played by language. Words like climate change, net zero or carbon neutral only resonate with a tiny fraction of the population, and we need to connect more deeply to the values people hold (Kaushal et al., 2022, p. 3583). That's why we framed this process as 'the Celebration of the Possible' to break down preconceptions that people had about sustainability (e.g. "that's the job of our climate manager, not me"). This completely changed the narrative when approaching organisations for support, rather than being dismissed as the 'crazy eco-group' they were seen as the innovative 'future thinkers'. This opened doors and improved dialogue with a whole range of different organisations including local councils, businesses, academic institutions and community groups, facilitating broader participation. However, scepticism remained amongst some, notably in parts of the business community with the question emerging 'What is in it for me?', highlighting their focus on the financial return, with less understanding of the benefits of non-financial returns (e.g. social value) whilst others, did not see themselves as providers of community value. Furthermore, it was a lengthy process to engage with a wide range of different political actors, as we have a range of different district authorities, plus an overarching county council. But political buy-in was an important piece of the puzzle to making the COP a success.

To enable the COP process to blossom deep collaborations and new partnerships were formed coming from a range of areas and offering insights into sectors and networks which aimed at democratising the process. Local groups like Support Staffordshire provided staff time to develop plans to connect the COP to individuals and community members. Local environment groups such as Moorlands Climate Action facilitated workshops in their areas. Sector-specific groups, including the YMCA and multi-faith groups, facilitated direct outreach to the most underrepresented cohorts (notably, these groups are often being those the most affected by climate shocks) (Adger et al., 2011). Staffordshire University provided space for the COP's seminal event. Leading environmental businesses and business leaders provided additional support, enhancing legitimacy with other business groups.

The Big Challenges…

Whilst cross-sectoral enthusiasm and engagement delivered much in-kind support, the funding required for the project delivery remained a major constraint. In a period of just 3 months, the COP team had secured enough funding (through public and private sector sponsors) to launch the framework with support including grants funding from Keele University, transforming the Trent Valley Landscape, with sponsorship from Refresh Britain, Cannock Chase Council and Stoke On-Trent BID, and in-kind support from Staffordshire University and Support Staffordshire. The next step in the project, post-conference is to secure a further long-term grant to enable the growth and development of the framework.

A major area of learning concerned participation by underrepresented groups. Even with specially devised strategies which included meeting groups where they were based, it was still a struggle to engage with a cross section of local community members. They have been working even harder to ensure their second round of consultations is more representative of the wider population with their social media campaigns and visual messaging helping to improve access for many groups around the COP.

Finally, as a small non-profit team, resources remained a constant challenge. However, this has been overcome through the development of a delivery partnership matrix, with different resources spanning several organisations including Globe and Support Staffordshire. In addition they were able to draw on their committed team, partners, volunteers and community members to co design, consult, organise, run and manage the COP event.

Successes and How Long It Took to Get There

The Staffordshire and Stoke-on-Trent COP was built on the back of six years of steady growth at Globe, seeing them develop from hyper-local litter picking group through to regional driver of change. When announcing the COP in October 2023 with a March deadline, they knew their aims were ambitious but achievable by completing the first six steps outlined above, ahead of officially launching the COP Framework and highlighting a potential vision of the future. Success manifested itself by engaging with such a wide range of stakeholders to develop their vision – informed by over 300 members of the Staffordshire and Stoke-on Trent community – and hosting their oversubscribed COP event attended by over 150 from all walks of life from students to CEOs, community members to local MPs. All those attending were asked to create a collaborative and impactful pledge by being asked to 'look beyond generic pledges' such as 'recycling more', to think deeply about systemic change. This, in turn, led them to identify specific individuals who would help them on their journey, finishing the day with over 50 transformative pledges.

Lessons to Share

For those looking to take on a similar Place-based COP Challenge, here are four key takeaways:

1. Partnerships are the key to success
2. Clear, exciting and fun communications can inspire the doubters into action

3. Small-scale pilots can create legitimacy and build momentum. Before launching the COP framework, there were naturally those who saw the challenges as beyond reach. But by demonstrating what was possible at a small scale, it was possible to inspire others to join in too.
4. Remain humble. Their journey across the region unearthed interesting stories and facilitating connections with local people. Finding out about the park which made people 'take the long way round', to the unique nature of Staffordshire's aquifers, it was clear that local people are the experts on their place.

Future Goals

What's next then? Now, the Staffordshire and Stoke-on-Trent COP framework exists it can grow as a mechanism for change. Their next step is articulated as creating a comprehensive 'Portrait of Place' – utilising the principles of Doughnut Economics – building on the snapshot from their preliminary research. In time this aims to provide a deeper dive into the area and provide some key-metrics of success. Importantly they look to further explore local histories and cultures informing the way people think about their communities, in turn, enabling them to come together to support action. The plans and visions which come from this portrait can be used to create a collaborative roadmap to their co-created vision of the future, addressing who is responsible for which actions and how members of the community can hold them to account. Finally, they see an ongoing need to inspire and empower other regions to take similar action in helping them to also 'Celebrate What's Possible'.

For more information, visit staffordshirecop.com

References

Adger, W. N., Barnett, J., Chapin, F. S., III, & Ellemor, H. (2011). This must be the place: Underrepresentation of identity and meaning in climate change decision-making. *Global Environmental Politics*, *11*(2), 1–25.

Cornwall County Council. (2022). *Cornwall decision-making wheel*. https://letstalk.cornwall.gov.uk/11505/widgets/41725/documents/23255

Doughnut Economics Action Lab. (2022). *Doughnut unrolled: Introducing the four lenses*. https://doughnuteconomics.org/tools/doughnut-unrolled-introducing-the-four-lenses

Kaushal, S., Dhammi, S., & Guha, A. (2022). Climate crisis and language – A constructivist ecolinguistic approach. *Materials Today: Proceedings*, *49*, 3581–3584.

Raworth, K. (2017). *Doughnut economics: Seven ways to think like a 21st-century economist*. Chelsea Green Publishing.

Shaikh, O. (2020). Divisive politics and economic development. *Journal of Politics Economy and Management*, *3*(2), 22–30.

Turner, R. A., & Wills, J. (2022). Downscaling doughnut economics for sustainability governance. *Current Opinion in Environmental Sustainability*, *56*, 101180.

Part Three

Moving Forward

Chapter 14

The Economic and Political Wisdom of Achieving Net Zero

Vicky Pryce[a] *and Steven McCabe*[b]

[a]*Birmingham City University, UK*
[b]*DoctorateHub, UK*

Abstract

Implementation of initiatives intended to achieve net zero will require very considerable investment. Whilst there are undoubted potentially immense benefits that will result from the transition to an economy that is based around the principles of net zero, all governments recognise the dilemma of making announcements necessitating spending many billions on this objective. This chapter examines the economic logic underpinning the quest to deal with the calamitous consequences of implementing measures essential to reduce emissions causing global warming. Using the UK as an exemplar, the political challenge and consequences of implementing economic changes required to produce net zero is considered. As is described, short-term expediency is frequently adopted as a way to avoid making difficult decisions to achieve not only long-term economic gain but almost universally regarded as essential to arrest the dire consequences that will befall future generations if immediate and urgent action is not taken. Drawing on previous research justifying the need to act now, this chapter potentially examines ways for governments to derive additional revenue, most particularly carbon taxes and emissions-trading schemes (ETS) as a way to fund investment in net zero through capital investment. As analysis of contemporary events suggests, the urgency of intervention all too frequently becomes a casualty of the need by political parties to avoid confronting tough choices by postponing such decisions.

Keywords: Economic benefit; green investment; opportunities/costs; political choice; carbon revenue

Examining Net Zero: Creating Solutions for a Greener Society and Sustainable Economic Growth, 139–150
Copyright © 2025 by Vicky Pryce and Steven McCabe
Published under exclusive licence by Emerald Publishing Limited
doi:10.1108/978-1-83608-574-420251014

Introduction

In late March 2024, the following headline appeared in the right leaning British newspaper, *The Telegraph*:

> Labour's net zero plans 'will cost £116 billion'

As Genevieve Holl-Allen (2024) explains, the Labour Party's leader, Sir Keir Starmer, has pledged to decarbonise Britain's electricity grid by 2030. However, an analysis carried out by Aurora Energy Research, a company founded by academics at the University of Oxford for Policy Exchange, estimates that achieving the objective of a carbon-free national electricity grid will result in the government needing to invest an additional £116 billion. Every government must, in fulfilling any grand aspirations, ensure sufficient finance is available through investment, borrowing and, of course, from the receipts of taxation.

The clear implication of reporting the additional cost of the British Labour Party's stated aim to achieve decarbonisation of the national grid – five years sooner than the Conservative Party has promised – will potentially result in taxpayers needing to make up any shortfall. Such is the dilemma faced by all governments; doing what it believes to the right thing but in such a way that doesn't create undue stress on the country's finances. This chapter will examine the economic and political arguments vital to the quest in achieving net zero. In particular, the inevitable costs will be considered in direct comparison to the long-term benefits likely to accrue to current and future generations.

The Challenges of Understanding the Costs and Benefits of Net Zero – Analysing the UK

In terms of the presentation and interpretation of the importance of achieving Net Zero, the British press tends to be differentiated by the political line its proprietors assume aligns with its readers. But there is no doubt that, ultimately, the admittedly vast sums of expenditure that are required must be judged through a lens which recognises both the magnitude of the threat the planet faces from global warming – not universally accepted – and the immense benefits that are possible through investment.

Bob Ward (2023), Policy and Communications Director of the Grantham Research Institute on Climate Change and the Environment at the London School of Economics worries that basically ill-informed articles on net zero in the press are used to propagate a particular (political) perspective. In his view, more honesty by those in the public eye on costs (and not just the benefits) would help. Ward examines the way that former Chancellor of the Exchequer, Philip, now Lord Hammond, made public his view that the cost of achieving net zero emissions of greenhouse gases by 2050 will be £1 trillion (Hazell, 2023). In an article for the Times, Hammond (2023) argued that successive Conservative prime ministers have been 'systematically dishonest' about the true costs of achieving net zero. Moreover, he adds, there's a 'cross-party disease' of politicians not willing to tell voters the true cost of net zero because of the inevitable consequence of slower rising living standards.

However, Ward points out that in citing the figure of a trillion pounds, based on an annual investment of between £50 and £70 billion per annum, the equivalent of 1–2% of GDP (gross domestic product), Hammond ignored the saving and benefits that would be possible. Indeed, the influential Climate Change Committee (CCC), then known as the Committee on Climate Change, in its role to provide advice to government, in its 2019 report, *Net Zero – The UK's contribution to stopping global warming*, estimated that the annual cost of investment in 2050, assuming GDP has risen to £3.9 trillion by then, would be 1.3% of GDP (£50.7 billion).

As the CCC stated in this report, a number of 'co-benefits' are possible from investment in arresting climate change:

> Achieving net-zero GHG emissions in the UK will result in significant benefits to human health from better air quality, less noise, more active travel and a shift to healthier diets. Changes to land use and farming practices that cut GHG emissions can also improve air quality and water quality and benefit biodiversity, resilience to climate change and bring recreational benefits. Benefits could partially or fully offset costs.

Significantly, the independent Office for Budget Responsibility (OBR), which has responsibility for examining the financial advice and decisions taken by the UK government, considered the CCC assumptions in its July 2021 Fiscal risks report and concluded:

> In the balanced pathway, the CCC estimates the total net cost of abatement across all sectors of the economy between 2020 to 2050 at £321 billion – with £1,312 billion of investment costs mostly offset by £991 billion of net operating savings.

Moreover, the OBR noted:

> From 2040 onwards, net operating savings are projected to outweigh investment costs. And by 2050, the CCC projects a £19 billion annual saving relative to its baseline emissions scenario.

Critically, the OBR stressed, the long-term costs to all societies and economies throughout the world would be much greater than those needed to achieve net zero. Indeed, as Ward asserts, where potential savings to be continued after 2050, all investment costs required to achieve net zero would be 'completely offset by 2070' (OBR, 2021). Investment in net zero is, providing it is accepted that climate change caused through emissions is not a work of paranoid fiction, as deniers suggest is the case, may not only be entirely logical but economically sound.

Nonetheless, analysis conducted thus far demonstrably indicates the economic advantages that are already flowing from investment in net zero. Analysis by the

International Renewable Energy Agency shows the significant cut in technology costs for renewables such as solar and wind power which considerably improve the cost–benefit calculation. A PWC analysis on Financing Net-Zero points to the fact that leading technology firms have now also pledged to eliminate emissions across their entire value chain by 2030. Indeed, some pledge to get to the stage where they are 'carbon-negative' in their operations.

A report published in early 2024 by The Energy & Climate Intelligence Unit (ECIU) in collaboration with the Confederation of British Industry (CBI), The UK's net zero economy – *The scale and geography of the net zero economy in the UK*, argued that investment in mitigating climate change in the UK has resulted in the net zero economy as they defined it expanding by 9% in 2023, contributing some £74 billion in gross value added (GVA) to the overall economy, some 3.8% of GDP in their calculations some 765,700 full-time equivalent (FTE) jobs can be directly attributed to net zero, almost 3% of total UK employment. Moreover, such employment is geographically distributed and creates opportunities in areas that have suffered deprivation as a consequence of diminishment of 'traditional industries' (Carrington, 2024).

Such investment and jobs, the ECIU argues, have generated an additional £25 billion to the economy through the 218,500 jobs that have been created indirectly in terms of expenditure on suppliers and goods. As they contend, 'for every £1 million in GVA contributed by net zero businesses, nearly £2 million more was added through these wider economic contributions'. Equally importantly, because net zero activities are intrinsically 'high value' in nature,

> the jobs are 1.6 times more productive than the average UK job, each FTE in the net zero economy generating £114,300 per year on average. This higher productivity is reflected in average wages (£44,600) which exceed the UK average (£35,400) by 23% (ibid).

Examining the Economic Costs and Benefits from Achieving Transition to Net Zero

In the preface to *The net-zero transition, What it would cost, what it could bring* (2022), McKinsey Global Institute, in collaboration with McKinsey Sustainability and McKinsey's Global Energy & Materials and Advanced Industries Practices unequivocally state that the belief that urgent intervention is required to deal with the physical manifestations of a changing climate. Achieving net zero, consistent with 1.5 °C of warming, will necessitate 'a fundamental transformation of the world economy' through a range of economic and societal adjustments (p. 4). Crucially, it is stressed, significant change is needed to the seven energy and land-use systems responsible for producing the world's emissions:

- Power
- Industry
- Mobility
- Buildings

- Agriculture
- Forestry
- Other land use
- waste

McKinsey Global Institute estimates the annual cost of making essential economics, and societal alterations will be of the order of $9.2 trillion per year on average. This would produce a total bill of at least $275 trillion by 2050, though, it acknowledges, transition to net zero will result in significant 'growth opportunities' as well (p. 8). Such opportunities, it contends, would be 'across sectors and geographies [... and incorporate] new markets for low-emissions products and support services' (Krishnan et al., 2022). Resonant with other organisations that have carried out cost–benefit analysis of net zero, they believe operating savings will be achieved through reduced fuel consumption, improved material and energy efficiency and lower maintenance costs.

According to their analysis, cost reductions are likely to occur in a number of ways. By 2050, operating costs to generate power could decrease by 'more than 60 percent relative to 2020 as the energy mix shifts to renewables' and that total costs associated with ownership for electric cars could in most regions be cheaper by 2025, and even sooner in some regions, than for internal combustion engine vehicles.

Economic development and increased prosperity are difficult to achieve without access to steady-state employment. In every previous major development in technology, commencing with the shift from agrarian societies to manufacturing that was experienced as part of the industrial revolution, whilst there's inevitable fear that existing jobs will cease to exist, now opportunities are created. The transition to net zero is no different. McKinsey's analysis suggests that the net-zero transition could by 2050 be a net gain of 10 million jobs worldwide in operations and maintenance. Additionally, a net gain of additional 6 million jobs will be created due to increased spending on physical assets needed for the net-zero transition by 2050. In total they assert, net zero could create an additional 16 million jobs as a direct impact of the transition to net zero.

Not everyone agrees with this rather optimistic-sounding analysis, but a multitude of international organisations argue that achieving net zero is no longer optional if the world is to avoid the catastrophic impact of climate change. Crucially, though, recognising that additional – not insignificant – investment is required, the potential economic benefits can still be considerable. The International Monetary Fund, citing analysis carried out by the Network for Greening the Financial System, a group of 127 central banks and financial supervisors working to manage climate risks and boost green investment, 'Ensuring a lower-carbon future is not only necessary but also good for the economy' (Mehrhoff, 2023). The World Economic Forum's Future Focus Report: what the world might look like in 2025 (Eisenberg, 2022) argued that amongst other changes that are likely to occur through increased investment in the wider resilience to climate change as a result of achieving net zero by the middle of this century, there are likely also to be exciting opportunities for growth in a number of sectors. These are likely to include new opportunities for tourism, which could move from being considered by many as it currently is as an activity which could in fact be a threat to environmental sustainability, to one which could actually become 'sustainable' itself.

But there are worries still that many businesses which are very much judged by the markets in relation to short-term financial results, will be put off from investing because of the threat to profits during that journey for them, their customers and their investors. There is also now increasing evidence of investors shying away from Environmental, Social and Governance (ESG) minded investments as the returns are poorer in relation to more conventional shareholding. According to the Deloitte Sustainability Report (Blondaut, 2022), the main obstacles remain difficulties in measurement and monitoring and also lack of sufficient low emissions inputs for their production processes as well as costs which were perceived to be too high. And this of course may get worse. The EU as part of its own Green Deal is introducing a system of extra carbon tariffs known as the carbon border adjustment mechanism (CBAM), for goods imported from high-carbon emitting and less tightly regulated parts of the world which will raise input costs further. And it has just passed a directive that requires a much closer examination of firms' global supply chain rules with a close emphasis on environmental sustainability which big firms will have to monitor (Energy Advice Hub, 2024).

Monitoring remains a concern and some resolution will be needed. The cooling of the ESG momentum owes a lot not just to perceived poorer performance but also worries that what is measured is just a tick-box exercise which hides what is truly going on underneath in this area which may, in fact, be very little. Indeed, we can see that concern in the UK in the further tightening up of reporting requirements by financial institutions just announced to reduce that 'greenwashing' which is eroding trust in the area od sustainable investment (Financial Conduct Authority, 2024).

The Criticality of Intervention by Governments

So, government intervention matters. It can facilitate the transition through a system of regulations, but it can also offer support in the form of subsidies along the path to net zero and work together with firms to smooth that path. Indeed, a move to net zero if too rapid impacts on business costs and can backfire also for the consumer whilst threatening competitiveness if too out of step with other countries/regions. As a result, in September 2023, the UK government announced a series of measures aimed at easing the cost of transition extending by 5 years to 2035 a proposed ban on the sale of new petrol and diesel vehicles, bringing the UK into line with other EU countries, as well as relaxing a previously announced deadline of ceasing installation of new gas boilers by 2025. Although seen as a political move before the elections due in late 2024 (Parker et al., 2023), Prime Minister Rishi Sunak stressed that the changes were sufficiently 'pragmatic' to still enable Britain to achieve net zero for by 2050 but would not require households to ensure additional costs of '£5,000, £10,000 or £15,000'.

Sunak's announcements on net zero reflected the fact that in his view governments 'of all stripes' had not been honest about costs and trade-offs required by net zero. He also argued that: 'When our share of global emissions is less than one per cent, how can it be right that British citizens are now being told to sacrifice even more than others?' Businesses though complained that the announced changes added considerable uncertainty to their investment plans which had been based on earlier more stringent targets.

That is a serious concern looking ahead as private investment will be crucial to achieving any targets. But it also emphasises how crucial the interaction with government is in achieving the aim for carbon reductions. Such is the challenge all politicians must confront in articulating a compelling and persuasive narrative as part of creating support and collective action.

As it happens, British courts have not taken kindly to that either. The High Court just ruled (again after saying something similar in 2022) (May 3) that the current government's climate change proposals are unlikely to be met even though there is a legal obligation to do so (Horton, 2024). And this comes against the background of Labour's dropped investment promises of £28 billion a year in late February (Stacey & Harvey, 2024) should they form the next government in the UK.

And writing in the Financial Times on 'How net zero became an election issue around the globe', Attracta Mooney and Alice Hancock explain that 'Similar scenes are playing out across the world. As 2030 approaches – the year by which scientists say the planet must almost halve greenhouse gas emissions – governments face pressure to take rapid action'. In 2024, when this book is being written, 64 countries – representing about 49% of the world's population – are holding elections to decide the complexion of their governments (Ewe, 2023). The polices contained in political parties' manifestos concerning climate change will be one of the important aspects of the decision taken by voters. Consequently, collective wisdom amongst almost half the planet's population could have potentially profound implications for the ability of the planet to limit the impact of climate change.

And the truth is that even though there's ample evidence that people largely agree that climate change is an issue requiring action, when faced with the prospect that this may necessitate raised taxes as well as potentially having to dedicate additional expenditure, such support wanes. Mathieu Lefevre, chief executive of non-profit, more in common quoted in the Mooney and Hancock's (2023) article worries that 'Climate is being weaponised by some political opponents'.

The challenge for politicians is, it frequently seems, not the absence of evidence of what needs to be achieved, but in interpreting data in a way based on objectivity and rational analysis of what will produce the greatest impact but with least discomfort to people's pockets. The mantra of 'if it isn't hurting it isn't working' is a dangerous one to follow in politics at a time of cost of living, food security concerns and other crises the world has been experiencing of late. But there is no doubt that this is a global phenomenon and carbon emissions have huge externalities, not least for poorer countries and hence the need for coordinated actions that are consistent and not subject to alteration merely to achieve short-term national political gain.

In *Net Zero + Climate and Economic Resilience in a Changing World* the Organisation for Economic Co-operation and Development (OECD, 2023) stresses the importance of governments in developing and implementing 'policy basics' from the outset:

> This means establishing clear long-term policy frameworks, setting overarching goals and interim targets that align with these, and ensuring regular monitoring and review of progress. It also means considering the full range of climate policy instruments and tailoring the policy mix to national circumstances, including phasing out fossil-fuel subsidies. (p. 12)

Carbon Taxes and Other Fiscal Measures

As already indicated, political willingness to both support and, crucially, invest in net zero is considered essential if targets to achieve success are to be achieved. This is especially the case because, as Cran-McGreehin (2022) points out, the transition to net zero will impact negatively on certain sectors – most notably gas and oil – with implications for employment and local economies. Though Cran-McGreehin specifically refers to the UK, because taxation from such sectors, usually very significant, would correspondingly reduce, this will require any government to examine how it can alter its revenue-raising powers so vital for public expenditure including investment into net zero. A potential solution to a challenge that will undoubtedly become more acute is the implementation of carbon taxes. Intended to incentivise energy companies to generate cleaner power (electricity) by reducing the amount of carbon dioxide emitted, they also ensure revenue is generated whilst also incentivising companies that use energy to decarbonise themselves as much as possible. It is not costless of course and much of it may be passed on to consumers, so carbon taxes need to be developed intelligently and not end up disadvantaging less developed nations to whom a lot of production has been outsourced.

The European Green Deal aims to make the EU a 'climate neutral bloc by 2050' (European Commission, 2019). It is multi-faceted with a focus across a number of sectors decarbonising such as construction, biodiversity, energy, transport and food. Much of the NextGenerationEU fund is aimed at facilitating investment across countries in ensuring greater sustainability in the face of climate change. The EU's CBAM is another example of that endeavour. There are reporting obligations already which came into force in October 2023 but payment by importers for any embedded emissions in what comes into the EU will not start until January 2026. The UK has indicated that it may well introduce its own CBAM in due course (Dillon et al., 2024).

Though carbon taxes certainly serve a very useful purpose, there's concern that they should be used as part of a wider package of measures to achieve net zero. And of course, there is already concern that this will disadvantage less developed, poorer countries which rely on trade for growth and prosperity and to whom much of the emission-emitting production has been outsourced by the richer nations for decades. Indeed, the Economist in a provocative commentary, 'A net-zero world needs new markets and institutions', makes clear its belief that individual carbon dioxide reduction (CDR) initiatives used in isolation are insufficient (2023). And pricing carbon is a difficult business. In fact, we have ended up with many different carbon taxes rather than a global one. Carbon offsetting, for example is arguably under-pricing carbon- and that price anyway differs hugely from that implied by the EU ETS and the UK's own version of it since it left the EU. The American government meanwhile intends to implement a $180-a-tonne tax credit for direct-air-capture projects by the end of 2032 – which is described as 'generous' – as well as develop support for carbon-storage hubs and a small programme for buying removals directly.

In truth, national or regional plans, often diverging from each other, can be (a) confusing and (b) distorting as well likely to be limited in their impact as Brad Crabtree, Assistant Secretary for the U.S. Department of Energy's Office of Fossil Energy and Carbon Management (FECM) is quoted as saying in the article. Indeed Crabtree, who leads and organises research and development at the FECM, expresses the view that tax credits do not offer a 'long-term policy' to achieve the immense task of CDR necessary to achieve America's net-zero targets.

There is indeed widespread unease at the way in which 'the marketplace' is adept at exploiting systems to ensure operators can receive an advantage that does not always work to the collective interest – and therefore do not become responsible for the real externalities – that is the costs-associated with carbon dioxide emissions, not just to their immediate environment but also globally.

The use of 'cap and trade' is one such system according to The Economist whereby emitters 'mix allowances issued under the scheme and credits for durable CDR when working off their carbon debt' (ibid).:

> Some emissions-trading schemes (ETS) are open to the idea of allowing carbon-removal credits. But the political economy is treacherous. For such schemes to work in terms of net emissions, any credits added to the allowances must have a real effect on what is in the atmosphere. For schemes to be palatable to the industries operating under them, the credits need to be cheap and plentiful, which experience suggests means dodgy. Thomas Gresham, a 16th-century merchant, held that bad money drives out good. The same would prove true of carbon credits.

Conclusion – What Does All This Tell Us?

Governments have, if they wish, a range of methods by which they can intervene. Also, how they present the data not easy as more and more studies appear adding to the need to act. A study in May 2024 by Adrien Bilal of Harvard University and Diego Känzig of Northwestern University calculated that, in fact, the damages to the economy of climate change are likely to be much larger than originally calculated – in fact, six times larger! They estimate that, in fact, every 1 °C increase in global temperature leads to a 12% drop in world GDP with a huge social welfare loss if we carry on with business as usual. And it is the global temperature shocks that matter rather than those at the national level (Bilal & Känzig, 2024). They believe the social cost of carbon should be set at $1,056 per ton of carbon dioxide.

This suggests perhaps that national plans are less important than international coordination but of course they do contribute to the total level of emissions. And for the right national and international policies to be implemented, they require a degree of trust in politicians and also trust that those availing of incentives do so with integrity. As *The Economist* depressingly points out, because of its size and the amount of influence 'The fossil-fuel industry has a record of being duplicitous and unreliable when it comes to emissions reduction'. Criticism has been expressed that, in the UK, oil companies have, at times, been able to unduly influence government decision-making and influential reports on carbon taxes produced by think tanks (Bychawski, 2024).

However, we hear in opinion polls and as in the UK at least the local election results in May 204 showed voters are not impressed by the various net zero/green policy U-turns that scale back targets and ease regulations (Kenningham, 2024). One solution, that's been suggested by German economist Ottmar Edenhofer and his colleagues, is the removal of direct responsibility by politician for carbon removal by setting up a central 'bank' to oversee this process entirely comparable to the way in which monetary policy is controlled across the European Union. It may be argued that the CCC in the UK was established to achieve this objective. Nonetheless, the threat to economic as well as financial stability that flows from being unprepared for the changes caused by the impending threat of global warming should be so urgent as to make policymakers and business believe that collaborative effort is essential in adaptation and mitigation of existential risks that lie ahead whilst being cognisant of the exigencies of consumers who, significantly, are also voters.

In the aftermath of a general election held on 4th July in the UK, a change of government has altered priorities as far as investing in Net Zero is concerned. In order to adhere to stated fiscal rules, Labour jettisoned a commitment to spend £29 billion pa and replaced it with a newly created £7.5b National Wealth Fund for 'green' projects. Additionally, there will be a Great British Energy company combined with more stringent carbon reduction targets for industry and consumer as well as increased offshore energy generated by wind and support for investment in carbon capture, green hydrogen and battery storage. Importantly, The Department for Environment, Food & Rural Affairs (Defra) under Labour announced protection of the UK's natural environment, food system and communities from the impacts of climate change.

Labour's stance on Net Zero is to be applauded though there's concern about the costs to be borne (and by whom) and the impact of deadlines being reintroduced for cessation of manufacture of combustion engines ahead of other nations as well as banning new North Sea oil and gas licences. Unfortunately, the same cannot be said about what may happen should Donald Trump become President of the United States. Trump – whose stance is explicitly sceptical – argues that measures to avert climate change will hurt consumers and undermine the US's economy. Similar arguments are increasingly being made by right of centre parties in all developed nations including within the EU. Unfortunately, short-term political expediency appears to 'trump' investment in dealing with a problem with catastrophic long-term consequences.

References

Bilal, A., & Känzig, D. R. (2024, May 10). *The macroeconomic impact of climate change: Global vs. local temperature*. National Bureau of Economic Research Website. https://www.nber.org/papers/w32450

Blondaut, J. (2022, May 18). *A guide to achieving your ESG objectives*. SoftwareAG Website. Retrieved April 18, 2022, from https://blog.softwareag.com/sustainability-guide/?utm_source=google&utm_medium=cpc&utm_campaign=bt_aris&utm_region=hq&utm_subcampaign=stg-1&utm_content=stg-1_guide_achieve-your-esg-objectives&gad_source=1&gclid=Cj0KCQjwir2xBhC_ARIsAMTXk87IGZkj3nN4twcSFFoIwcZfRaAnrZQl3PA6ZHRfIKNeQ6wM1tQ6fgIaAibGEALw_wcB

Bychawski, A. (2024, May 8). *BP and shell 'Shaped' UK carbon tax proposals, private emails show*. DeSmog Website. Retrieved May 10, 2024, from https://www.desmog.com/2024/05/08/bp-shell-shaped-uk-carbon-tax-proposals-private-emails-policy-exchange/

Carrington, D. (2024, February 27). UK's net zero economy grew 9% in 2023, report finds. *Guardian*. Retrieved April 3, 2024, from https://www.theguardian.com/environment/2024/feb/27/uk-net-zero-economy-grew-in-2023-report-finds

Cran-McGreehin, S. (2022, January 21). *Net zero: Economy and jobs*. Energy & Climate Intelligence Unit. Retrieved April 3, 2022, from https://eciu.net/analysis/briefings/net-zero/net-zero-economy-and-jobs#:~:text=A%20net%20zero%20economy&text=Economies%20do%20not%20stand%20still,the%20economy%20will%20be%20reduced

Dillon, A., Burnett, N., & Jozepa, I. (2024, March 5). *Carbon border adjustment mechanism*. House of Commons Library Research Briefing No 9935. UK Parliament, London.

Eisenberg, J. (2022, June 30). *Here are 5 things to look forward to in the future – according to 1,000 experts*. World Economic Forum (WEF). Retrieved April 2, 2022, from https://www.weforum.org/agenda/2022/06/here-are-5-things-to-look-forward-to-over-the-next-3-years-according-to-1-000-experts/

Energy Advice Hub. (2024, May 1). *EU approves new sustainable supply chain rules*. Energy Advice Hub Website. Retrieved April 2, 2024, from https://energyadvicehub.org/eu-approves-new-sustainable-supply-chain-rules/#:~:text=The%20directive%2C%20approved%20on%2024,human%20rights%20and%20the%20environment

Energy & Climate Intelligence Unit. (2024, February). *The UK's net zero economy – The scale and geography of the net zero economy in the UK*. CBI Economics. Retrieved April 3, 2024, from https://ca1-eci.edcdn.com/cbi-eciu-netzeroec-February2024.pdf?v=1709026812

European Commission. (2019 December). *The European Green Deal*. https://ec.europa.eu/commission/presscorner/detail/en/ip_19_6691

Ewe, K. (2023, December 28). The ultimate election year: All the elections around the world in 2024. *Time Magazine*. Retrieved April 5, 2023, from https://time.com/6550920/world-elections-2024/

Financial Conduct Authority. (2024, April 23). *FCA confirms anti-greenwashing guidance and proposes extending sustainability framework*. Financial Conduct Authority Website. Retrieved May 2, 2024, from https://www.fca.org.uk/news/press-releases/fca-confirms-anti-greenwashing-guidance-and-proposes-extending-sustainability-framework

Hammond, P. (2023, 1 August). Politicians have to come clean about full net zero costs. *Times*. Retrieved March 25, 2023, from https://www.thetimes.co.uk/article/politicians-have-to-come-clean-about-full-net-zero-costs-8kq6bbl6x

Hazell, W. (2023, July 29). Tory PMs 'systematically dishonest' about £1 trillion cost of net zero, says Lord Hammond'. *Telegraph*. Retrieved March 25, 2023, from https://www.telegraph.co.uk/politics/2023/07/29/tory-pms-systematically-dishonest-1-trillion-cost-net-zero/

Holl-Allen, G. (2024, March 25). Labour's net zero plans 'will cost £116 billion'. *Telegraph*. Retrieved March 25, 2024, from https://www.telegraph.co.uk/politics/2024/03/25/labours-net-zero-plans-will-cost-116-billion-analysis/

Horton, H. (2024, May 3). Britain's climate action plan unlawful, high court rules. *Guardian*. Retrieved May 4, 2024, from https://www.theguardian.com/environment/article/2024/may/03/britain-climate-action-plan-unlawful-high-court

Kenningham, L. (2024, May 9). *Sunak's green U-turn has been a strategic mistake*. City AM Website. Retrieved May 10, 2024, from https://www.cityam.com/sunaks-net-zero-rollback-strategic-mistake/?utm_source=CityAM&utm_campaign=e59af25c7b-EMAIL_CAMPAIGN_2024_05_11_02_54&utm_medium=email&utm_term=0_-e59af25c7b-%5BLIST_EMAIL_ID%5D

Krishnan, M., Samandari, H., Woetzel, L., Smit, S., Pacthod, D., Pinner, D., Nauclér, T., Tai, H., Farr, A., Wu, W., & Imperato, D. (2022, January 25). *The economic transformation: What would change in the net-zero transition*. McKinsey Sustainability Website. Retrieved March 26, 2022, from https://www.mckinsey.com/capabilities/sustainability/our-insights/the-economic-transformation-what-would-change-in-the-net-zero-transition

McKinsey Global Institute. (2022, January). *The net-zero transition, What it would cost, what it could bring* [Executive Summary]. McKinsey Global Institute in collaboration with McKinsey Sustainability and McKinsey's Global Energy &Materials and Advanced Industries Practices. Retrieved March 27, 2022, from file:///C:/Users/mccab/OneDrive/Documents/Net%20Zero%20and%20Green%20Economy%20book%20proposal/the-net-zero-transition-executive-summary.pdf

Mehrhoff, J. (2023, December 5). Benefits of accelerating the climate transition outweigh the costs. *IMF Blog*. Retrieved April 2, 2023, from https://www.imf.org/en/Blogs/Articles/2023/12/05/benefits-of-accelerating-the-climate-transition-outweigh-the-costs

Mooney, A., & Hancock, A. (2023, September 21). How net zero became an election issue around the globe. *Financial Times*. Retrieved April 4, 2023, from https://www.ft.com/content/f6667506-d38f-43c2-8e75-b39c72112a41

OBR. (2021). *Fiscal risks report – July 2021*. Office for Budget Responsibility. https://obr.uk/frs/fiscal-risks-report-july-2021/

Organisation for Economic Co-operation and Development. (2023, May). *Net Zero+ Climate and Economic Resilience in a Changing World*. OECD Environment Directorate. Retrieved April 2, 2023, from https://www.oecd.org/climate-change/net-zero-resilience/Policy-Highlights-Net-Zero-climate-and-economic-resilience-in-a-changing-world.pdf

Parker, G., Fisher, L., & Ackard, J. (2023, September 20). Rishi Sunak announces series of U-turns on net zero pledges. *Financial Times*. Retrieved April 4, 2023, from https://www.ft.com/content/02ecb92e-1e67-4db1-ad73-6c0e76bdc6ca

Stacey, K., & Harvey, F. (2024, February 8). Labour cuts £28bn green investment pledge by half. *Guardian*. Retrieved April 5, 2024, from https://www.theguardian.com/politics/2024/feb/08/labour-cuts-28bn-green-investment-pledge-by-half#:~:text=Labour%20has%20cut%20its%20green,turn%20of%20Keir%20Starmer's%20leadership

Ward, R. (2023, August 3). *Costs and benefits of the UK reaching net zero emissions by 2050: The evidence*. Grantham Research Institute on Climate Change and the Environment. Retrieved March 25, 2023, from https://www.lse.ac.uk/granthaminstitute/news/costs-and-benefits-of-the-uk-reaching-net-zero-emissions-by-2050-the-evidence/

Chapter 15

Transporting Nations to Net Zero

Beverley Nielsen

Centre for Brexit Studies, Birmingham City University

Abstract

Transport is responsible for around a quarter of global emissions. It is 91% fossil fuel dependent for energy, with emissions remaining stubbornly high, increasing in the EU since 1990 and falling since then by just 15% in the UK. The UK's National Infrastructure Commission (NIC), in producing its second assessment, a major strategic overview for the next 30 years, emphasises a near universal dependency on electricity and hydrogen to decarbonise transport emissions. Locally distributed energy solutions are not considered part of their approach and neither do they consider where the products proposed for mass adoption – electric vehicles (EVs) are to be manufactured. Embodied carbon emissions are not taken into account, with emissions analysis focused on zero tailpipe emissions. Green gases which can be used in combustion engines and hybrids, harnessing existing supply chains and maintenance service provision, are also not seen as part of the solution, even during transition. Manufacturers are concerned that legislation and policy approaches, such as the Zero Emissions Vehicle Mandate, will lead to off-shoring of production. Zero Emissions Vehicles do not consider tyre emissions, which some research has shown to be many times higher than tailpipe emissions with devastating impacts on ecosystems. The chapter proposes the need for a greater holistic and circular approach to be taken to embodied carbon, mineral and resource utilisation together with biodiversity and planetary impacts.

Keywords: Electric vehicles; battery electric vehicles; zero emission vehicles; green gases; biomethane; hydrogen; distributed energy systems; particulate emissions; integrated transport

Examining Net Zero: Creating Solutions for a Greener Society and Sustainable Economic Growth, 151–164
Copyright © 2025 by Beverley Nielsen
Published under exclusive licence by Emerald Publishing Limited
doi:10.1108/978-1-83608-574-420251015

Introduction

The International Energy Agency (IEA) has highlighted the requirement for CO_2 emissions from the transport sector to fall by more than 3% a year to 2030 to meet 2050 global Net Zero targets, with transport continuing to rely on fossil fuel oil products for almost 91% of its energy, down only 3.5% since the early 1970s (Teter & Voswinkel, 2023). Transport was responsible for about a quarter of the EU's total CO_2 emissions in 2019, with 71.7% from road transportation, and it was the only sector where greenhouse gas emissions increased in the past three decades, rising 35.5% across the EU between 1990 and 2019 (European Parliament, 2023). In the UK, transport is responsible for 26% of CO_2 emissions or for 109 MtCO2e. Whilst energy emissions have fallen by 48% since the 1990s, domestic transport emissions have decreased by just 15% in this period in spite of more efficient combustion engine design.

The NIC Second National Infrastructure Assessment (NIA, 2023), a substantial strategic report providing a 30-year overview of infrastructure priorities for the UK, makes clear that their proposed solution for UK decarbonisation lies in '*switching from fossil fuels to a mix of electricity, hydrogen and fossil fuels abated with carbon capture and storage*'. As 80% of the UK's energy requirement is from fossil fuels, the NIC, like the IEA and European Parliament, highlights the scale of this challenge. By 2035, modelling for the Commission suggests that around 60 GW of offshore wind and 70 GW of solar generation will be needed.

Linking Energy and Industrial Strategies

Getting the UK on track to meet the climate targets set out in the Sixth Carbon Budget requires a reduction in UK emissions of 78% by 2035 relative to 1990, or a 63% reduction from 2019. The NIC anticipates the near universal adoption of heat pumps and EVs by residents, forecasting a halving in energy costs for households in the longer term, whilst simultaneously promoting the need for government funding to provide household support during the earlier transition stages whilst these options remain more expensive.

The UK is highly car dependent in terms of travel to work. Whilst on average 68% of worker commuting is estimated to be by car, if London is extracted, then average regional commuting by car increases to over 75% (Department for Transport, 2017), whilst 72% of car journeys are under five miles (Department for Transport, 2021a, 2021b) and modal shift is a priority for these. Accelerating charging point installations for EVs is seen as an immediate priority by government given UK 2030 targets to reach 300,000 public charge points. Growing at 38% year on year, by August 2023, there were around 45,500 UK public charge points, of which 8,700 were rapid chargers, with around 75,000 required by 2029. In France, by 2023, there were 118,000 public EV charge points, in Germany 87,155 and in Spain around 25,000 (Statista, 2024).

Whilst continued devolution of transport budgets to all local authorities responsible for strategic transport is recommended, the NIC does not spell out any role for locally distributed energy to be prioritised by these administrations as a potentially diversified set of off-grid energy solutions given the challenges faced by the electricity network capacity limitations.

Similarly, the NIC does not evaluate where the products they propose for mass adoption are going to be made. Nor is there a focus on localising production to save emissions, shorten supply chains and improve resilience, with few mentions of prioritising the circular economy in this latest assessment.

With gas boilers heating around 88% of the almost 30 m British homes due to be phased out and replaced by heat pumps and around 32 m fossil-fuelled cars which could be potentially replaced one for one with EVs, the scale of the changes proposed in the NIC's assessment is vast. The solution proposed by Carl Arntzen of Bosch Thermotechnology Ltd as a UK-based boiler and heating products manufacturer is for hybrid gas boiler and heat pumps, deliverable at 20% of the cost of heat pumps and reducing CO_2 emissions by 80%, an option which is not considered or promoted, even during the transition phase.

The Catapult Energy Systems report, 'Innovating to Net Zero' (2024) highlights the challenges around meeting electricity requirements at times of low renewables and peak demand and the impact of this in determining the cost of our future energy system. They emphasise this 'peak heat' challenge as 'the biggest system innovation challenge for Net Zero' stating that alongside:

> Fabric efficiency, a significant increase in thermal storage and other energy demand managing technologies such as smart controls will be needed. We also need to develop an energy system which is as flexible as possible, allowing us to use different sources and vectors of energy at different times to keep the overall system cost down. However, these can only go so far. Our modelling finds system value in the use of hybrid heating systems combining electric heat pumps with the supply of gaseous energy (natural gas) through the existing gas network, as we transition the system. (Catapult Energy Systems, 2024)

As Mr Arntzen points out, there is no analysis linking current consumer demand to the sales targets proposed through the Clean Heat Market Mechanism, especially as heat pumps are considerably more expensive and often less effective given the state of UK housing stock. The same dilemma facing the home heating market is shared by EV manufacturers, providing what is seen as 'the future of road transport' by the NIC, and promoted as being zero emission and cheaper to run EVs.

To make progress on cars, the UK government has instigated a 'Zero Emission Vehicle Mandate'. As with home heating, government has set sales targets for at least 22% of all new cars sold in the UK to be 'zero emissions class' in 2024, rising to 80% in 2030 and 100% by 2035. However, in setting these sales targets, Carlos Tavares, CEO of Stallantis (producing brands including Peugeot, Citroen, Vauxhall, Fiat, Alfa Romeo, Chrysler and Jeep), notes that whilst his business is committed to decarbonisation policies, forcing them to sell more EVs beyond what he has termed 'natural demand' will simply render them unprofitable given the £15,000 fines imposed for every vehicle short of these targets. With demand for Stallantis EVs at 11% and the government target sitting at 22%, the business is facing the imposition of a significant fine. Although battery electric vehicles (BEVs) account for 16% of national registrations, fleet operators have been taking advantage of company car tax breaks impacting national sales, with estimated demand from private motorists sitting closer to 10% (Lea, 2024).

Mr Tavares stated in April 2024:

> The ZEV [Zero Emission Vehicle] mandate promotes the self-destruction of the industry. I am not going to sell cars at a loss. If the UK is sincere about having manufacturing activity in the UK and protecting it, then something must be done. (Lea, 2024)

Mr Tavares' colleague, Linda Jackson, Brand Chief Executive, Stellantis, has called for increased consumer incentives, including reducing the costs of EVs, rather than imposing corporate fines (O'Donoghue, 2023). However, from June 2022, the Plug-In Car Grant (PCG), which previously made funding available towards the purchase of EVs, was wound up, with any resulting savings shifted into funding the public charging network. The PCG grant, responsible for making £1,500 discounts off the cost of new EVs below £32,000 price mark and running since 2011, had been part of a range of Department for Transport (DfT) EV subsidies. It was reduced to £1,500 in December 2021 from the original £5,000 and cut completely in June 2022 in a move which has left the UK as the only country in Europe without any upfront electric car purchase incentives (Cinch, 2024) and with France, for example, having introduced social leasing as a means of making EVs accessible.

Manufacturers have also expressed frustration that the Zero Emissions mandate, rather than incentivising growth in EV sales, increased the threat from China where they were able to produce cars for sale at 25–30% lower price points. Professor David Bailey at University of Birmingham has observed that the UK government removed these incentives far too quickly, given that EVs were still more expensive than either petrol or diesel cars (Lawson, 2024). Companies like Stellantis and Bosch Thermotechnology, manufacturing in the UK, have been asking for more emphasis on UK manufacturing and its contribution to the UK economy, through the balance of payments made by their exports, whilst appealing to government for support in lowering energy costs or providing more consumer incentivises to help make UK manufacturing more competitive with Chinese car makers. These manufacturers are concerned that the current policy approach will lead to off-shoring of production to economies without such stringent net zero legislation.

Matthew Rhodes, former Chairman of Energy Capital West Midlands, speaking in an interview with Nielsen B, 1 May 2024, said:

> The challenge for the UK is that energy policies should go hand in hand with an industrial strategy, especially for English regions, such as the West Midlands, which is an energy-based industrial region. We need to stand up and recognise this, otherwise the market will simply go to China.

Renewable Energy Generation – National or Local?

Given the current strategy which focuses primarily on electrification in delivering a decarbonised economy and with half our electricity currently supplied through renewable sources (Morley, 2024), the UK needs to accelerate renewable energy production. Whether this is best done through a national approach, as indicated in the NIC report, or drawing on regional energy generation requires further assessment.

Local authority leaders have highlighted the crisis holding back regional growth due to their inability to access the national grid infrastructure in a timely manner (Tapper, 2024). The National Grid's electricity systems operator (ESO), responsible for managing power distribution, has emphasised that the queue requesting grid connection has 'grown at an unprecedented pace'. Britain's power stations generate around 75 GW of electricity, with the country expected to need at least twice as much by 2050 as people switch to EVs and heat pumps. However, the ESO has said the queue of projects waiting to be connected to the national grid could reach the equivalent of 800 GW by the end of 2024 – far more than the country is expected to need. Under the first-come, first-served system, developers can pay to jump ahead and block the queue (Tapper, 2024). With many applications awaiting determination, Ofgem has had to approve three-month delays until developers are able to find out when they can achieve a grid connection. Considering these challenges, projects which do not need to be connected to the grid and can supply power to local projects have clear advantages as Heart of England Community Energy outlined in their chapter with energy from local solar arrays available at up to 60% lower prices than electricity from the grid.

John Baldwin, Managing Director, CNG Services Ltd, working to support the installation of a biomethane refuelling station network across the UK, said in an interview with the author (Nielsen, 2024):

> As the CEO of Daimler Truck recently observed, the first Battery Electric Vehicle truck is relatively easy to charge; a hundred trucks are difficult, a thousand very expensive. And for 15,000, it is almost impossible. With fuel cells, on the other hand, it is the other way around.

Matthew Rhodes, former Chair of West Midlands Energy Capital, has noted that a decarbonised economy should lead to changes in previously firmly held economic assumptions through the measurements of 'embodied carbon' in products and services which are required and which should incentivise more circular economy approaches, encouraging companies to maximise locally available resources where possible. This should include making use of local waste streams, encouraging design of products and services for re-use and minimising transport costs (Braungart & McDonough, 2002), with a need to start thinking about national and regional economic and industrial strategies in new ways as a decarbonised world is fundamentally more localised (Nielsen & McCabe, 2021, p. 87).

Matthew Rhodes added in a recent interview with Nielsen (2024):

> The marginal cost of solar is one tenth the cost of gas and where it can be generated close to use it can be a lot cheaper than grid electricity. Supplying some of your electricity from a megawatt of solar panels on your factory roof is always going to be more cost-effective than buying grid electricity. In addition, government should be incentivising this kind of investment by making connections easier and paying good rates for exported power, rather than the opposite.

Circular economy considerations should play a greater role, given IEA statements highlighting that solar and wind farms, EVs, batteries, all require more minerals to build than their fossil fuel-based counterparts (IEA, 2022a, 2022b, 2022c). An electric car needs six times the minerals of a conventional car. Onshore wind needs nine times more mineral resources than a gas-fired plant. Since 2010, the average minerals needed for a new unit of power generation capacity have increased by 50% as renewable energy use has risen.

Hundreds of new mines will need to be opened to meet current plans for Net Zero. IEA forecasts that for some minerals such as lithium and cobalt, surpluses are expected in the near term; however, looking further ahead to meet climate goals, supplies from existing mines and projects under construction are forecast to meet only half of projected lithium and cobalt requirements and 80% of copper needs by 2030 (IEA, 2022a, 2022b, 2022c).

In slowly moving from fossil fuel dependency to 'green' electricity, the mineral supplies required for clean electric energy are impacting our environment, biodiversity, local populations and resulting in the exploitation and dispersal of local communities. Mining, production and processing of mineral resources such as cobalt, copper and lithium have led to a variety of high-profile environmental and social challenges with human rights abuses recorded, local communities displaced and biodiversity threatened in a wide range of places including the DRC, Argentina, Chile, India and China (Amnesty International, 2023; Jemio, 2024; Kay & Parkin, 2024; Kurmayer, 2024). Given increasing concerns amongst consumers and investors for companies to use sustainably sourced minerals, the IEA warns that this may be challenging given there may simply be insufficient quantities of appropriately sourced minerals to meet demand (IEA, 2022a, 2022b, 2022c).

By contrast, hydropower and bioenergy have low mineral intensities accounting for only about 2% each of the total demand for copper from low-carbon power additions in 2040.

Green Gas – Adding to the Energy Mix for Heavy Vehicles

In the UK, where the centralised national electricity grid is projected as the primary energy source to meet increased demand, there also exists a range of other distributed energy solutions including renewable green gases able to ease electricity grid capacity pressures.

Biomethane (also referred to as Bio Compressed Natural Gas, Bio-CNG, and Renewable Natural Gas, RNG), is a purified version of biogas, produced naturally as organic matter breaks down through the process of anaerobic digestion. The methane created, instead of escaping into the atmosphere as a greenhouse gas with a warming impact 86 times stronger than CO_2 per unit of mass over a 20-year period, is captured as a valuable energy source. Harnessing these emissions, in turn, contributes to Global Methane Pledge signed by 155 nations including the UK, to reduce global methane emissions by 30% from 2020 levels by 2030, with methane recognised as the second-largest contributor to global warming after CO_2 and 2021 seeing the second largest annual increase in methane emissions since global monitoring began four decades ago (Climate and Clean Air Coalition, 2024; IEA, 2022a, 2022b, 2022c).

John Baldwin, Managing Director, CNG Services, speaking about the advantages of using biomethane in sequestering carbon added in an interview with the author (Nielsen, 2024):

> The anaerobic digestion (AD) plant produces around 45% bio-CO2 in the biogas, which is separated in the biomethane production process. It used to be vented off, but it's now always liquefied and taken from site by road. Initial use is in industry but, from 2027, it may be sent to CCS (Carbon Capture and Storage) facilities, unlocking the potential to deliver greenhouse gas removals (GGR). This means, when generating 100 GWh of biomethane from AD, 14,000 tonnes of bio-CO2 could be captured and permanently removed from the atmosphere. If we have 10 TWh of biomethane per annum then that is 1.4 million tonnes of 'dinosaur era' CO2 removed per annum.

Biomethane provides a circular economy model with energy produced locally from organic wastes, such as manure, food scraps or damaged and crop residue, or algae such as seaweeds. It is a form of waste management offering the security of supply, very low minerals requirement, a stable pricing structure and has a significant role to play in the decarbonisation of transport, particularly for long-distance trucks and ships, where electrification is more difficult and expensive. The EU is targeting increased biomethane production targets to reach 35 billion cubic metres (350 TWh) per year by 2030, a 12-fold increase in output (European Commission, 2024; IEA, 2022a, 2022b, 2022c).

The rapid deployment of Bio-CNG in Sweden has proved a successful part of their solution in moving towards clean mobility. Biomethane has one of the lowest greenhouse gas-intensive pathways when the whole emissions lifecycle is measured (Arnau, 2022). The Swedish example highlights concerns that when nations implement bans on internal combustion engines to cut the use of fossil fuels, they are also blocking the opportunity for the affordable use of biomethane in transport. Instead, Arnau suggests, legislation should stimulate the deployment and availability of renewable fuels such as Bio-CNG with CO_2 emission performance standards, taking into account the whole lifecycle, not just the vehicle's tailpipe emissions. In Sweden, a combination of national, municipal and private investments supports the development and consumption of biomethane, together with related technologies and infrastructure. These prove useful considerations when considering cost comparisons and technology readiness levels of combustion engines and supply chains, compared with battery electric or fuel cell technologies. Given the resource and energy implications they suggest policy makers should consider all available renewable energy options rather than ruling out certain alternatives.

In the UK, the Climate Change Committee (CCC, 2016a, 2016b) has anticipated a limited role for Bio-CNG. Their Technical note of 2016 states,

> biomethane could be used to displace some … natural gas to offer … significant savings, but in the long term supply will be limited and there will be competition from other sectors […] our assessment suggests that the total biomethane resource is likely to remain significantly lower than total natural gas demand, such that any increase in demand for gas from HGVs would be met by fossil natural gas at the margin.

The CCC's central estimates for available biomethane resource suggest around 20 TWh, which could displace about 5% of fossil natural gas in 2050. Alternative sources contest these estimates, suggesting that the UK has the potential for 200 TWh (Baldwin, 2024). The particular relevance of biomethane is its energy density which, being over four times greater than that of hydrogen, makes this green gas an option for use by heavier transport, including heavy goods vehicles (HGVs), buses, trains and trams.

John Baldwin, CNG Services, notes the challenges for the UK economy, currently burning 800 TWh of gas a year, if reduced to a binary choice of electrification and hydrogen. With the CCC working towards its seventh budget, he highlights a range of green gases, targeting 100 TWh of green gas by 2035. With Denmark, Sweden and France in particular harnessing biomethane effectively, Mr Baldwin suggests a growing range of green gas options including E-methane (made from wind and bio-CO_2) and biosynthetic natural gas (made by gasifying waste and converting the syngas to methane) along with the potential to import biomethane by pipeline from Ukraine as part of GB's imported LNG cargoes. The Renewable Energy Association has been working up, '*credible targets for production of these green gases for submission to the CCC ahead of their Seventh budget*' (Baldwin, 2024). Using the gas grid, plant and storage capacity, these renewable green gases offer a low-cost option to add to the energy mix, particularly if produced at greater scale and are particularly valuable for heavier transport (HGVs, freighters, tractors, excavators, buses, trains and trams). Hydrogen is also proposed as an alternative, but as volumes produced of green hydrogen are very low, it will still require a vast investment in hydrogen pipelines, centrifugal compressors, salt cavity storage (with big gas reciprocating compressors), hydrogen pressure reduction stations and hydrogen generation plant (Baldwin, 2024).

Given these green gas options, the old plateau number of around 10–20 TWh for Biomethane is stated as being too low, indicating that green gas can provide a valuable additional resource to power heavy transport vehicles currently not well served through Battery Electric.

Rail – Alternatives to Pure Electric

Whilst the continued use of Bio-CNG by HGVs and buses is anticipated, it has not been promoted as an option for rail-based transport where electrification is seen as the primary driver. As part of UK government's plans to decarbonise transport, a target to remove all diesel-only trains (passenger and freight) from the network by 2040 has been set by government (DfT, 2021a, 2021b). This plan notes the government's support for battery and hydrogen trains as well as use of '*technology to clean up diesel trains until they can be removed altogether*' although there is no specific mention of biofuels (DfT, 2021a, 2021b).

The UK rail network is 38% electrified, and government plans to increase this to 51% over the next 10 years, according to the Rail Industry Association which sees potential for battery electric for around one-third of the remaining network (Flaig, 2024). This will, however, continue to increase pressure on the grid given the charging requirements and infrastructure needed to support any battery electric trains.

Biofuels have been proposed as an alternative, building on the experience of HGVs and buses. In the USA, OptiFuel Systems recently announced that they had started testing their prototype 5,600 hp Total-Zero™ Renewable Natural Gas Line Haul Locomotive along with a 2,500 hp Total-Zero™ Powered Tender with a 7,500 diesel gallon equivalent capacity. The RNG-powered line haul locomotive produces 5,100 hp from zero emission Cummins RNG engines using their modular technology with zero Well-to-Wheel nitrogen oxides and particulate matter emissions and Negative Carbon Intensity. This is intended to improve fuel costs and operating range by 25%. The company has been working as lead technical partner with GTI Energy, the formal applicant to the US Department of Energy with other partners including Cummins, BAE Systems, Luxfer Gas Cylinders, TMV Control Systems Inc., ENSCO, CAF Group, New York Air Brake and Powerhouse, a Marmon Rail Company.

Given their involvement in the design and build of fuel cells, hydrogen storage and battery modules for the Sierra Northern Railway's hydrogen hybrid switcher locomotives, OptiFuel have stated that they are '*uniquely qualified to understand the strength and weakness of battery-electric and hydrogen fuel cell hybrid locomotives*'. Scott Myers, OptiFuel President added:

> However, we now believe that RNG is the preferred path to zero emission line haul locomotives and tenders due to the physics of energy storage, overall operating cost, operating risk, fuel availability and cost over the next 20 years. A 4500 hp line haul locomotive requires continuous high power for extended hours, something that neither battery-electric nor hydrogen fuel cell hybrid line haul locomotive solutions will be able to do. (Businesswire, 2024)

Additional advantages include being able to use standard components in the RNG vehicles enabling economies of scale in production and lower maintenance costs with a CAPEX saving projected at around $150 billion over 25 years through the decarbonisation of 38,000 freight vehicles (Businesswire, 2024).

Ultra Light Rail Partners Ltd (ULRP) is a small startup whose team members have been involved in designing and producing the Stourbridge Shuttle. This service has been operating for the past 15 years, run by Pre Metro Operations Ltd (PMOL) as the UK's smallest Train Operating Company serving Stourbridge Town (population 57,000) to link the mainline rail and the bus stations. PMOL have, during this time, been running the UK's only gas-powered train, using LPG (a cleaner fuel than diesel) and harnessing kinetic energy through its on-board flywheel. They have carried over 7 million passengers demonstrating the viability of a rail-based shuttle in a small town. Since the formation of ULRP (chaired by the author), the company has been awarded three grants by Innovate UK, the UK's innovation agency, to pilot a UK first-of-a-kind biomethane train operating with a flywheel, delivered in 2020, alongside designs for a biomethane and flywheel operated train (2021), a tram (2021) and transportable refuelling station (2023). The intention has been to trial and demonstrate ultra light rail as an affordable sustainable rail-based service for smaller cities and towns enabling significant modal shift.

Following a recent meeting (9 April 2024) between ULRP and the UK Minister for Transport, Anthony Browne MP, along with DfT officials, it became clear their views were moving beyond the promotion of a primary electric solution. The Department highlighted their acceptance of all available renewable energy options for rail-based transport, including trams, stressing they were '*technology agnostic*' when it came to renewable, low and zero carbon fuels used in their powertrains as we push to meet Net Zero targets. They emphasised that the decision-making for any particular project, along with their choice of fuel, is one for local transport authorities to make, assuming they were renewable options. Where they might opt for biomethane, for example, the Department emphasised they would support this option (Nielsen, 2024).

This approach ties in with the more active devolution of funding to local and regional transport authorities, most recently demonstrated by City Region Transport Settlements (familiarly known as 'CRuSTS') with £16 bn of this funding already devolved.

Phil Evans, Managing Director of PMOL, noting the DfT's shifting attitude stated:

> Having operated the Stourbridge Shuttle for the past fifteen years, carrying over 7 million passengers and achieving a 99.6% reliability track record as the only train operating company in the country to use LPG (up to 70% cleaner than diesel) combined with a flywheel, we are very pleased to hear the DfT is 'technology agnostic'.
>
> We see a great future for a diversified energy portfolio drawing on the particular features, attributes and strengths of local economies.

> We agree with the National Infrastructure Commission (NIC) that the government should 'carry out a more comprehensive analysis of capacity needs in smaller cities to see which ones should be prioritised'. But unlike the NIC we believe there is a great opportunity for ultra light rail, and not only buses, to service these smaller towns and cities as we have amply demonstrated in Stourbridge. This town of 57k people has proven that rail connectivity can be viable in smaller places and make a great contribution to the local economy, CO2 emissions reductions, visitor experience and air quality. (Nielsen, 2024)

The NIC second infrastructure assessment calls for an integrated transport strategy to include active travel and trams as a connectivity option for larger cities, with buses providing solutions for smaller cities, towns and more rural areas. Investing in sustainable trips within and between English cities together with the need for more and safer active travel is required, they state, for England's transport systems to support economic growth over the next 20–30 years, with under investment and poor connectivity highlighted as holding back productivity. A full array of park and ride, walking and cycling corridors linked with local multi-modal hubs will be required with UK government targeting '*half of all journeys in towns and cities will be cycled or walked by 2030*' (Department for Transport, 2021a, 2021b).

The impact of bus and car tyres on public health and ecosystems more generally has not been considered when referring to 'Zero Emission vehicles'. When this term is used it simply refers to tailpipe emissions. Emissions Analytics research (2022) shows that tyre particulate emissions are up to 1,850 times greater than tailpipe emissions.

For BEVs, Emissions Analytics state:

> Half a tonne of battery weight can result in tire emissions that are almost 400 more times greater than real-world tailpipe emissions, everything else being equal. (Emissions Analytics, 2022)

Ocean pollution by plastics and microplastics has become an increasing source of concern with an estimated 14 million tonnes of plastic entering our oceans each year and an estimated 358 trillion microplastic particles floating close to the surface of our world's oceans and more on the seabed (Davison, 2024). Some research by the Pew Charitable Trust suggests that tyre particulates account for 78% of microplastics pollution of the oceans affecting ecosystems and, in particular, plankton and micro-organisms at the base of the food chains (Euronews Green, 2023).

Research conducted by Andreas Stohl, from the Norwegian Institute for Air Research, published in the Journal Nature Communications, indicated that 550,000 tonnes of particles smaller than 0.01 mm are deposited each year, with almost half ending up in the ocean. Tyre and brake pollution is forecast to get worse before it improves as electric cars become more widely adopted. Being heavier than internal combustion engine cars, there would be more wear on tyres and brakes with more tyre emissions (Carrington, 2020).

Following recent research by the British Antarctic Survey, Dr Clara Manno, a marine ecologist and lead scientist on the CUPIDO project stated:

> Krill and salps play an important role in slowing down climate change. The Southern Ocean is a hugely important carbon sink and these animals play an integral part transferring atmospheric CO2 into the deep oceans. Interactions with microplastics have the potential to interfere with the amount of carbon these organisms can take down and trap in the deep ocean. (British Antarctic Survey, 2023)

Trams with steel wheels on steel rails are far more energy efficient with a durability of three times compared to buses and offer a solution to the detrimental impacts of tyre emissions and microplastics contaminating the marine sea surface microlayer which absorbs and concentrates these chemicals. These, in turn, kill or negatively affect krill and other zooplankton, and given short food chains, are 'highly likely' to transfer these microplastics to larger predators such as whales, penguins and seals, impacting entire food chains.

It would appear, therefore, that to combat Climate Change effectively and protect our biodiversity along with the planet's ecosystems, rather than simply off-shoring emissions, developed economies will need to take a much more holistic, circular approach to transport. Distributed and localised energy systems should play a more significant role, along with investments in public transport solutions including greater train and tram use, prioritising the integration of these options with active travel and multi-modal hubs.

References

Amnesty International. (2023, September 12). *Democratic Republic of the Congo: Industrial mining of cobalt and copper for rechargeable batteries is leading to grievous human rights abuses*.

Arnau, A. (2022, March 14). *Biomethane for decarbonising transport: The Swedish example*. Energy Post.

Baldwin, J. (2024). *Offshore energies, heatability that's the beauty of gas*. Issue 58 Winter 2024.

Braungart & McDonough. (2002). *Cradle to cradle: Remaking the way we make things*. Vintage.

British Antarctic Survey (BAS). (2023, March 29). *Microplastic found in Antarctic Krill and Salps*. BAS Natural Environment Research Council.

Businesswire. (2024, January 11). *OptiFuel's Total-Zero™ 5600 hp RNG-electric line haul locomotive and RNG-powered tender are on track for testing at the federal railroad*. Administration's Transportation Technology Center. Retrieved May 12, 2024, from www.businesswire.com/news/home/20240111675553/en/OptiFuel's-Total-Zero™-5600-hp-RNG-Electric-Line-Haul-Locomotive-and-RNG-Powered-Tender-are-on-Track-for-Testing-at-the-Federal-Railroad-Administration's-Transportation-Technology-Center.

Carrington, D. (2020, July 14). Car tyres are major source of ocean microplastics – Study. *The Guardian*.

Catapult Energy Systems. (2024, June 3). *Innovating to net zero 2024, innovating to net zero 2024 – energy systems catapult*.

Cinch. (2024). https://www.cinch.co.uk/guides/electric-cars/what-grants-can-you-get-for-electric-cars-in-the-uk

Climate and Clean Air Coalition. (2024, May 17). *Methane*. www.ccacoalition.org/short-lived-climate-pollutants/methane

Climate Change Committee. (2016a) *Technical Note, Biomethane*. Retrieved May 17, 2024, from www.theccc.org.uk/wp-content/uploads/2016/12/2016-PR-Biomethane-Technical-Note.pdf

Climate Change Committee. (2016b). Technical Note: Biomethane, supporting the transport chapter of the report Meeting Carbon Budgets – 2016. Progress Report to Parliament, Committee on Climate Change.

Davison, T. (2024, March 18). *How much plastic is in the ocean?* Clean Hub.

Department for Transport. (2021a). *National Travel Survey 2021: Mode share, journey lengths and public transport use*. Retrieved May 24, 2024, from www.gov.uk/government/statistics/national-travel-survey-2021/national-travel-survey-2021-mode-share-journey-lengths-and-public-transport-use#:~:text=In%202021%2C%2025%25%20of%20trips,under%205%20miles%20in%202019

Department for Transport. (2021b). *Decarbonising Transport, A Better, Greener Britain*. Department for Transport.

Department for Transport, Statistical Release. (2017, December 17). *Transport Statistics Great Britain*.

Emissions Analytics. (2024, May 3). *Gaining traction, losing tread pollution from tire wear now 1,850 times worse than exhaust emissions*. www.emissionsanalytics.com/news/gaining-traction-losing-tread

Euronews Green. (2023). *Toxic tyre dust: This source of microplastic pollution could be the worst of all*. Retrieved May 24, 2024, from www.euronews.com/green/2023/10/02/toxic-tyre-dust-this-source-of-microplastic-pollution-could-be-the-worst-of-all

European Commission. (2024, May 3). *Energy, climate change, environment, biomethane*. https://energy.ec.europa.eu/topics/renewable-energy/bioenergy/biomethane

European Parliament. (2023). *CO2 emissions from cars, facts and figures*.

Flaig, J. (2024, April 17). *Could battery trains decarbonise a third of the UK rail network?* Institution of Mechanical Engineers, Engineering News. Retrieved May 3, 2024, from www.imeche.org/news/news-article/could-battery-trains-decarbonise-a-third-of-the-uk-rail-network

IEA. (2022a). *Global Methane Tracker 2022*. The Global Methane Pledge. Retrieved May 17, 2024, from www.iea.org/reports/global-methane-tracker-2022/the-global-methane-pledge

IEA. (2022b). *Scaling up biomethane in the European Union: Background paper*. IEA.

IEA. (2022c, March). *The role of critical world energy outlook special report minerals in clean energy transitions*. International Energy Agency.

Jemio, G. (2024, January 28). *The rise of lithium mining threatens the Andean Flamingo in Argentina*. El Pais.

Kay, C., & Parkin, B. (2024, May 11). Endangered Rare Great Indian Bustard threatened by green energy. *Financial Times*.

Kurmayer, N. J. (2024, February 16). *Solar PV industry caught up in China forced-labour controversy*. Euractiv.

Lawson, A. (2024, March 15). Honda and Nissan join forces on electric car technology to chase Chinese rivals. *The Guardian*.

Lea, R. (2024, April 26). Car Chief warns green quota is threat to British manufacturing. *The Times*.

Morley, K. (2024). *National Grid: live*. https://grid.iamkate.com

National Infrastructure Commission. (2023, October 18). *Second National Infrastructure Assessment, An Assessment of the UK's Infrastructure Needs to 2055 and beyond*.

Nielsen, B. (2024, May 22). *Delivering Modal Shift – Shuffling reluctant motorists out of their cars: Can it be done?* Centre for Brexit Studies Blog. centreforbrexitstudiesblog.wordpress.com/2024/05/22/delivering-modal-shift-shuffling-reluctant-motorists-out-of-their-cars-can-it-be-done

O'Donoghue, D. (2023, September 23). *Interview with Linda Jackson, CEO, Peugeot, Completecar.ie*. Retrieved May 24, 2024, from www.completecar.ie/features/post/12710/Interview-with-Linda-Jackson-CEO-of-Peugeot

Rhodes, M. (2021). The implications of decarbonisation for regional identities: Can the centre hold? In B. Nielsen & S. McCabe (Eds.), *Exploring the green economy* (Ch 8, pp. 87–92). Bite Sized Books.

Ritchie, H. (2023, September). *How much more electricity will the UK need to switch to electric vehicles? Sustainability by numbers*. www.sustainabilitybynumbers.com/p/uk-ev-electricity-demand

Statista. (2024, May 3). *Volume of public electric vehicle chargers in France from 2014 to 2023, and Number of publicly accessible charging points for electric vehicles in Germany from January 2017 to October 2023*.

Tapper, J. (2024, March 10). Capacity crunch on national grid is delaying new homes in UK by years. *The Observer*.

Teter, J., & Voswinkel, F. (2023, July 11). *iea50 transport energy system*. Retrieved May 17, 2024, from www.iea.org/energy-system/transport

Chapter 16

An Evidence Based Pathway to Net Zero Ready Homes

Mike Leonard and Monica Mateo-Garcia

Birmingham City University, UK

Abstract

In the UK, the Future Homes Standard (FHS) will be used to achieve reductions in greenhouse gas emissions by 75–80% in newly constructed houses as part of the effort to achieve net zero by 2050. This chapter explains what this means in practice through design and building of houses by a housing association and speculative housebuilder. Research carried out by the Centre for Future Homes at Birmingham City University (BCU) has enabled a deeper understanding to emerge in how technology and collaborative approaches to production by all participants engaged in the supply chain can ensure attainment of carbon emissions. Crucially, the research has incorporated analysis of the experiences of occupants of innovative houses in altering behaviour and interaction with technology including heat pumps and ventilation systems. Findings from the research will be widely disseminated to assist others in appreciating the potential for housing, built with traditional locally available labour materials to be part of the effort to arrest climate change through proactive carbon reduction.

Keywords: FHS; innovation; emissions; carbon reduction; resilience; collaboration; occupants

Introduction

The built environment faces significant challenges in achieving climate change that will ensure, critically, safer buildings we live in. The contribution of the

Examining Net Zero: Creating Solutions for a Greener Society and Sustainable Economic Growth, 165–173
Copyright © 2025 by Mike Leonard and Monica Mateo-Garcia
Published under exclusive licence by Emerald Publishing Limited
doi:10.1108/978-1-83608-574-420251016

housing market to carbon emissions is significant. The global building stock accounts for over 40% of total global greenhouse gas emissions (IEA & OECD, 2015; UNEP, 2023). In 2019, 17% of heating emissions emanating from buildings originated in homes (HM Government, 2021). Recognising this, improving energy efficiency in buildings is essential to reduce energy consumption, and greenhouse gas emissions.

To address this problem, the UK has set a target to reduce greenhouse gas emissions to net zero by 2050. Though buildings account for 37% of total energy consumption, heating them in the UK accounts for almost one-third of the UK's annual carbon footprint. The UK set an emission reduction target of 34% by 2020 and 80% by 2050, below the 1990 baseline (Climate Change Act, 2008). In order to achieve these targets, in 2019, the UK government announced the development of a FHS with the aim that all new homes built from 2025 will produce 75–80% less carbon emissions than homes built under 2013 regulations. To achieve these carbon reductions, FHS aims to incorporate more energy-efficient fabric, with higher levels of insulation, higher-specification windows, increased levels of airtightness, to reduce heat loss, and low-carbon heating systems. The government introduced an interim enhancement in 2021 requiring new homes to produce 31% less emissions, as a stepping stone to the implementation of FHS in 2025.

As new building standards focus on energy conservation, increasing the thermal insulation and the air tightness, therefore reducing the air exchange from the exterior, further analysis is needed to avoid any unintended consequences before implementation of the regulation in the journey to net zero ready homes that provide comfortable and healthy spaces for its occupants. Achievement of change requires a major shift in design, construction, and operation of buildings, as well as the need to engender cultural and behavioural change. A vital part of the process of change is the education of those who occupy buildings as well as all who work in the construction sector. Accordingly, this chapter examines work being undertaken by a team of researchers at the BCU Centre for Future Homes to explore the impact of designing and building net zero homes as well as lessons learnt for future implementation.

Background to Research

The existing housing crisis has made newly built construction a priority in the UK. This is predicted to produce momentum that will translate into aligned input to cope with the even greater challenge of reducing carbon in existing buildings. The government's response to new build homes has been the proposed introduction of the 'Future Homes Standard' supported by the 'Home Energy Model', which will involve the use of electricity instead of gas for home heating and cooking as well as improvements to the building fabric and ventilation to improve energy efficiency and prevent overheating. The Home Energy Model is intended to replace the Standard Assessment Procedure, which is the methodology currently used in the UK to assess the energy performance of homes.

Crucially, construction, an industry that is highly varied and includes huge diversity and complexity in the way it carries out processes, must play a key role in delivering net zero ready homes. However, given the scale of the issues, there is worrying paucity of data (as well as critical insights), a key requirement enabling policy makers, informed by the industry, in making evidence-based decisions and avoiding the danger of unintended consequences. To help address this evidence gap, BCU has established the Centre for Future Homes. This centre aims to carry out primary research underpinning highly relevant and critical change in the development of net zero ready homes, addressing the challenge of climate change combined with the need of increased building safety for housing resilience. In order to address these challenges, BCU's research team is involved in applied research into areas such as impact of new building regulations (FHS) in the energy performance of houses, improvement of indoor air quality and overheating mitigation, low-carbon heat performance (heat pumps), embodied and operational carbon, single life plastics in the construction sector, fire safety for resilient homes, and the retrofit of existing homes and buildings. This experience has led the Centre for Future homes to establish a 'Home Energy Model Task Group' to act a 'critical friend' and support government to make sure that energy performance assessment tools for compliance are fit for purpose before the new regulation comes into force, avoiding unintended consequences.

Developing a strong industry collaborative network has been critical to the success of the centre, as has the focus on putting the occupier/consumer, at the heart of research. The main goal is to understand and analyse the performance of real houses lived by real people in real time, delivering real impact and producing information and data explicitly intended to change behaviours and enable policymakers to arrive at evidence-based decisions. As part of evidence gathering, researchers at the Centre for Future Homes have partnered with home developers and housing associations providing net zero ready homes meeting 'Future Homes Standard'.

One of those projects is Eco Drive, developed by social housing provider Midland Heart on what's known as Project 80. This project has built 12 dwellings in Handsworth in Birmingham in compliance with the FHS. Another project covered in this chapter is Gedling Green, developed by the home builder Keepmoat who, supported by Homes England, Lloyds Bank, and Leeds Building Society, have delivered houses for sale built to the FHS. Both projects provide insights from real performance of net zero ready homes as well as occupant behaviour. Some of the tasks undertaken include advise and monitoring on cost, design, construction, commissioning, sales, and handover of properties, followed by two-year post-occupancy evaluation of the homes. The post occupancy evaluation intends to better understand the customer 'journey', including operation and maintenance of these new homes, inherently more complex. This has been achieved by the use of sensors coupled with interviews carried out regularly to ascertain the lived experience of occupiers.

The objective is to elicit data that will accurately inform, create influence, and lead to policy and implementation adhering to the principle of net zero whilst making people's lives better. This includes the team working closely with UK government departments engaged in the home development process, hosting site visits and sharing data and lessons learnt with policy makers and industry. Subsequent to publication of an interim report of findings from Project 80 (Mateo-Garcia et al., 2023), in the Spring of 2024, the team presented the current findings at eight NHBC *Building for Tomorrow* conferences across the UK attended by over 2000 construction industry professionals.

Project 80 Eco Drive, Handsworth

In 2019, Midland Heart Housing Association declared its intention to build Eco Drive development in Handsworth, Birmingham. Originally designed to attain the 2013 building regulations, the decision was taken to enhance the design and construction to comply with regulations that would be introduced in 2025. To this purpose, three alternative designs were proposed to test the impact. This demonstrator project provided an opportunity to consider how traditional architectural design, using traditional masonry materials and methods, can achieve the FHS and actively respond to dramatic challenges posed by climate change.

The Eco Drive research project sought to understand the impact of designing, building, and living in new homes compliant with the new standard for housing. Importantly, the programme included three different buildable and affordable high-specification designs to provide homes that are 'future-proofed' and enhanced experience for occupiers. This adaptive approach would, it was believed, ensure the demonstrator project to provide data and have a greater opportunity for learning including how a traditional architectural design in masonry can be adapted to meet the climate change challenges. The research examined the decision-making process around the design to ensure conventional masonry houses are fully compliant with the projected standard and analysed the success of the construction and operation phases since completion in 2022. It also analysed how the building specification influenced wall construction to reduce air permeability, occupant experience of controls, heat pumps, thermal comfort, and ventilation.

The main findings from the research were that FHS can be cost effectively delivered and the carbon reduction target exceeded using locally produced masonry materials and a range of heating and ventilation options. There remains a challenge in scaling-up installation of electric heating systems, as well as ensuring building UK manufacturing achieves capacity and ability to commission. Effective commissioning that ensures full understanding by home occupiers of how the systems operate will potentially influence behaviour to underpin the most efficient use of the technology in homes built to the FHS. Key lessons from this demonstrator project are included in the interim report. These have been shared with policy makers and industry to drive impact and facilitate a smooth transition to net zero ready homes and optimum occupier engagement and satisfaction.

Design Specification

House types one and two were designed to go beyond the indicative 2025 standard with lower air permeability and MVHR ventilation. Type one was designed with a Baxi heat pump for space and water heating. Type two was a two-bed house in which 'the space load' was considered minimal and designed with Glen Dimplex electric panel radiators for space heating and a water only heat pump. Type three included Vaillant heat pumps for space and water heating. The ventilation in Type three included filterless extract fans in wet rooms with a low background rate. All 12 houses had a PV array of 2.2 KW, beyond the standard, to help reduce energy costs.

One of the key requirements of new regulation is the use of thicker walls to accommodate extra levels of insulation. In the Eco Drive project, due to site's arrangement of plots, this extra thickness could not be implemented without reducing site density or house space, so a 352-mm wall with a fully filled cavity with high-performance PIR insulation was selected. The fire aspects of this specification were fully considered with the inclusion of brick and block non-combustible elements and fire cavity barriers. Junction details were carefully designed to reduce thermal bridging and heat loss. Polymer wall spray was used in Type one and Type two houses to increase airtightness. As well as thicker walls, internal space for the hot water cylinder needed to be considered the new standards do not allow the use of gas boilers.

Regarding the window specification, enhanced double glazing was selected instead of triple glazing due to a number of practical considerations including availability, replacement, weight, cost, ease of maintenance, frame size, and light transmission. High-specification double glazing was considered the simpler solution with the losses in energy performance balanced out by tighter criteria on other elements including the walls and roof.

The most significant change was the move to electric heating resulting in several key decisions, including where to position a heat pump and a hot water cylinder, the length of the pipe run and security as the air source heat pumps were placed outside of the properties. The PV panels were considered a useful addition to help occupants with their electricity costs although they were not at the time a requirement of the FHS. The controls and inverter for the PV panels were installed in the roof space, ensuring access for maintenance. Table 16.1 shows the specification of each housing type and the design energy performance. Passivhaus values have been included only for comparison as these houses were built to meet FHS indicative specification.

Supply Chain Collaboration

A unique feature of the project was the extensive collaboration between all the stakeholders involved in the project despite being a typical 'design and build' project. Intensive discussions and negotiations occurred to shape the final specification, which included two different fabric solutions with low *U*-values and different levels of air tightness, three low-carbon heating systems, and two ventilation solutions, adding extra complexity to the construction. All the project team, including those engaged in building control, collaborated in a spirit of openness and cooperation. Project review meetings were organised monthly with the aim of delivering a trailblazer development and share lessons learnt. Suppliers' knowledge and

Table 16.1. Design Performance of Each House Type.

Element/ Specifications	Indicative FHS Specification	Type 1	Type 2	Type 3	Passivhaus
Floor *U*-value ($W/m^2.k$)	0.11	0.11	0.11	0.11	0.15
External wall *U*-value	0.15	0.13	0.13	0.13	0.15
Roof *U*-value	0.11	0.1	0.1	0.1	0.15
Window *U*-value	0.8	1.2	1.2	1.2	0.8
Door *U*-value	1.0	1.2	1.2	1.2	0.8
Air permeability ($m^3/h/m^2$)	5.0	1.5	1.5	5	0.6
Heating	Low-carbon heating	ASHP	Panel heater, HWHP	ASHP	–
Ventilation	Natural (with extract fans)	MVHR	MVHR	Natural (with extract fans)	MVHR
PV	None	Yes	Yes	Yes	–
Wastewater heat recovery	No	Yes	Yes	Yes	–
Y-value	0.05	0.028	0.0274	0.028	0.01
CO_2 reduction		85%	80%	90%	

experience were extremely useful to ensure the best use of materials and systems as well as calculating the thermal bridging junction details required to meet the FHS. BCU academic team's role in these meetings was to examine background material, provide expert advice, and develop an in-depth monitoring strategy throughout all the process.

The project identified and recognised the key role of subcontractors in meeting the new standard. In this case, the main contractor subcontracted some of the main work packages but collaborated with them to ensure a model delivery due to the demonstrator nature of the project. This required subcontractors to work with new materials and to greater accuracy in more complex details, disturbing workflows.

User Experience

User experience and satisfaction were monitored for one year after occupants moved into the houses. To achieve this, occupants filled out activity diaries and were interviewed to provide feedback on their experience of living in low-carbon homes, particularly around thermal comfort and indoor environment, daily patterns and behaviours, and usability of low-carbon systems. All occupants expressed satisfaction with their homes and the performance of the homes, particularly around thermal comfort. In addition, they were excited about playing their part in tackling climate change by living in net zero ready homes built to future standards.

Although occupants identified that their homes required minimal effort to achieve acceptable levels of comfort, these could come from high electricity consumption as some occupants were living at high temperatures. They admitted not having modified their lifestyles to take advantage of the maximum efficiencies of their low-carbon heating systems. Some households also disclosed not having experienced any respiratory health conditions, including asthma, since moving into the new homes, highlighting the health benefits of net zero ready homes, as better insulation and ventilation have the potential to create healthier indoor spaces.

Cooking was identified as a source of air pollutants in kitchens. Most households reported using not just cookers, but also other appliances such as microwave, air fryers, and toasters. Culturally influenced cooking patterns and ingredients used seem to influence the level of air pollutants, including particulate matter and volatile organic compounds. Although data from air quality sensors showed high spikes in these pollutants during cooking, this pattern was followed by a quick decay, possibly due to occupants opening windows to increase ventilation.

Residents were not confident with heating controls, preventing them from using them in the most efficient way. Research showed that occupants need assistance in understanding the way new homes should 'operate', so they can take greater responsibility in adapting their behaviours to achieve anticipated efficiencies FHS should allow.

Keepmoat Gedling Green, Nottingham

Gedling Green is a 33-home development, featuring zero carbon ready, two-, three-, and four-bedroom homes and offers the first new homes for private sale in the UK built to the anticipated FHS. These houses were launched for open market sale in 2023. The BCU team research aim is to understand occupants' experience of the homes of the future by assessing energy usage in the new properties over a two-year period. The study will examine how Keepmoat's properties will enable homeowners to use an estimated 51% less energy compared to the 2013 building regulation standards, reducing significantly their energy bills and maximising the benefits of their new homes. There is also a desire to encourage behaviour change and educate the homeowners on the optimum way of interacting with their home.

As well as working with BCU, Keepmoat has partnerships with a number of organisations engaged in development including Homes England, Gedling Borough Council and Arcadis, Lloyds Banking Group, and Leeds Building Society. This will allow Keepmoat to be confident of 'lending capacity' by finance through mortgage for green home that are energy efficient home and affordable. Maintenance of confidence by potential purchasers is essential for speculative housebuilders.

Design Specification

Built using locally produced brick and block and designed to last at least 150 years, Keepmoat's homes built in accordance with the 2025 FHS, will deliver a 91% reduction in carbon emissions when compared to 2013 regulations.

The building envelope is formed of non-combustible brick and block and concrete roof tile construction with mineral wool insulation. The inclusion of high performing double-glazed windows and doors ensures that heat loss is reduced to the minimum. All the new homes at the development feature air source heat pumps, solar PV panels, increased levels of insulation, EV charging points, and smart hot water cylinders with AI technology to understand how much hot water people living in the home use on average in order to identify ways to reduce waste.

The ground floor benefits from underfloor heating which adds to the comfort and maximises space. The inclusion of an effective ventilation system ensures the air quality providing a comfortable and healthy indoor environment.

Conclusion

The FHS provides a blueprint to other jurisdictions who are looking to progress to net zero ready be homes. Research conducted in the two case studies into the behaviour patterns of occupation of the homes will assist designers in considering and incorporating future trends. Most particularly, it will allow developers to showcase how sustainable technologies and renewable energy solutions can be utilised to inform how homes in years to come can be powered more efficiently whilst, critically, contributing to reduction of emissions as part of the UK's net zero pledge.

The research will assist organisations within the UK house-building sector to identify robust, scalable, and sustainable solutions to modern house-building challenges. This will ensure the sector can contribute to the economic development, reduce inputs, and improve outputs. The research will provide data and insights enabling policy makers to base future decisions on evidence and avoid unintended consequences through learnt lessons from collaboration with practice. Further, research will examine the design, construction, commissioning, sales, financing, occupation, and maintenance of housing to achieve zero ready homes by putting occupiers at the heart of this critical transition.

The research undertaken by BCU has and will continue to identify key issues that need to be addressed to ensure a smooth transition supported by a skilled workforce. It's critically important to avoid unintended consequences, drive quality and understand that. As Albert Einstein famously claimed, '*The only mistake in life is the lesson not learned*'.

References

HM Government. (2008). *Climate Change Act*. https://www.legislation.gov.uk/ukpga/2008/27/pdfs/ukpga_20080027_en.pdf

HM Government. (2021). *Heat and buildings strategy, business, energy and industrial strategy*, London.

IEA (International Energy Agency) and OECD (Organisation for Economic Co-operation and Development). (2015). *Energy efficiency market report 2015*. Paris.

Mateo-Garcia, M., Aboagye-Nimo, E., Cheung, F., Weng, K., Leonard, M., Hopkin, T., & Boyd, D. (2023). *Project 80-Eco Drive Handsworth: Future homes standard case study-interim report*. Birmingham City University. https://bcuassets.blob.core.windows.net/docs/fhsproject80casestudy2023bcu-133343996058952751.pdf

United Nations Environment Programme. (2023). *Building materials and the climate: Constructing a new future*. United Nations Environment Programme, Industry and Economy Division, Energy and Climate Branch, Paris, France.

Chapter 17

Delivering Net Zero and Beyond: Addressing the Financing Challenges for UK Green SME Transition

Robyn Owen and Amy Burnett

Centre for Enterprise, Environment and Development Research (CEEDR), Middlesex University, UK

Abstract

The transitional challenges to delivering a green growth economy, particularly for small- and medium-sized enterprises (SMEs), presented by the twin concerns of climate and biodiversity are considerable. This chapter examines the UK case, where extensive public and private investment is required, in combination, to deliver the UK Government's desired green growth enabled by green innovation and business transition towards environmentally positive business models. The chapter draws on a contemporary literature review and qualitative interview evidence from UK financiers, entrepreneurial innovators and policymakers. We examine how they influence the emerging UK green finance escalator that relates to providing finance for green enterprise from an initial idea through to commercialisation, scaleup expansion and maturity. The findings suggest that this green transition requires a clear SME finance roadmap to deliver coherent public policy and regulation and sufficient knowledge of the environmental risks and opportunities presented. We provide a blueprint framework that can provide the finance for net zero and, beyond this, the wider environmental changes needed for a sustainable green economy transition.

Keywords: Net zero; biodiversity; SME; innovation; finance; policy

Examining Net Zero: Creating Solutions for a Greener Society and Sustainable Economic Growth, 175–185
Copyright © 2025 by Robyn Owen and Amy Burnett
Published under exclusive licence by Emerald Publishing Limited
doi:10.1108/978-1-83608-574-420251017

Introduction

The UK's hosting of the climate-related Conference of the Parties (CoP)[1] in 2021 was a watershed event for the nation's finance markets but also for its SMEs, which account for 99% of UK businesses. During that year, the British Business Bank, the government agency responsible for financial support to smaller businesses, commissioned a study of small business and net zero readiness (British Business Bank, 2021). This revealed moderate awareness and good intentions amongst small business owners but also considerable concerns as to the investment costs for change. Suddenly, smaller businesses were on the UK finance market's radar, with high street banks starting to develop green lending products and the state business bank supporting climate finance. Likewise, the biodiversity-related CoP15 in 2022, which involved the UK signing up to the Kunming-Montreal Agreement to protect 30% of land and water by 2030 (30 × 30), raised the stakes for the UK to develop a more holistic green economy (CBD, 2022). This led to a revision of the UK Green Investment Strategy (HM Government, 2023) which now includes the joint aims of creating a 'green growth' economy that addresses net zero through carbon reduction and biodiversity preservation. However, despite these good intentions, a clear roadmap for SME 'green', environmentally positive, finance in the UK remains elusive.

This chapter examines the evolving landscape of UK SME green finance markets through the lens of the finance escalator, which presents the availability of different types of finance (public, private, grant, equity, debt) through the stages of business growth (Baldock & Mason, 2015). We address the concerns of SMEs and their financiers regarding investment in new green innovation and the transition to greener, more environmentally positive business models. A major question is how policymakers, financiers and businesses, the triple nexus axis of the SME green economy, can determine what is good for the environment and the public good versus what is advantageous to the business bottom-line and economic growth (Harrer & Owen, 2022). Here, sustainability economists present the Malthusian limits to growth concerns (Wrigley, 1988) that traditional concepts of increasing labour productivity and material consumption to deliver wealth are unsustainable under the current capitalist system unless checked by public good (health and environmental) policy considerations (Burnett, 2022; Jackson, 2017; Raworth, 2012). We draw on: (i) the combined evidence of contemporary academic and policy literature review; (ii) extensive interviews with policymakers, public and private SME financiers and their supporter organisations and (iii) in-depth case studies of green innovative SMEs to expose the challenges and opportunities to financing the UK SME green growth economy.

Focusing on the UK green economy, which purports to be a global leader and the context of its evolving green finance escalator to support innovation, we highlight why green innovation finance is high cost, high risk and highly problematic. This is particularly the case for the wider environmental business model changes

[1]General Assembly policymakers forum to address climate change through the UN Framework Convention on Climate Change (UNFCCC).

required, such as protecting biodiversity, to enable effective sustainable economic solutions. Here, the spotlight is on SME innovations to provide the science-based targets (SBTs) to facilitate improved UK and global finance market risk assessment of the environmental impacts of business models. We conclude by discussing our key findings and how these relate to establishing a clear and effective UK SME green finance roadmap.

The Emerging UK Green Finance Escalator

The UK has a mature SME finance market which underwent fundamental changes after the 2007 Global Financial Crisis (GFC) when traditional bank lending debt finance options and venture capital (VC) equity options retreated from start-up and earlier stage business finance. North et al. (2013) and Baldock and Mason (2015) explain these UK post-GFC changes through the lens of the finance escalator. The finance escalator is underpinned by Berger and Udell's (1998) theory of financial opacity which states that as businesses progress up the escalator from start-up, they develop a trading track record which reduces their opacity and the higher levels of information asymmetry that make younger businesses too risky to finance. The post-GFC UK finance escalator featured the rise of crowdfunding through public donation, product and service reward agreements, peer-to-peer (P2P) debt funding and public smaller-scale equity investment opportunities. It also saw the emergence of business hothousing accelerators, notably in tech start-up areas such as London's Shoreditch 'Silicon Roundabout' (Harrison & Baldock, 2015) and the rise of business angel networks, which remained resilient as the main source of UK start-up investment through the GFC period (Mason & Harrison, 2015).

The finance escalator offers a dynamic model for assessing private finance availability and where government policy interventions, such as public–private co-funds are required to leverage private financing into funding gaps (Baldock & Mason, 2015). These often occur at earlier stages of business development, where information asymmetries are greatest. Owen and Mason (2016) review the example where UK government-led co-funding made a difference post-GFC by encouraging business angel networking syndicate investing which the national Angel Co-fund could support equally 'pari-passu', thus doubling the amount of investment into early-stage potential high-growth businesses and sharing the higher risk between more investors.

More recently, a UK 'green finance escalator' has emerged, accelerating during the COVID-19 Pandemic and the post-CoP26 period, driven by raised public awareness for public health and the environment. This has seen, for example, a trebling of the numbers of business angel investors to over 300 high net-worth individual members in the Green Angel Syndicate (GAS), forming the UK's largest environmental impact investment network by Autumn 2023. This period also witnessed increasing numbers of specialist cleantech and agricultural tech (ag-tech) VC and a surge in equity crowdfunding investment for sustainable and environmental mission start-ups and earlier-stage UK SMEs (O'Reilly et al., 2023; Owen et al., 2023).

Why Green Investment Is Problematic

Green finance, which funds businesses with missions for positive impact on the environment (Gao et al., 2018), faces particular problems. Firstly, there are the information asymmetries which Harrer and Owen (2022) argue are greater for green start-ups because they present disruptive new business models that are difficult to understand and because, for example, investors do not know what a 'high-return nature-positive business' looks like. Whilst global movement through the Taskforce for Nature-Related Financial Disclosures (TNFD, 2023) and the development of green taxonomies in the UK[2] and the EU are increasingly shaping such definitions, critically, currently SME financiers find that it is difficult to demonstrate what the commercial value of green impact will be.

Secondly, there are so-called deeptech disincentives because many green innovations require long-horizon, deep pocket multi-million capital investments into research and development (R&D) to provide commercial demonstrators. Mazzucato and Semieniuk (2018) state the need for government policy intervention to address this long-horizon funding deficit to help green businesses overcome their extended *valley of death period*, where businesses fail because they run out of R&D finance.

Thirdly, Polzin (2017) finds that there is a green dividend deficit whereby investors are never fully remunerated for the public good (e.g. reduced public health costs) delivered by green businesses, which may include social enterprises.

Fourthly, market instability caused by economic downturns (Cowling & Liu, 2023) and poor government policy co-ordination (Uyarra et al., 2016) leads to uncertainty and underinvestment. The UK's poor environmental policy mix points to the need for decisive and clearly supportive environmental governance with regulation that guides positive environmental outcomes. This has been lacking in the UK since the GFC[3] and exacerbated during the recent Brexit period where European Regional Development Funds were replaced by the UK government Shared Prosperity Funds. Owen (2023) also points to a lack of joined up thinking between government agencies and departments in developing and delivering effective funding programmes for the UK green finance escalator, pointing to historical disconnect between Innovate UK (a public start-up grant funding agency) and the British Business Bank. Furthermore, the UK Government's separation of environmental (Department for Environment, Food and Rural Affairs – DEFRA), business (Department for Business and Trade – DBT) and energy-related climate affairs (Department for Energy Security and Net Zero – DESNZ) creates frictions and lack of policy cohesion between climate and biodiversity. This is particularly the case for SME innovation since the overarching strategic Green Finance Institute (GFI) focuses delivery of the UK's Green Finance

---

[2]See https://www.greenfinanceinstitute.com/programmes/uk-green-taxonomy-gtag/.

[3]Examples of UK green governance failure include the removal of the renewable energy feed-in tariff incentive in 2019 and incoherent and patchy support for local government green business policy. Though despite this, local government is seeking to innovate in the delivery of localised green growth approaches (see LGA, 2023).

Strategy (2023) mainly through large-scale business and infrastructure. Although there is interest in supporting SMEs, GFI does not have a mandate to do so.

Arguably, it is important to stimulate new green innovation and its adoption through a supportive and stable regulatory environment (Owen et al., 2023). The current lack of environmental reporting requirements and standards for smaller UK businesses with less than 500 employees and £500m annual turnover[4], means that many of UK SMEs are either not aware of their environmental risks and the value of adopting environmental practices, or are not incentivised to go green. A further pertinent example is the danger of negative regulation and signalling of government policy to the finance markets, such as the delay in implementing Biodiversity Net Gain (BNG).

Biodiversity Net Gain

BNG is a global leading flagship policy introduced by the UK Environment Act (2021), brought into implementation in February 2024. The evolution of BNG provides an important insight into the development of UK green finance markets since, like the operation of voluntary carbon and biodiversity markets, it requires a financial valuation of land, environmental mitigation and evidence-based improvement activity. Unlike voluntary markets, BNG is a statutory legal obligation which demands a standardised financing and operational structure, outlined in the Statutory Biodiversity Metric (DEFRA, 2024) and its small sites metric counterpart. This summarises the size and value of land habitat, hedgerow and water unit quality and the process by which valuation should be undertaken, prescribing timelines and the differentiation between on-site and offsite arrangements.

The principle of BNG is to ensure that UK development requiring a planning consent delivers at least a 10% net gain in biodiversity to the equivalent land quality and type, and in some cases, local authorities are seeking a higher minimum uplift, such as in Wiltshire and Guildford through policies in their local plans. This is permitted if sufficiently justified, but not necessarily advised by BNG planning practice guidance.

Whilst it may be seen as a significant contribution to '30x30', a key contentious issue of BNG is that habitat is treated as a simple proxy for 'nature' but neglects key issues such as ecosystem integrity and co-dependencies, which can be disrupted through development. Whilst not ideal from an ecological perspective, BNG does provide a standardised framework for the scaling of ecological assessment by ecologists (who are typically required to apply the BNG metric). However, the small sites metric and the complementary 'Joe Blooms' BNG tool also

---

[4]Mandatory reporting of climate impacts is in place for larger companies. On nature-related reporting the TNFD, whilst relevant to SMEs, does not provide specific guidance to them yet though this is in development. In October 2024, the Institute of Environmental Management and Assessment (IEMA) released guidance to support SMEs to align to the TNFD.

offer a potentially more affordable route to measurement. There is also potential to widen the involvement of communities in the measurement of ecological services, such as through community-led 'citizen science' approaches. BNG is also complementary to the the wider protections afforded to irreplaceable habitat (e.g. ancient woodland) and endangered species (e.g. great crested newts).

BNG has created a finance market in two distinctive ways. Firstly, it requires the financialisation of the quality of a land unit (calculated based on ecological factors and biodiversity value). The demand for BNG units may vary across sites, the type of habitat being created or restored and the demand for BNG units by investors and developers. Secondly, it may require offsetting, where on-site BNG is not feasible. This has opened up a market for developers requiring offsetting who seek to purchase BNG units as a measure of the future biodiversity value arising from development. The sale of which is mediated through an intermediary or a local authority and secured through a 30-year land management agreement with landowners. The principle of offsetting is to find land of similar size, type and quality which is close to the development land. This process requires intermediary ecological services to monitor land and for arrangements to be put in place to ensure that the improvements are delivered and maintained over time. In some cases, landowners (i.e. estates and farmers as well as local authorities) are seeking to capitalise on BNG funds to support farmer-led or wider community-based investment models for environmental action, such as in Malvern Hills District Council or the Environmental Farmers group. Whilst still nascent, BNG indicates the role of regulation in standardising approaches from which place-based actors and green investors can innovate to deliver nature-positive outcomes, working through emerging local nature recovery partnerships (see Environment Act, 2021). Whilst this is a first step, more needs to be done to adequately measure biodiversity and understand the impacts of environmental management.

The Need for Science-Based Targets

Globally, state central bankers (NGFS, 2022) have asked for SBTs that can inform financiers of the risks and opportunities for green investment. They recognise that climate change carbon management can be measured on a global standard of tonnes of carbon dioxide or equivalent greenhouse gas reduction (*tCO2e*). However, for biodiversity, as demonstrated by BNG, this is far more complex to measure, as it is place-based and habitat and species specific. Thus, the global TNFD has reviewed current approaches and produced a framework which incorporates different domains (marine, freshwater, land, climate services and state of nature) with a specific emphasis on bringing together climate, biodiversity, material conservation and indigenous people's social justice (TNFD, 2023). This has been hugely challenging and highlights the role of a holistic approach to environmental measurement to inform financial market risk assessment.

It also highlights the complexity of measuring biodiversity which ideally requires: species counts for abundance and variety; a focus on key apex species (as indicators for multiple supporting species); endemic and endangered protected species and potentially threatening non-native species. A further dimension is to improve understanding of how habitat management can mitigate environmental harm, restore and improve the state of nature to operate effectively.

SME Case Studies – Translating Environmental Impact into Financial Risk Assessment

Some UK SMEs are addressing the TNFD's nature positive and biodiversity measurement requirements as providers of ecological services technological innovations. Here, we highlight three more advanced case studies relating to species presence, soil and water quality that have attracted investment, which is often supported through government grants, investor tax breaks and co-financing programmes. These have considerable potential to shape finance markets in these critical areas of nature positive investment. However, since as one interviewee suggested '*…there is no single silver bullet tech solution*', different innovators need to collaborate for more effective holistic solutions.

NatureMetrics

NatureMetrics, established in 2013, is a fast-growing global leading SME that has received over £20m in external funding (including initial seed funding from GAS, followed by VCs and more recently Robert Downey Junior Foundation funds) to develop and commercialise eDNA testing kits for measuring species presence and abundance in land and water. The company was set up by ecologists aiming to deliver SBTs. Like many of the new nature technologies, the tools can be consistently repeated over time, reducing boots on the ground time and the risk of human error during in-person observation techniques. The approach works particularly well for soil and water samples, where the kit can be used to collect snapshot geographical positioning system (GPS) located samples from which subsequent lab work can reveal species presence, abundance and variety and whether DNA came from live or dead matter.

A drawback for SMEs and citizen scientists is the cumulative cost since each test kit costs £200 and can only provide one-off samples for a specific area. Multiple samples are required to cover areas of more than 2 hectares, whilst regular sampling is required to map the impacts of mitigation practices. Large-scale projects for railways, renewable energy wind farms and mining companies have cost upwards of £20,000. A major advantage of this approach is that over time, NatureMetrics have monitored the impacts of high-risk commercial activities, such as mining company mitigation practices for land restoration and developed dynamic virtual mapping and artificial intelligence (AI) predictive algorithms for biodiversity change in specific locations and habitats. This is described by the company as an example of where '*Technology is ahead of policy*' and notably BNG.

Whilst NatureMetrics offer a web-based platform to raise awareness and guide potential customers through their land and water-based biodiversity measurement solutions, it faces drawbacks in relation to affordability for smaller businesses/projects, real-time data, air quality/biodiversity measurement and acknowledge that there is scope for collaborative working between different types of ecological services to deliver more holistic solutions.

Watr.Tech

Watr.Tech started trading in 2019 after a decade of related tech development by the founders. They received international financing from a Hong Kong accelerator, UK business angels and equity crowdfunding, eventually amounting to £750,000 to design and develop a water monitor with the needs of business customers in mind. The product had to be robust, self-powered, portable and easy to install with a remote application programme interface for real-time data monitoring, which can be viewed on a smartphone. Key water measurements are captured through a multi-probe sensor system that collects data on pH, oxygen, water level, temperature, turbidity (opacity), flow rates and pollution levels (i.e. from agricultural field run-off and heavy metals from industry), such as nitrates and phosphates.

The equipment was successfully used in trials in Devon with water utilities companies and local farmers to determine the extent of field pollution run-off and guide improved farm practices. A key finding from these studies was that public dog-walking footpaths were a source of water pollution during periods of heavy rainfall. Watr.Tech offers a niche complementary solution to NatureMetrics by offering real-time water condition monitoring. The technology has helped water companies to improve the management of water courses and prepare for storm floods, as well as deliver early detection of pollution and its sources. Customers have tended to be large water companies and river trusts in the UK. A major project involves working with desalination plants and 'The Line' development in Saudi Arabia, where strict environmental codes are required. Yet at £60, the basic equipment is also affordable for citizen science groups.

BX Tech

BX Tech, successfully monitored the increased carbon content of Bardsley apple farm, enabling it to become the first verified carbon neutral farm in the UK. Notably, for many investors, including the supermarket supply-chain that supported the project, carbon capture is a significant and in many cases overriding measure in nature positive financing which justifies investment because it is relatively easy to measure and conveniently ticks the 'climate change impact investment' box. However, this narrowly focused approach – also known as carbon tunnel vision – is holding back wider nature positive environmental impact investment, suggesting that the sooner there is a scientific basis for investing in biodiversity (informed by the TNFD and green taxonomies), the more likely there will be a more effective approach to environmental investment (in SMEs) within the UK and global finance markets.

Conclusions – A Blueprint for a Sustainable Green SME Finance Roadmap

This review has focused on the evolving UK SME green finance escalator, demonstrating that it is a crucial part of delivering the UK's net zero and wider environmental biodiversity protection commitments. Notably, leading innovations in the UK, if not globally, are improving environmental measurement and informing policy and finance markets which are being developed by SMEs. However, these innovations often remain highly dependent upon public funding. There is a need for more widespread recognition, through raising public and private investor awareness, of the vital role that SME green innovation investment can play in developing the UK as a global leader in developing a prosperous and sustainable green economy.

Drawing on these findings, we can summarise that to deliver net zero and beyond, the UK will require a vastly improved green finance roadmap for SMEs (Owen et al., 2023). Furthermore, the blueprint for this roadmap will need to bring together the essential policy, finance and SME enterprise elements to deliver a cohesive and coherent approach. This will effectively develop the synergies of a holistic environmental policy (Dasgupta, 2021) that acknowledges that to deliver a sustainable green economy all public and private finance should cornerstone investment decisions on environmental risks and opportunities (NGFS, 2022). Key points for our blueprint are set out below.

- Effective green policy requires an overarching strategic body. This body or cluster of organisations should bring together key public agencies to holistically address net zero, circular economy (regenerative) approaches and biodiversity. This should set out a roadmap for SME green finance and especially SME green innovation (Mazzucato & Semieniuk, 2018).
- To enable UK global leadership, public funding for SME green innovation is required through a suitable mix of grants, investor tax incentives and co-financing to attract earlier stage private finance, share risk, upskill green impact investors and provide demonstration that the market is investible (Owen, 2023), through successful examples like NatureMetrics.
- To deliver SME green finance at scale, there also needs to be consistent government policy which provides stable and coherent policy and regulations (Uyarra et al., 2016) to support environmental innovation and provide confidence in its adoption by businesses and the public.
- Finally, a priority must be to support the innovative SME ecological services solutions that will guide future finance and green transition business models. These, if effectively supported within an open innovation (Bogers et al., 2018) setting can deliver the rapid development of SBTs to inform the UK and global finance markets. In turn, this will most likely unlock the vast amounts of public and private financing required to deliver sustainable economic targets.

Acknowledgements

Our UK SME Nature Positive Finance research (2022–2024) is part of the Natural Environment Research Council's Integrating Finance and Biodiversity (IFB) programme.

References

Baldock, R., & Mason, C. M. (2015). Establishing a new UK finance escalator for innovative SMEs: The roles of the Enterprise Capital Funds and Angel Co-Investment Fund. *An International Journal of Entrepreneurial Finance*, *17*(1–2), 59–86.

Berger, A. N., & Udell, G. F. (1998). The economics of small business finance: The roles of private equity and debt markets in the financial growth cycle. *Journal of Banking and Finance*, *22*(6–8), 613–673.

Bogers, M., Chesbrough, H., & Moedas, C. (2018). Open innovation: research, practices, and policies. *California Management Review*, *60*(2), 5–16.

British Business Bank. (2021). *Smaller businesses and the transition to net zero*. British Business Bank Plc report with IPSOS, October, Sheffield. https://www.british-business-bank.co.uk/research/smaller-businesses-and-the-transition-to-net-zero/

Burnett, A. (2022). Operationalising performance measurement and incentives for 'regenerative value' to improve net sustainability outputs. In G. Vélez-Cuartas & O. Romero-Goyeneche (Eds.), *Transformative metrics: Contributions to the studies for monitoring and evaluating how science, technology, and innovation can address social and environmental challenges*. University of Antioquia. https://bibliotecadigital.udea.edu.co/bitstream/10495/31313/1/VelezGabriel_2022TransformativeMetricsContribitions.pdf

CBD. (2022). *COP15: Nations adopt four goals, 23 Targets for 2030 in landmark UN biodiversity agreement*. https://www.cbd.int/article/cop15-cbd-press-release-final-19dec2022

Cowling, M., & Liu, W. (2023). Access to finance for Cleantech innovation and investment: Evidence from UK small and medium-sized enterprises. *IEEE Transactions on Engineering Management*, *70*(3), 963–878. https://doi.org/10.1109/TEM.2021.3066685

Dasgupta, P. (2021, February). *Final report – The economics of biodiversity: The Dasgupta review*. Final report of the Independent Review on the Economics of Biodiversity for HM Treasury, London.

DEFRA. (2024, February). *The statutory biodiversity metric: User guide*. Department for Environment, Food and Rural Affairs. Open Government Licence, Crown copyright, published online. https://assets.publishing.service.gov.uk/media/65c60e0514b83c000ca715f3/The_Statutory_Biodiversity_Metric_-_User_Guide_.pdf

Gao, Y., Tsai, S.-B., Xue, X., Ren, T., Du, X., Chen, Q., & Wang, J. (2018). An empirical study on green innovation efficiency in the green institutional environment. *Sustainability*, *10*(3), 724.

Harrer, T., & Owen, R. (2022). Reducing early-stage cleantech funding gaps: An exploration of the role of environmental performance indicators. *International Journal of Entrepreneurial Behavior Research*, *28*(9), 268–288.

Harrison, R., & Baldock, R. (2015). Financing SME growth in the UK: Meeting the challenges after the global financial crisis. *Venture Capital: An International Journal of Entrepreneurial Finance*, *17*(1–2), 1–6.

HM Government. (2023, March). *Mobilising green investment: 2023 green finance strategy*. Crown Copyright. https://assets.publishing.service.gov.uk/media/643583fb877741001368d815/mobilising-green-investment-2023-green-finance-strategy.pdf

Jackson, T. (2017). *Prosperity without growth: Foundations for the economy of tomorrow* (2nd ed.). Routledge.

LGA. (2023). *Identifying and promoting green growth opportunities*. Local Government Association. https://www.local.gov.uk/publications/identifying-and-promoting-green-growth-opportunities

Mason, C. M., & Harrison, R. T. (2015). Business angel investment activity in the financial crisis: UK evidence and policy implications. *Environment and Planning C: Government and Policy*, *33*(1), 43–60.

Mazzucato, M., & Semieniuk, G. (2018). Financing renewable energy: Who is financing what and why it matters. *Technological Forecasting and Social Change*, *127*, 8–22.

NGFS (Central Bankers and Supervisors). (2022). *Central banking and supervision in the biosphere: An agenda for action on biodiversity loss, financial risk and system stability*. Final report of network for greening financial systems NGFS-inspire study group. NGFS-INSPIRE-Central-Banking-and-Supervision-in-the-Biosphere.pdf

North, D., Baldock, R., & Ullah, F. (2013). Funding the growth of UK technology-based small firms since the financial crash: Are there breakages in the finance escalator? *Venture Capital*, *15*(3), 237–260.

O'Reilly, S., Mac an Bhaird, C., & Cassells, D. (2023). Financing early-stage cleantech firms. *IEEE Transactions on Engineering Management*, *70*(3), 991–1005.

Owen, R. (2023). Lessons from government venture capital funds to enable transition to a low-carbon economy: The U.K. case. *IEEE Transactions on Engineering Management*, *70*(3), 1040–1054.

Owen, R., Lodh, S., Pierrakis, Y., Botelho, M., Bhaird, C., Hussain, J. G., & Scott, J. (2023). Editorial: Entrepreneurial finance for green innovative SMEs. *IEEE Transactions on Engineering Management*, *70*(3), 942–949.

Owen, R., & Mason, C. (2016). The role of government co-investment funds in the supply of entrepreneurial finance: An assessment of the early operation of the UK Angel Co-investment Fund. *Environment and Planning C: Government and Policy*, *35*(3), 434–456.

Polzin, F. (2017). Mobilizing private finance for low-carbon innova1on – A systema1c review of barriers and solu1ons. *Renewable and Sustainable Energy Reviews*, *77*(C), 525–535.

Raworth, K. (2012). *A safe and just space for humanity. Can we live within the doughnut? Oxford discussion paper*. Oxfam. https://policy-practice.oxfam.org/resources/a-safe-and-just-space-for-humanity-can-we-live-within-the-doughnut-210490/

TNFD. (2023, September). *Task force on nature-related financial disclosures (TNFD) recommendations*. Version 1.0. https://tnfd.global/publication/recommendations-of-the-taskforce-on-nature-related-financial-disclosures/#publication-content

Uyarra, E., Shapira, P., & Harding, A. (2016). Low carbon innovations and enterprise growth in the UK: Challenges of a place-blind policy mix. *Technology Strategy and Social Forecasting*, *103*, 264–272.

Wrigley, E. A. (1988). The limits to growth: Malthus and the classical economists. *Population and Development Review*, *14*, 30–48. https://doi.org/10.2307/2808089

Chapter 18

The Elephant in the Net-Zero Room: Why Advocating Benign Population Reduction Is Taboo

Conall Boyle

Independent Researcher

Abstract

Population control as a state-sponsored activity came into prominence following the publication of Ehrlich's *The Population Bomb* in 1968. This was taken up by the IPCC, but by 1994, this changed and any mention of population reduction as a part-solution to CO_2-induced global warming became taboo. Later, when drastic reductions in birth rates as measured by Total Fertility Rates (TFR) were observed in economically advanced countries, books were written to celebrate the fact. The population bomb, it seems, had been defused spontaneously, or so it was claimed. The new problem for many states was the decline of their native populations, and the aging workforce triggering the need for mass immigration to fill the gaps. This chapter traces the ebb-and-flow of Population Policy related to climate change and net-zero. The current 'hands-off, the problem is solved' policy is a grievous mistake and may hasten the *Major 'Population Correction'* (he means catastrophic near wipeout) described by William E Rees in 2023. If States and inter-governmental organisation would get behind a policy of non-coercive population reduction, then the goal of net-zero can be achieved quicker and more easily.

Keywords: carbon footprint; coercive population limitation, women's/girls' equality and education; IPCC; Ehrlich; PopulationMatters.org; population crash

Examining Net Zero: Creating Solutions for a Greener Society and Sustainable Economic Growth, 187–196
Copyright © 2025 by Conall Boyle
Published under exclusive licence by Emerald Publishing Limited
doi:10.1108/978-1-83608-574-420251018

Introduction

It should be obvious that one way of reducing the human carbon footprint[1] would be to reduce the number of foot-printers. If only we could contrive a world with fewer people, then the journey towards Net Zero would be easier and swifter. You may agree, but for some reason, none of the obvious proponents such as the Green Party or the IPCC in its Reports, will countenance, let alone advocate a policy for population reduction. Politicians are reluctant even to suggest that slowing down population growth would be a good idea.

There is no need, as yet, to forecast some kind of Apocalypse. Because of the overshooting of human populations beyond the Earth's carrying capacity, there may be a future in which widespread famines, virulent pandemics or nuclear wars will drastically reduce the number of humans on this planet to one-fifth or one-tenth their present number of eight billion souls. There are conspiracy theorists who believe that powerful secretive figures are plotting this awful Nemesis[2]. Instead, the type of population reduction policy proposed in this chapter is progressive, working with the needs and aspirations of families.

Progressive population policies

PopulationMatters.org (PM) is a UK charity promoting these humane and progressive policies which have the effect of reducing birthrates. As its Patron Sir David Attenborough says

All our environmental problems become easier to solve with fewer people, and harder – and ultimately impossible – to solve with ever more people.

There are proven and reliable means which have the effect of lowering birthrates. By far the most important is economic development. Raising people up from extreme poverty, hopefully to a modest standard of life leads families to choose to have fewer children. Policies specifically directed at improving the lives of women and girls are vital. Free and universal access to contraceptive knowledge and products is one. Implementing proper schooling for girls should also be part of policy. The outcome is that these educated women and girls will choose to have far fewer children and will also have the means to do so. One other freedom is access to quick and safe abortion, which is controversial.

Environmental advocates near-silent on population limitation

Who would be against these highly desirable benign and positive policies? (apart from the abortion bit perhaps). Yet most politicians and policy implementers

[1]A person's 'Carbon Footprint' is a powerful visual image, and a clever way of bringing home the Climate Change crisis. Your footprint is the amount of environmentally damaging Carbon and other gases you produce by your activities. It can be extended to visualise the damage caused by organisations, cities, countries, etc.

[2]See, for example The Corbett Report blog.

avoid mentioning it. Those at the forefront of combatting Climate Change are strangely silent when it comes to effects of overpopulation and the benefits of having fewer people.

The Green Party of England and Wales: In its programme they make no mention of the over-population issue, but it does include this:

> Transforming lives through international aid: We are one of the richest countries in the world, we can and should take the lead in sharing the world's wealth more fairly. We will increase the international aid budget by a third and will increase the proportion of aid given directly to families and communities, putting the best aid tools in the hands of those best qualified to use it.[3]

Could that include family planning? Ensuring equal access to schooling for both boys and girls? No specifics are given. Elsewhere there is plenty on the topic of animal welfare, but no reference to re-wilding, making space for nature and animals. This ignores the devastating impact of over-population on species' habitats especially in the high birthrate countries of the less developed world.

The International panel on climate change (IPCC): The most recent IPCC meeting – COP28 was in December 2023. The following extract was derived from their very comprehensive statistical publication, outlining the threats to the environment: *IPCC Report 2023: Climate Change Synthesis Report*

'The drivers of urban GHG emissions are complex and include *population size* [my italics], income, state of urbanisation and urban form. (high confidence)' GHG = are stated in CO_2-equivalents (CO_2-eq) using the Global Warming Potential with a time horizon of 100 years. (p. 10)

'Depending on levels of GHG mitigation, modelled emissions scenarios based on the SSPs can be consistent with low or high warming levels' and then buried in a footnote

> High mitigation challenges, for example, due to assumptions of slow technological change, *high levels of global population growth*, [my italics] and high fragmentation as in the Shared Socio-economic Pathway SSP3, may render modelled pathways that limit warming to 2 °C (>67%) or lower infeasible (medium confidence). (p. 20)

So it is quite clear that the policy makers and agenda setters at the IPCC are well aware that high levels of population and its growth are a 'challenge'!

One searches in vain for any mention of the population footprint challenge, let alone any proposal to deal with it. In a lengthy final memorandum *Outcome of the first global stocktake*. The word 'population' occurs only once (para 122).

---

[3]From their website www.greenparty.org.uk 'Our political programme'.

> Recognizes the importance of particularly vulnerable developing countries and segments of the population that are already vulnerable owing to geography, socioeconomic status, livelihood, gender, age, minority status, marginalization, displacement, or disability, as well as the ecosystems that they depend on, in responding to loss and damage associated with climate change impacts;

Not a hint that the sheer weight of numbers is having a devastating impact on the local environment. Nor any recognition that burgeoning populations have no choice but to make a living in such imperilled locations nor that their only other choice might be mass migration.

Why Such Fear of Mentioning Population Reduction?

It was not always like this. The publication in 1968 of the Ehrlich's *The Population Bomb* created world-wide concern. Governments began to take vigorous action. It struck a chord too, with many couples in affluent societies choosing to have fewer children, or in extreme cases, none at all. There have been, of course many other reasons besides concern for the planet causing family size to drop. In the literature, Goodhart and Pradhan (2020) cite economic development, women's rights, and access to contraception as the main factors driving down fertility rates. The extent of maternal support and the sheer complexity of juggling jobs and childcare make having babies a daunting prospect. But still part of the sub-conscious for many is the environmental awareness of population overshoot.

Ehrlich's 1968 prediction of 'standing room only' did not happen. That was not because his forecast was wrong at the time, but because trends in fertility have since changed, not least because of his warnings. Then, sometime around 1994 governments and environmentalists breathed a sigh of relief. This was one less awkward topic they had to deal with. The population overshoot problem had somehow solved itself and could be left to others to deal with.

The unattractive side of population control policies: The experiences of coercive population control have cast a dark shadow over attempts by governments to reduce their population. China's one-child policy is one such, where a highly authoritarian regime clamped down hard on women who tried to evade the 'one-child' edict. The Indian example is just as bad with undoubted human rights violations committed in the pursuit of sterilisations and vasectomies.

Another aspect of population reduction which creates much dissent is the reliance on abortion as a birth control mechanism. For the USA, as a donor nation for humanitarian aid, domestic politics dictate that no money must be given for abortion programmes. Many other countries have influential religious groups whose beliefs do not approve either.

Is it racist to advocate population limitation? Even Ehrlich admits[4] that there is a danger it will be seen that way. The accusers point to the obvious fact that the overwhelming burden of CO_2 damage has been created by affluent white western

[4] In a 4 Mar 2022 interview on Nate Hagens 'The Great Simplification' blog.

economies. Shouldn't they be the ones who take the remedial action, not the populations in the still under-developed world? Niger is the country which has the world's highest birthrate, with women having an average of 6.5 births each[5] in 2022. But each child in Niger will only create the tiniest of carbon footprints, because the average income in Niger is a mere $533 *per annum*. Compare that with the UK at $46,586 per person, or even newly enriching China at $10,409 per person on average. Why make Niger feel guilty about having too many children when it's the affluent white countries who have done most damage?

According to Jane O'Sullivan, an Honorary Senior Research Fellow at the University of Queensland[6]

> These days we're encouraged to believe birth control efforts did nothing but breach human rights, but this is a gross misrepresentation. Almost all national family planning programs were voluntary and based on improving people's lives by delivering better health and contraception services. They also worked to break down many of the patriarchal traditions that relegated women to childbearing, such as child marriages and son preference, and to ensure girls' access to education. By slowing population growth, they were able to improve job prospects and access to services such as electricity and sewage. Gradually, it became a virtuous cycle. It didn't happen because they were richer or better educated, but because they gave family planning a high priority. For example, Thailand was much poorer and less developed than the Philippines in 1970, but is far better off now, and a major rice exporter, thanks to its family planning program. Bangladesh was the poorest of the poor, but promoted family planning while Pakistan didn't. Now it has overtaken Pakistan, where worsening conditions are leading to political instability.

Comment: Eventually global economic development should lift up every child to a decent standard of living. To condemn a large swathe of humanity to everlasting grinding poverty just to keep their carbon footprint small is a wicked idea. Hopefully, in 50–80 year's time, the whole of humanity will achieve a decent minimum that no group will be left behind just to keep their carbon footprint low for the benefit of the wealthy.

When Did Environmentalists Stop Worrying About Overpopulation?

Here is an explanation for this deliberate amnesia, from a PopulationMatters.org 2024 publication *Breaking Silos*. It harks back to a 1994 Conference in Cairo

---

[5]This is widely referred to as the Total Fertility Rate. A value of 2.1 children, on average, results in a static population, just about replacing itself. Above that means population increases, below 2.1 will *eventually* lead to population decline.

[6]In an interview in Resilience.org 24 Mar 2024

when concern for women's and girl's reproductive autonomy and the need for educational equality was divorced from the impact of population on development and the environment.

> There remains, however, profound resistance to acknowledging the linkage between population and environmental destruction. This rejection of evidence and scientific consensus is profoundly harmful to those most vulnerable to these effects, including, of course, women and girls.

A New Reason to Ignore the Over-population Issue.

The population problem is not only fixed, soon there'll be too few of us! It wasn't until 2010 that I encountered an author of some standing who claimed that the population problem was 'solved' and therefore could be ignored. Fred Pearce is the environment consultant of the New Scientist magazine. He says in *People-quake* (2010) that,

By late in the century, when some threats such as climate change are expected to become most serious, our population may be falling. If population was the only thing we had to worry about, we might be OK. (p. 241)

Concern that the environmental problem is so urgent, and that population control will take too long to be effective i.e. sufficiently reduce the number of carbon footprinters, has also been voiced by Bradshaw and Brooke (2014). They worked through a range of future population scenarios and concluded that the effect of demographic momentum leads to, at best a world population that peaks mid- to late-century and only drops back to today's level by 2100. The outlook has somewhat improved since they wrote their paper. Birthrates are falling even faster than expected. Even so, this suggests that more draconian population limitation policies may prove essential. A complete ban on immigration from the third world is mentioned by the authors. Dystopian science-fiction suggests some of the more extreme remedies which might be enacted, for example nuclear war in *The Handmaiden's Tale*, causing near-universal female infertility.

Falling Population in a Nation-state: A Melancholy Prospect?

Overwhelmingly, commentators see a shrinking population as an economic and social disaster. First there are the burdens of an ageing population: health costs, care home costs and pension costs. The economy suffers because of fewer customers, less spending by the old. There will be less dynamism in the economy because of fewer workers in the younger entrepreneurial age group. One bright side might be that the reduced workforce will achieve better wages and the wage rises will be more evenly distributed.

The social outcomes of falling and ageing populations don't look too rosy. The countryside empties out, schools will close and villages become deserted. It will be a duller society too because of mono-ethnicity, less diversity of diet, entertainment, culture. Nationalists worry that there will be not enough men for an army. Niall Ferguson illustrates an article[7] on de-population with a picture of a literally soulless Chinese housing estate, with the implication that this lifeless place is a 'melancholy' place for humans.

Comment: If shrinking populations lead to such a miserable society and an ineffective economy why not apply some thought to making it more palatable? Skirbekk (2022) in his *Decline and Prosper! Changing Global Birthrates and the Advantages of fewer Children* makes some attempt to do so. This is a topic which deserves much more study during our journey to net zero.

An Extreme Push-back Against the Imminent Planet-saving Population Reduction

Environmentalists generally are people who advocate moves towards net zero carbon emissions. Does that make them part of a 'death cult' hell-bent on wiping out nearly all of human life on this planet of ours? In a bizarre quote from Elon Musk (who is a notorious pro-natalist, and one who practices what he preaches – he has 11 children by several partners)

> I'm pro-environment but if you take environmentalism to an extreme, you start to view humanity as a plague on the surface of the earth, like a mould or something ... The environmental movement – and I'm an environmentalist – has gone too far. They've gone way too far. If you start thinking that humans are bad then the natural conclusion is that humans should die out.[8]

Musk went on to point out that while there were explicit extinctionists at the fringes of the environmental movement, the sentiment behind the 'death cult' had pervaded the movement as a whole. Musk has some credentials as an environmentalist, risking his personal fortune to build Tesla, the global leader in the production of electric cars. But overall, he seems to believe that when it comes to population numbers 'the more the merrier'. He could also be dubbed the Prince of Techno-Hopium, believing that when we exhaust this planet we can fly away and colonise some of the millions of other planets. This matters, because Musk has the platform (X formerly Twitter) to spread his views.

What to Do – Don't Bother, too Controversial?

The prevailing climate of opinion seems to confirm that the earlier decisions to stop seeing population size as a problem were correct. Instead, we are assailed by warnings that we are approaching the opposite – the dire consequences of

---

[7]Ferguson, Niall 'Global Population Crash Isn't Sci-Fi Anymore' Bloomberg 10 Mar 2024

[8]I found this at the blog of the Daily Skeptic 5/11/2023 Ian Price. Also reported in The Standard newspaper 1/11/2023

below-replacement birthrates and falling populations. In an excellent and original 2023 report '*Migration, Stagnation, or Procreation: Quantifying the Demographic Trilemma*', (Morland and Pilkington, 2023) lay out the well nigh-insoluable 'problem' of falling populations thus:

- economic stagnation, caused by ageing, dependent populations, shortage of labour and lack of entrepreneurial vigour,
- need for immigrants to care for the elderly and fill the gaps in the labour market. But this comes at the price of changing the culture of the host society and
- the seemingly irreversible behaviour of women world-wide to have fewer children, at a TFR of less than the replacement rate of 2.1.

Comment: Left to our own devices, falling TFRs might, indeed, be 'irreversible'. But this trend could just as easily stop or go into reverse. TFRs have varied quite a bit, even in a stable and developed country like the UK. In the 1930s, the TFR for the UK dropped to 1.79 and then rose to 2.81 by 1965. It has now settled back down to around 1.87 since 1980[9]. A major study in The Lancet (2024) forecasts that this decline will continue, dropping to 1.38 in 2050 and 1.3 in 2100.

This sounds like the classic 'if current trends continue' trap. Today's sub-replacement level of TFR need not be baked-in. Pro-natalist rhetoric could rapidly take hold leading to human populations choosing bigger families. Those celebrating the population crash may find that history proves their forecasts to be just as wrong as Ehrlich's did.

Going Forward with a Benign Non-coercive Population Reduction Campaign

Prudence dictates that we should encourage the downward trend in TFRs. In a best case scenario, a policy which accelerates the downward trends in TFR will take us to our goal of net-zero all the sooner. At the very least, public policy should recognise and may be even celebrate responsible parents. They should be congratulated for making net-zero easier to achieve. But it will take courage for politicians to endorse population reduction as 'good for the planet'.

Putting money into programmes of overseas aid such as girls' education and provision of contraceptives *specifically to curb population growth* is more difficult, but equally necessary. Raising billions of people in the developing world out of poverty is a laudable aim. Great strides have been made in reducing the numbers in deep poverty – those living on \$1 or \$2 a day. The Chinese Communist regime has been particularly successful in this regard. But, the fight against poverty is not over. Even as the World's population climbs past six, then seven and now more than eight billion there always seems to be an irreducible 800 million stuck in grinding poverty. This matters because it is among those in the direst poverty that extremely high rates of fertility persist.

---

[9]https://www.statista.com/statistics/1033074/fertility-rate-uk-1800-2020/

Full and equal citizenship for women is not a given although most countries would be expected to aspire to it. The consequences of girls being excluded from education, being hidden from view by head-covering or purdah directly results in higher TFRs. This is why patriarchal, pro-natalist societies are content to leave such repression in place. Even more than rising affluence, full access to education is an even more effective means of reducing TFRs. Well-educated women aspire to be something more than baby-making machines, and rightly so. More controversial is access to 'Modern Family Planning', as PopulationMatters.org coyly calls it. Most countries allow access to contraceptives of various kinds, but access is not enough. It should be easy and widespread access if it is to be adequate. Ideally, it should be free of charge too. Although religious objections to this have abated, some pro-natalist countries are trying to make contraceptives and abortions difficult to obtain.

Conclusion

On its own, population reduction will not fix climate change, nor will it be quick. But, every step will make a contribution. Each nation, each state has to make its contribution, but for the sake of the Planet, it would be best if that happened in the most affluent resource-hungry countries soonest. Trying to fix labour shortages by shipping immigrants into affluent countries works in an altogether wrong way. Each country will have to adapt to a falling population with its own people. Japan is achieving great success in this regard. Does this mean Japan as a nation is about to fizzle out? Not really. Japan's population reached a high of 128.5 million in 2008 and is predicted to fall to 100.6 million by 2050. But that is the same as the population of Japan in 1967.

On our journey to Net Zero politicians must speak up for the goal of population reduction. They must tackle the taboos. It is not an impossible task, as the 'Woke' movement shows, minds can be changed. It would be a dereliction of duty if this, the simplest and cheapest strategy to tackle Climate Change was eschewed. Many organisations and all governments claim to be working towards net-zero. Without an open and well-supported population policy such claims are dishonest. The biggest ultimate cause of climate change is that there are just too many people. All the technological fixes in the world are just 'virtue signaling' unless the contribution of overpopulation is acknowledged and acted upon. I will truly believe in the sincerity of the save-the-planet types when they dump their 'Just Stop Oil' banners and are seen with placards demanding 'Just Stop Having Babies'!

References

Bradshaw, C. J. A., & Brooke, B. W. (Adelaide) (2014). Human population reduction is not a quick fix for environmental problems *Proceedings of the Natural Academy of Science* https://doi.org/10.1073/pnas.1410465111

Eherlich, P. (1968). *The population bomb*. Ballantine.

Ferguson, N. (2024, March 10). *Global population crash isn't Sci-Fi Anymore*. Bloomberg. https://www.bloomberg.com/opinion/articles/2024-03-10/global-population-collapse-isn-t-sci-fi-anymore-niall-ferguson?utm_source=website&utm_medium=share&utm_campaign=twitter

Goodhart, C., & Pradhan, M. (2020). *The great demographic reversal: Ageing societies, waning inequality, and an inflation revival*. Palgrave Macmillan.

Green Party of England & Wales, The website.

IPCC. (2023a). *Outcome of the first global stocktake*. https://unfccc.int/sites/default/files/resource/cma2023_L17_adv.pdf

IPCC. (2023b). *Climate change synthesis report*. Contribution of Working Groups IPCC Geneva. https://www.ipcc.ch/report/ar6/syr/downloads/report/IPCC_AR6_SYR_LongerReport.pdf

Lancet. (2024, March 20). *The Global fertility in 204 countries and territories, 1950–2021, with forecasts to 2100: A comprehensive demographic analysis for the Global Burden of Disease Study 2021*. https://doi.org/10.1016/S0140-6736(24)00550-6

Morland, P., & Pilkington. P. (2023). *Migration, stagnation, or procreation: quantifying the demographic trilemma*. https://www.arc-research.org/research-papers/the-demographic-trilemma

Pearce, F. (2010). *Peoplequake: Mass migration aging nations and the coming population crash*. Eden Project Books.

Rees, W. E. (2023). *The human ecology of overshoot: Why a major 'Population Correction' Is Inevitable*. https://www.mdpi.com/2673-4060/4/3/32

Skirbekk, V. (2022). *Decline and prosper! Changing global birthrates and the advantages of fewer children*. Palgrave Macmillan.

Statistics generally: Found at Statista and OurWorldinData websites.

United Nations (2023). *Framework convention on climate change*, 13 December 2023.

Chapter 19

Concluding Thoughts: An Impassioned Call for Intervention to Produce a Greener, Cleaner Future

Alex de Ruyter[a], Steven McCabe[b] and Beverley Nielsen[a]

[a]*Centre for Brexit Studies, Birmingham City University*
[b]*DoctorateHub, UK*

When confronted with crisis, we instinctively look for solutions. It's the way that humans have, of all creatures on this planet, been able to survive and thrive. The history of human endeavour is replete with impressive examples of ingenuity and resourcefulness. However, as the preceding chapters in this book make clear, human activity is the very reason we are confronted with the threat of a rapidly warming environment that will, if allowed to continue unchecked, undermine the ability of many millions to survive. Climate change has the potential to create an environmental calamity that will devastate the lives of many millions of people around the globe.

Alterations in weather patterns, rising temperatures and increased pollution are not mere coincidence. It's the result of human activity and the fact that the world's population requires a steady flow of energy to produce the goods we so readily consume every day, in heating (or cooling) homes and workplaces. Food and produce we buy is transported vast distances from where it's grown and manufactured to our shops. The emissions produced by such activities have steadily built up – particularly in recent decades – to produce a greenhouse effect that's so destructive to life on earth. There has to be a better way to ensure the billions of earth's inhabitants can continue to exist healthily whilst ensuring the planet is not made increasingly uninhabitable for future generations.

A greener and cleaner economy, as explained by many of the contributors to chapters in this book, as well as ensuring we avoid the calamitous impact of climate change, has the added advantage of being collectively good for societies

Examining Net Zero: Creating Solutions for a Greener Society and Sustainable Economic Growth, 197–200
Copyright © 2025 by Alex de Ruyter, Steven McCabe and Beverley Nielsen
Published under exclusive licence by Emerald Publishing Limited
doi:10.1108/978-1-83608-574-420251019

in every country. As international consultancy group Arup (2024) explain, a green economy is based on an economic model that purposely aims to reduce the harmful consequences of production and consumption on the environment but to create a 'virtuous relationship between economic growth and environmental wellbeing'. How a green economy and the importance of circularity is dealt with in McCabe's chapter. In our quest to reduce emissions and avoid the worst effects of climate change, we must think about how we reuse and recycle the earth's resources and, in particular, as Nielsen explains in her chapter, make a greater effort to measure embodied carbon in all we produce and to focus on sustaining our biodiversity.

Significantly, according to Arup, a greener economy in achieving the primary objective of a cleaner environment will lead, crucially, to secondary economic and societal benefits, including:

Economic benefits of a green economy

- Foster jobs and skills
- Fuel economic growth
- Spur innovation
- Trade competitiveness

Social benefits of a green economy

- Reduce poverty
- Foster inclusivity/equity
- Ensure wellbeing
- Enforce labour rights

In stressing how important a green economy can be in stimulating economic growth, Oxford Economics (2023) calculate the transition to a net zero emissions environment by 2050 would create new industries and employment opportunities worth $10.3 trillion (5.2%) to the global economy. This would be through the adoption of initiatives that will produce a cleaner environment. Equally, new 'green' products and markets will emerge as innovative technology creates a fertile environment for entrepreneurs and disruptors. This would follow the pattern of every previous industrial revolution. Finally, to quote once again from Arup, 'productivity gains will be made as regions adversely affected by climate change and unsustainable use of natural resources, see those negative effects reversed, leading to a global economy built on a more sustainable footing' (Oxford Economics, 2023).

The University of Liverpool's Heseltine Institute for Public Policy, Practice and Place, an interdisciplinary public policy research institute, and aiming to facilitate collaboration between academics, policymakers and practitioners to develop sustainable and inclusive cities and city regions recently produced an informatively crucial report. *Net Zero Manifesto: Scaling Up Green Prosperity* provides 'a roadmap for future governments to deliver green growth and maximise the LCR's remarkable potential' (University of Liverpool, 2024).

Whilst *Net Zero Manifesto: Scaling Up Green Prosperity* (2024) is aimed at influencing the change required to achieve a greener and cleaner environment and economy in Liverpool and its surrounding area, the five objectives forming the manifesto are applicable to every region in the United Kingdom and, we contend, every country across the globe. These are:

1. *Future energy generation*: We need a sustainable, consistent and long-term plan to achieve clean, green energy in the Liverpool City Region
2. *Better, greener, healthier housing*: Devolve the funding and powers to retrofit and build green homes
3. *Invest in transport*: Unlock connectivity, accessibility, affordability and greener journeys across the LCR by investing in low carbon technologies and integrated transport
4. *Unlock net zero innovation*: We need long-term investment to realise the potential of local innovation and build on our assets to accelerate green growth
5. *Future-proof green skills and jobs*: Dedicated funding, programmes and responsibilities to scale up green skills in existing and new sectors and future proof the jobs we need

Net Zero Manifesto: Scaling Up Green Prosperity explicitly aims to provide an achievable roadmap for the implementing measures that will create a green economy in which growth for collective good occurs. As we acknowledge, success is impossible without coordinated and consistent policymaking by politicians at all levels, most especially in government. As economists Vicky Pryce and Steven McCabe explain argue in their chapter, the confluence of committed politicians who dedicate sufficient financial support is critical. As *Net Zero Manifesto: Scaling Up Green Prosperity* makes clear in its conclusion, 'A more stable, consistent, and long-term national policy framework for net zero is required to facilitate effective local action' (University of Liverpool, 2024).

Everything that needs be said about the urgency of responding to the rapidly developing crisis that's climate change and could affect every citizen is contained within the preceding chapters of this book. The concluding thoughts presented here are made with the urgency of individuals who passionately wish to see a better future for all. Nevertheless, as we've seen across the globe, because of the desire to ensure support from voters at the next election, those who can genuinely influence the radical intervention required to deal with climate chance, namely politicians, appear to believe the costs of action outweigh the risks confronting all citizens and are likely to become considerably worse.

Ignoring how phenomenally devastating these risks are is entirely erroneous, not to say dangerous for millions who will suffer if climate change is not dealt with. Besides, we assert, though the costs are undoubtedly considerable, the economic benefits and payback will be, at worst, equitable and very likely more than the price tag of intervention made now. To borrow from the title of the much-covered song first recorded in 1949 by Guy Lombardo and His Royal Canadians, whilst we continue to 'enjoy' ourselves, with regards to the threat of climate change and the need to protect our planet from emissions and waste, it's far later than we think.

References

Arup. (2024, May 30). *Defining the green economy*. Arup Website. https://www.arup.com/perspectives/a-new-understanding-of-the-green-economy

Liverpool City Region All Party Parliamentary Group (APPG). (2024, May). *Liverpool city region: A manifesto for net zero, scaling up green prosperity*. The Heseltine Institute for Public Policy, Practice and Place, Liverpool, United Kingdom.

Oxford Economics. (2023). *The global green economy: Understanding and capturing the opportunity*. Oxford Economics, Oxford, United Kingdom.

University of Liverpool. (2024, May 17). *University develops Net Zero manifesto for Liverpool City Region*. University of Liverpool Website. Retrieved May 30, 2024, from https://news.liverpool.ac.uk/2024/05/17/university-develops-net-zero-manifesto-for-liverpool-city-region/

Afterword

As former President of the CBI and Chair of the All-Party Manufacturing Group's Manufacturing Commission, responsible for producing their report on *Manufacturing Resilience*, (2021), I've been acutely aware of the appetite amongst our UK manufacturers to meet the challenges posed by net zero and the delivery of a sustainable economy, as aptly illustrated by the case studies in this book.

One of our central messages in 2021 was a plea for Government to put manufacturing at the centre of our plans for a green economy. In the run up to COP26, we were greatly encouraged by Government's intentions for a green recovery primed, in particular, by the 10-Point Plan for a Green Industrial Revolution (2020) and the Net Zero Strategy, Build Back Greener (2021), with further policies introduced in 2023 through Powering Up Britain: Net Zero Growth Plans. But as those of us in business know, important as they are, we'll need more than new policies, laws and regulations, to tackle climate change as emissions and temperatures continue to relentlessly increase, causing disruption for millions around the world, biodiversity and ecosystem loss and economic upheaval.

I remain as focused as ever on championing our UK manufacturers who power our country's tech, ingenuity and creativity, offering the solutions to the challenges of climate change. They must be at the forefront of our efforts to create a more sustainable, prosperous world, and our policies and laws should consider where these solutions are going to be produced and the implementation of a circular economy, providing the necessary resilience to contend with future shocks.

With a recent report (2023) by the Energy and Climate Intelligence Unit and CBI highlighting 9% growth in the net zero economy, compared to just 0.1% in UK GDP that year, this sector alone is responsible for £74bn in goods and services and 765,000 jobs. The report showed these jobs are, on average £10,000, better paid than the UK average of £35,400, and 50% more productive, generating £114,300 in economic activity overall. COP 26, hosted in Glasgow, was illuminating and as Mark Carney announced then, there's a wall of investment, backed by firms with $130trn in assets, standing ready to help drive sustainable growth. Our challenge remains to provide the policy stability required to create an attractive business environment, essential, if we are to entice investors to unleash these funds to fuel clean growth. Now, more than ever, we need political clarity and long-term policy stability, so our businesses can get on and produce the sustainable future which upcoming generations are depending on our leaders to deliver and which are amplified so clearly in this book.

Karan Faridoon Bilimoria, Baron Bilimoria

Printed and bound by CPI Group (UK) Ltd, Croydon, CR0 4YY

18/09/2026

14965027-0001